Historical Materialism
research in critical marxist theory

No.3 Winter 1998

Symposium: Political Organisation and the Legacy of

Editorial introduction

After decades of mockery and excoriation, Marx's corpse is being exhumed once more by pundits and columnists. Faced by the intractability and apparent inscrutability of capitalism's inherent tendency to devastating crisis, bourgeois economists and commentators have rediscovered the virtues of Marx's critique. Seemingly, the years of neoliberal extremism and excess were a 'mistake', and the market can no longer be credited with the capacity for self-regulation and infinite profit making. So the spirit of Marx is once more invoked in the desperate hope that lessons can be gleaned which will allow the system to be saved.

But the point remains to change it. While Marxists may reap a grim satisfaction from the renewed fashionability of Marx, it should not be forgotten that it is only his analysis of capitalism that is being gingerly examined, and not his prescriptions for revolutionary transformation – for these have, it is claimed, been 'disproved' in bloody and unqualified manner by the fate of the Eastern bloc. Indeed, one might even say that while more and more now claim to be 'Marxian', it is unfortunately still rare to define oneself as 'Marxist', and rarer still is it to recognise the continuing vitality of the classical Marxist tradition as a whole.

It is with these considerations in mind that *Historical Materialism* has organised the first of what we hope will be a series of symposia. Having received two articles, from Simon Clarke and Howard Chodos and Colin Hay, which engaged – in very different ways – with the problems of organisation, the political, and the Bolshevik tradition, we felt that in addition to their intrinsic interest, they would serve well as springboards to a wider discussion of the issues involved.

Gathered here, then, are five critical discussions of the two lead articles by Marxists from varied traditions and outlooks, which Clarke, Chodos and Hay may choose to reply to in a future issue. We hope that, while we intend to carry a substantial debate on crisis theory in our next issue, the current issue will initiate a much-needed process of reflection on the concrete tasks of passing beyond capitalism.

Was Lenin a Marxist? The Populist Roots of Marxism-Leninism

Simon Clarke

Populism and the origins of Russian Marxism

Lenin's name has been coupled with that of Marx as the co-founder of the theory of 'Marxism-Leninism'. However, despite his emphasis on the role of revolutionary theory, Lenin's original theoretical contributions to the development of Marxism were very limited. His talents were those of a determined revolutionary, in the populist tradition of Chernyshevsky, and a brilliantly effective propagandist and political organiser. His contribution to 'Marxism-Leninism' was to modify Marxist orthodoxy in such a way as to integrate the political and organisational principles of revolutionary populism into Marxism, on the basis of Plekhanov's 'dialectical materialism', whose distinctive interpretation of Marxism was Lenin's constant guide and inspiration. In this paper I want to argue that Lenin never broke from the theoretical and political traditions of Russian populism, but completed Plekhanov's project by assimilating Marxism to the very different theoretical framework of populism.

According to Marxist-Leninist orthodoxy, populism and Marxism-Leninism constitute two radically opposed political and theoretical traditions. However this is a completely misleading characterisation, for Russian Marxism emerged directly out of populism, and the distinctiveness of Marxism-Leninism can be traced directly back to the theoretical traditions of Russian populism.

The development of Marxism in Russia took place not against but within the populist movement. The early populists were romantic critics of capitalism, who drew heavily on the Hegelian philosophy of history, and particularly on the Young Hegelians' revolutionary interpretation of Hegel's historical dialectic as a process of negation and transcendence. Although they were romantic critics of capitalism, the early populists were fierce opponents of idealism, which was associated with the tyranny of religion and the autocracy. So they developed a materialist interpretation of the Hegelian dialectic according to which the values of freedom, equality and community were not derived from any spiritual world, but were inherent in the existing institutions of peasant life, and above all in the peasant commune; a materialist interpretation of history which was supplemented in the 1860s by Darwin's evolutionism. The most influential philosopher was Ludwig Feuerbach, whose naturalistic materialism was the direct inspiration for both Belinsky and

Chernyshevsky, who, nevertheless, like all the populists, combined their materialism with a romantic utopianism.

The theoretical problem which the populists faced was that of relating their own utopian vision to the more mundane aspirations of the peasantry, whose conditions of life were supposed to provide the material base for the realisation of that vision, but whose ignorance and limited cultural horizons prevented them from making the socialist vision their own. Thus, while the material base might be the aspirations of the peasantry, the values and ideals of the new society were those of the intelligentsia. This problem provided the basis for the principal division within the populist movement, which was between those who believed that socialist values were immanent in the conditions of life of the mass of the population, and so put primary emphasis on agitation, and those who believed that the realm of values was the specialist realm of the intellectual, and so put primary emphasis on education.

It is important to emphasise that the division within populism expressed different solutions to a single ideological and political problem, that of legitimating and realising socialist values which are held by only a small minority of the population, the intelligentsia. In this sense they were both variants of what Marx characterised as 'utopian socialism'. Populism looked to the material needs of the peasantry to provide the popular base for a political movement which could realise these values, and in this sense it was committed to a 'materialist' philosophy, but these 'material needs' were themselves defined ideologically by the intelligentsia, for what the populists sought to realise was not the aspirations of the peasantry, but the intellectuals' own values, and in this sense populism was committed to a philosophy which was just as idealist as that which it opposed.

In the 1870s, this division separated the anarchists, inspired particularly by Bakunin, from the 'subjective sociologists', inspired particularly by Lavrov and Mikhailovsky, but this was primarily a tactical and even rhetorical division within the populist movement, as both factions moved into the villages to propagandise amongst the peasantry. It was only with the collapse of the populist faith in the peasantry, following the famine of 1890–1, that this division came to assume much greater significance, coming to separate the social democrats from the 'legal Marxists', on the one hand, and the anarchists and 'economists', on the other.

Marxism had been influential in Russia from an early stage in the development of populism, for Marx provided the most powerful critique of modern capitalism, and the strongest of arguments for resisting its advance. But the greatest importance of Marxism was that it provided the ideological bridge from romantic populism to modern socialism, providing a scientific theory which could both explain the failures of populism, and point a new way forward. Marx's 'political economy' established the possibility of the advance of capitalism, against the populist belief that the lack of markets made capitalist development impossible in Russia, while also showing the limitations of capitalism, and identifying in the proletariat the social force which would overthrow it. Ultimately, however, the Marxists of the 1890s were as little concerned with the conditions of the proletariat as the populists of the 1870s had been concerned with the conditions of the peasants. The turn from peasantry to proletariat did not come about because the suffering of the proletariat was greater than that of the peasantry, and still less because the proletariat constituted a majority of the population, but because the proletariat was identified as the new vehicle for the old populist hopes, the 'material base' for the realisation of socialist values. In this sense, Russian Marxism developed directly out of Russian populism, in response to changing economic, social and political circumstances.

Plekhanov's Marxism developed in the context of the debates within Russian populism in the 1880s, as Plekhanov turned from the peasantry to the proletariat as the basis of his revolutionary hopes. The laws of historical materialism guaranteed that the development of capitalism, which was destroying the immediate hopes of the populists, would give rise to their ultimate realisation, so that the revolutionary movement could embrace the development of capitalism as a necessary stage on the road to socialism. However this did not mean that revolutionaries had to sit back and wait for the inevitable revolution. Plekhanov's Marxism stressed the active role of ideas and of political organisation in determining the pace of historical development. On the other hand, it was not possible to achieve socialism until the historical process had matured. Thus Plekhanov vehemently opposed the voluntarism of the 'subjective sociologists'. The freedom of action open to the revolutionary movement was not defined by the ability of the subject to transcend its determination by historical laws, but was rather defined by the ability of the revolutionary movement to come to know those laws, and so to accelerate (or retard) the pace of historical development – this was the difference between scientific and utopian socialism. Following Engels's interpretation of Hegel, Plekhanov defined freedom as the knowledge of necessity, and so the ability to control the laws of nature and of history, which had hitherto operated as blind forces. This idea lay at the heart of Plekhanov's reconciliation of a rigidly deterministic materialism with a vigorous political activism. Plekhanov called the philosophy which he developed to express this idea 'dialectical materialism', which opposed both the fatalism implied by a 'mechanical materialism' and the voluntarism implied by 'subjective sociology'.

Plekhanov's philosophy of history: the populist foundations of dialectical materialism

Although Plekhanov invented the term, the exposition of the philosophy of 'dialectical materialism' is often attributed to Engels.[1] However, Plekhanov's characterisation of 'dialectical materialism' is significantly different from Engels's characterisation of the 'materialist dialectic', and from Marx's own critique of bourgeois philosophy. The difference is quite fundamental, for Plekhanov's 'dialectical materialism' is nothing less than the philosophical materialism of the populist followers of Feuerbach, which was precisely the philosophy against which Marx and Engels directed their most devastating criticism.[2]

Plekhanov criticised eighteenth-century materialism for its inconsistent adherence to materialist principles, exemplified by the contradiction between the view that *'the opinions of men are determined by their environment'* and the view that *'the environment is determined by opinions'*.[3] It therefore fell back into a view of opinions and the environment, manners and the constitution, as mutually interacting forces, without any understanding of the 'historical factor which produced both the manners of the given people and its constitution, and thereby *created the very possibility of their interaction'*.[4]

The French historians of the Restoration period advanced beyond this dualism, to locate both manners and the constitution in the *civil condition* of men, in which particular property relations determined particular class interests. However this did not resolve the contradiction, since property relations were seen as essentially legal and political relations; the historical development of property relations being explained in terms of the spiritual development of humanity from the infantile age of feelings, through the adolescent age of passions, to the mature age of reason.

The utopian socialists, and above all Saint-Simon, had an inkling of the solution to the puzzle, in relating the development of property to the development of production. However, the development of production was ultimately seen as a further expression of human intellectual development, expressing the development of scientific and technical knowledge, repeating the Restoration historians' identification of the

---

[1] Plekhanov used the term the term 'dialectical materialism' in an 1891 article in *Neue Zeit*. Lenin adopted the term in his 1894 *What the 'Friends of the People' Are*. The phrase 'the materialist conception of history' dates from Engels's 1859 review of Marx's *Critique of Political Economy*, but the term 'historical materialism' was only introduced in his 1892 Special Introduction to the English edition of *Socialism, Utopian and Scientific*.
[2] There is a link between Engels and the populist roots of Plekhanov's philosophy, for Engels in his adolescence was a member of the group of Young Hegelians and followers of Feuerbach who provided the philosophical inspiration for the first generation of Russian populists. Indeed, one of Engels's own youthful articles, developing a Feuerbachian critique of Hegel, had a significant impact in Russia in the 1840s.
[3] Plekhanov 1956, p. 21.
[4] Plekhanov 1956, p. 24.

historical development of human nature with the development of the individual from infancy through adolescence to maturity.

All of these different formulations of a materialist conception of history fell at the last hurdle, reducing historical development to the moral and intellectual development inscribed in human nature. The result was a profound ambivalence as to the role of human agency in the making of history, as they oscillated between an extreme fatalism and an extreme subjectivism. The belief that moral and intellectual development was subject to determination by natural laws led to fatalism. On the other hand, knowledge of those laws provided the basis for utopian schemes to reform human institutions in accordance with human nature, without any regard for historical laws or institutional constraints. The utopian preoccupation with 'what ought to be' was accordingly associated with a profound disregard for what is. In particular, existing political institutions and political conflicts were seen as merely an expression of an outmoded stage of moral and intellectual development, irrelevant to and inappropriate for the realisation of the utopian schemes, which depended not on the mobilisation of material and political interests, but on the realisation of an *idea*. Thus in the last resort materialism, rather than submit to a paralysing fatalism, reverts to idealism.

The importance of Hegel for Plekhanov was that it was he who broke through the contradiction at the heart of 'metaphysical' materialism in adopting the point of view of dialectics, 'which studies phenomena precisely in their development and, consequently, in their interconnection'.[5] The dialectical study of an historical process 'presupposes an attentive attitude to its *real* course in *actual fact*' so that dialecticians 'do not content themselves with *abstract conclusions from abstract principles*'.[6] The importance of Hegel's dialectic is that, in showing that everything is useful in its right place and at the right time, but then becomes harmful, Hegel dispels all utopias, which claim to provide an ideal valid for all places and all times. Similarly Hegel destroyed the foundations of utopianism in destroying the idea of an invariant human nature. Hegel certainly retained a universal historical principle, the principle of reason; but this was not at all the human reason of the *philosophes*, but rather an objective reason, of which the philosopher can only become aware *ex post*, through the scientific study of its manifestations. For Hegel 'reason governs history ... in the sense of *conformity to law*'.[7] This leads to a fundamentally different conception of intellectual development from that of the metaphysicians, who each believed that they had achieved the truth against which all other systems of thought were simply false. Intellectual development is no less subject to historical laws than is any other human institution, adapting to changing historical needs. Thus *'Philosophy is the*

---

[5] Plekhanov 1956, p. 92.
[6] Plekhanov 1956, p. 101. See also pp. 108–9.
[7] Plekhanov 1956, p. 126.

intellectual expression of its own age ... every philosophy is true for its own age, and mistaken for any other'.[8]

The Hegelian dialectic is undoubtedly idealist. But more importantly it is *monistic*, avoiding the dualism into which previous forms of materialism had always degenerated in trying to recover a role for consciousness and subjectivity. For consistent idealists, including Leibniz and Spinoza as well as Hegel, the human and natural world is universally governed by determinate laws which operate independently of human consciousness and human will. However, the fact that historical development is governed by such laws in no way undermines human freedom. 'The laws of material necessity themselves are nothing else than the laws of action of the spirit. *Freedom presupposes necessity, necessity passes entirely into freedom*'.[9] Thus Hegel's rigorous commitment to determinism simultaneously provides a far wider scope for freedom than do the dualists who, 'when trying to delimit *free* activity and *necessary* activity, ... thereby tear away from the *realm of freedom* all that region ... which they set apart for *necessity*'.[10]

This apparent paradox is resolved when it is appreciated that the possibility of any effective exercise of my freedom depends on an understanding of the *necessity* which governs the consequences of my action. The exercise of freedom is only possible on the basis of an understanding of necessity. '*The possibility of the free (conscious) historical activity of any particular person is reduced to zero, if at the very foundation of free human actions there does not lie necessity which is accessible to the understanding of the doer*'.[11] While I am not conscious of the necessity which governs the consequences of my actions, those consequences will turn out to be other than those I intended, and so will be determined not by my free will, but by necessity. The necessary outcome of such acts will in turn modify the situation of the individual actors, determining new aims which they will freely pursue. Thus freedom and necessity are not the mutually exclusive categories posited by the dualists, but are inter-penetrating opposites. The consequences of the free acts of individuals are determined according to necessary laws, the outcome of which provides the grounds for new forms of free conscious activity. This interpenetration of freedom and necessity '*also takes place according to definite laws, which can and must be discovered by theoretical philosophy*'.[12] However, once theoretical philosophy has discovered 'the laws of social and historical progress, I can influence the latter according to my aims'[13] – freedom can only grow out of knowledge of necessity.

Hegel's monism provides the only firm foundation for a science of history. However Hegel reduced the history of social relations to the

---

[8] Plekhanov 1956, p. 127.
[9] Plekhanov 1956, p. 130.
[10] Plekhanov 1956, pp. 130–1.
[11] Plekhanov 1956, p. 132.
[12] Plekhanov 1956, p. 134.
[13] Plekhanov 1956, p. 135.

history of the Idea, which cannot be the determining cause of historical development, since it is no more than the 'personification of our own logical process',[14] the outcome of our reflection on history. All that remains is to set Hegel's philosophy on materialist foundations. The way forward was shown by Feuerbach, who replaced Hegel's Idea by the category of Matter, inverting the Hegelian relationship between thinking and being, a point of view which 'was adopted by Marx and Engels and was by them made the foundation of their materialist conception of history'.[15] But Feuerbach's materialism was incomplete, and still suffered from the defects of those which had preceded it. For Feuerbach, the relationship between being and thought was purely contemplative, thought being a passive reflection of matter, so that the laws of history were once again reduced to the laws of nature. Marx finally solves this problem in his *Theses on Feuerbach*, where he 'develops and amplifies Feuerbach's ideas'[16] in insisting that the relationship between man and nature is not a *contemplative* but a *practical* relationship, practice providing the key to historical development. Human nature is not an unchanging phenomenon since, as Marx noted in *Capital*, '[b]y acting on nature outside himself, and changing it, man changes his own nature'.[17] The laws which govern historical development cannot be found in the unchanging human nature of the bourgeois materialists, nor in the disembodied Spirit of Hegel, but must be located in the concrete material interaction between humanity and nature, in the development of *production*. It fell to Marx to provide a materialism which was both monistic and historical in locating the common foundation of social and political institutions, that which determined their substantive content and the forms of their interaction, in the development of the *means of production* which mediate the relation of humanity to nature, and provide a materialist explanation for the development of human society by determining the social relations within which production must take place.

Plekhanov is unequivocal in seeing the progressive and autonomous development of the productive forces as playing the determining role in historical development.[18] The foundation of Plekhanov's historical materialism is not the 'economic' relations of society, since

> the economy of society and its psychology represent two sides of one and the same phenomenon of the 'production of life' of men, their struggle for existence, in which they are grouped in a particular way thanks to the particular state of the productive forces. The struggle for existence creates their economy, and on the same basis arises their psychology as well. Economy itself is something derivative, just like psychology ... [O]nly in a popular speech could one talk about economy as the prime cause of all

---

[14] Plekhanov 1956, p. 137.
[15] Plekhanov 1929, p. 7.
[16] Plekhanov 1929, p. 11–12.
[17] Quoted in Plekhanov 1929, p. 13.
[18] Cf. Plekhanov 1956, pp. 156–7, p. 187, p. 188, p. 197, p. 198, p. 229.

social phenomena. Far from being a prime cause, it is itself a consequence, a 'function' of the productive forces.[19]

For Plekhanov the inadequacy of Feuerbach's materialism lay in its failure to find any principle of historical change in the material world. Marx's great advance was to introduce an historical principle into nature, locating that principle in the development of the forces of production. Thus Marx's materialism was not qualitatively distinct from that of Feuerbach, or from previously existing forms of bourgeois materialism; it merely completed and perfected the philosophy of materialism.

Plekhanov claims that his critique of bourgeois philosophy is that of Marx and Engels. However, he does not develop his critique by reference to the works of Marx and Engels. In part he can be excused such a neglect, since, of course, many of the early works of Marx, in which he developed that critique, were not available to Feuerbach. Nevertheless, although Marx's critique of bourgeois philosophy is largely contained in those unpublished early works, he devoted his life's work to developing the critique of the most developed and sophisticated exposition of bourgeois materialism, classical political economy, and Plekhanov almost completely ignores the significance of this critique for his characterisation of Marxist philosophy. Had he done so, he could not have avoided recognising that his critique of Hegelian idealism and of French materialism is not that of Marx, but that of the classical political economy of Smith and Ricardo and the philosophy of Feuerbach. Plekhanov remained clear throughout his life that Marx merely developed Feuerbach's materialism to its conclusions. In *In Defence of Materialism* Plekhanov argued clearly that

> none of the fundamental ideas of Feuerbach's philosophy are refuted. Marx is content to amend them, and to demand that these ideas should be applied more consistently than they were applied by Feuerbach ... [T]he materialist views of Marx and Engels have been elaborated in the direction indicated by the inner logic of Feuerbach's philosophy.[20]

In *Materialism and Empiro-Criticism* Lenin went even further than Plekhanov in reducing Marxism to a vulgar materialism, a literal inversion of Hegelian idealism, and a simplistic identification with Feuerbachian materialism. Lenin condemned Plekhanov as an inconsistent materialist, because Plekhanov believed that ideas were symbols or 'hieroglyphs' of reality, rather than literal 'copies of real things'.[21] Thus Lenin notes, following Plekhanov, that Engels criticised hitherto existing materialism for its mechanical (ie. its attempted

---

[19] Plekhanov 1956, p. 207. Plekhanov also falls back into a geographical determinism, for which his Soviet editors administer a stern rebuke. Plekhanov 1956, pp. 161–3, pp. 270–1.
[20] Plekhanov 1956, pp. 21–2.
[21] Lenin a, p. 238.

reduction of chemistry and organic nature to the principles of mechanics) and undialectical character (ie. its failure to grasp the relation between absolute and relative truth),[22] and its residual idealism in the realm of social sciences. Lenin is emphatic: *'Exclusively* for these three things and *exclusively* within these limits, does Engels refute both the materialism of the eighteenth century and the doctrines of Büchner and Co.! On all other, more elementary, questions of materialism ... *there is and can be no difference* between Marx and Engels on the one hand and all these old materialists on the other'.[23]

That Plekhanov's misinterpretation cannot be attributed to his ignorance of much of Marx's early work is shown clearly by the critique of David Ryazanov, who was clear on the limitations of Feuerbach's argument in his Preface to *In Defence of Materialism*, where he denies Plekhanov's assertion that Feuerbach provides the philosophical basis of Marxism. Plekhanov claims that Feuerbach's thesis that 'thought is conditioned by being, not being by thought. Being is conditioned by itself, has its basis in itself' is the 'view of the relations between being and thought which was adopted by Marx and Engels and was by them made the foundation of their materialist conception of history. It was the most important outcome of the criticism of Hegelian idealism which, in its broad lines, had been made by Feuerbach himself'.[24] However, Ryazanov qualifies this assertion, noting that

> Marx radically modified and supplemented Feuerbach's thesis, which is as abstract, as little historical, as the "Man" Feuerbach put in the place of "God" or of "Reason"' and then, quoting Marx's sixth thesis on Feuerbach, concludes that 'the basic error of all philosophical systems endeavouring to explain the relations between thought and being, is that, like Feuerbach, they have ignored the fact that 'the abstract individual analysed by them really belongs to a specific form of society'.[25]

It is not surprising that Ryazanov was disposed of by Stalin.

Against the common interpretation of Marx as a 'materialist', it is essential to be clear that Marx did not oppose materialism to idealism. In the *German Ideology* and elsewhere, Marx characterised his starting point as 'materialist', but the term referred not to a philosophical materialism, but to the premise of 'real individuals, their activity and the

---

[22] The Machians believe that because truths are relative there can be no absolute truth independent of mankind. They do not understand that 'absolute truth results from the sum-total of relative truths in the course of their development; that relative truths represent relatively faithful reflections of an object existing independently of man; that these reflections become more and more faithful; that every truth, notwithstanding its relative nature, contains an element of absolute truth' – a purely Hegelian and idealist conception of science. Lenin a, p. 247.
[23] Lenin a, p. 247.
[24] Plekhanov 1956, p. 7.
[25] Ryazanov in Plekhanov 1956, p. xiii.

material conditions under which they live' which can 'be verified in a purely empirical way',[26] a perspective which Marx identified as that of the *'practical* materialist, i.e., the *communist'*.[27] Engels typically characterised Marx's work as 'materialist', but in the sense of assimilating it to the movement of modern science, which 'no longer needs any philosophy standing above the other sciences',[28] the task of philosophy being only to formalise the 'materialist dialectic', which Engels saw as the characteristic method of modern science. Marx believed that the opposition between materialism and idealism was a false one, since 'matter' is no less idealist a concept than is the 'idea', so that *'abstract materialism* is the *abstract spiritualism* of matter'.

Marx sought to overcome this false opposition by focusing on *society* as the mediating term between the 'material' and the 'ideal', but society understood not as yet another abstraction, but as the everyday practical activity of real human beings. It is the divorce of individual from society which underlies the false antitheses of the Enlightenment, in eliminating the mediating term between humanity and nature, between the ideal and the material, between subject and object. Thus, in his early works, Marx criticised materialism and idealism alike from the standpoint of *'sensuous human activity, practice* ... "practical-critical activity"',[29] 'human society or social humanity',[30] characterising his own position not as a materialism but variously as a humanistic naturalism, or a naturalistic or real humanism: 'Consistent naturalism or humanism is distinct from both idealism and materialism, and constitutes at the same time the unifying truth of both'.[31] Similarly, Marx rejected the equally false antithesis between humanity and nature: *'Society* is the complete unity of man with nature ... the accomplished naturalism of man and the accomplished humanism of nature',[32] a formulation which should not be interpreted as proposing a 'sociologistic' solution to a philosophical problem, but of transforming the problem from a philosophical to a socio-historical one. Marx declared not the triumph of materialism over idealism, but the triumph of social science over philosophy.

Marx's early critique was directed at both Adam Smith and Hegel, but he certainly did not support the 'materialist' Smith against the 'idealist' Hegel. Marx's position was that the two theories were equally idealist in resting on the categorical oppositions of matter and idea, individual and society, humanity and nature – oppositions which Marx argued were empty abstractions, empty because they are concepts which do not correspond to any determinate existence, and so can have no determinate effects. But this is not only a critique of Smith and of

---

[26] Marx and Engels 1964, p. 31.
[27] Marx and Engels 1964, p. 56.
[28] Engels 1962a, pp. 39–40.
[29] Marx 1975b, pp. 421–2.
[30] Marx 1975b, p. 423.
[31] Marx 1844, p. 336.
[32] Marx 1844, p. 298.

Hegel, for these conceptual oppositions are constitutive of bourgeois thought in general, as that has come down from the Enlightenment.

For Marx, the weakness of bourgeois materialism was that it sought to explain social relations by referring them back to a material foundation, which was seen naturalistically, defined by the physical conditions of production. This led it to naturalise what were in reality historically specific social relations, constituted on a particular *social* foundation. Thus Marx, and later Engels, criticised the earlier materialism for its lack of a systematic and historical perspective, in having a naturalistic view of the world which could not embrace history. To this extent Plekhanov's characterisation of Marx's critique of Feuerbach's materialism is correct. But Marx attributed Feuerbach's errors not to his being insufficiently materialist, in locating history outside nature, but for being *too* materialist, in reducing history to the history of nature. Certainly Marx criticised Feuerbach's static view of nature, but Feuerbach's was not the last word in bourgeois materialism. While Feuerbach's materialism was restricted in having an unchanging view of human nature, that of classical political economy was not so limited.

It is very significant that in Plekhanov's extensive discussions of the history of materialism he completely ignores the role of classical political economy, and the historical materialism of the Scottish Enlightenment, for the latter proposed a philosophy of history which corresponds exactly to Plekhanov's characterisation of Marx's philosophical revolution. Against the various forms of racial, demographic and climatic determinism proposed by continental materialism, the Scottish Enlightenment offered a philosophy of history which explained the development of manners, morals and constitutions precisely in terms of the stages of development of the 'mode of subsistence' – although the latter was not so crudely reduced to the means of production, nor to geographical conditions, as it was by Plekhanov – thus offering precisely the 'historical' materialism which Plekhanov characterises as that of Marx. Marx, in his tenth thesis on Feuerbach, addressed the limits of this form of materialism in noting that 'the standpoint of the old materialism is civil society; the standpoint of the new is human society, or social humanity'. The error of hitherto existing materialism for Marx was *not* identified with its adoption of the standpoint of human nature, but of the abstraction of the human individual from 'the ensemble of social relations' (sixth thesis), which is the historical characteristic of bourgeois society. Marx's standpoint is not that of the act of material production, it is that of 'human society, or social humanity'. Thus Marx did not defend the materialism of political economy against the idealism of Hegel, but criticised both as equally idealist theories of history.

Similarly, the philosophers of the Scottish Enlightenment had precisely the Hegelian view of the relation between freedom and necessity which Plekhanov characterises as that of Marx, which is why they turned to the study of political economy, as the science which could reveal the laws of development of society. Against the romantic idealism of the French *philosophes*, the political economists believed that the only basis of social reform was the knowledge of the material foundations of history provided by their new science. However 'science' for Marx provides no solution to the dualisms of bourgeois materialism for, as he remarked in his third thesis on Feuerbach,

> [t]he materialist doctrine concerning the changing of circumstances and upbringing forgets that circumstances are changed by men and that it is essential to educate the educator himself. This doctrine must, therefore, divide society into two parts, one of which is superior to society.[33]

For Marx knowledge is undoubtedly a weapon in the revolution, but it is not knowledge which makes the revolution, but the proletariat, and knowledge only constitutes a revolutionary weapon when it is embodied in the proletarian movement. The philosophical roots of Bolshevik politics can be traced directly back to Plekhanov's fundamental misunderstanding of the significance of Marx's critique of political economy.

In Hegel's work, bourgeois reason finds its summation and its most systematic expression. The great merit of Hegel, according to Marx, was that he pushed bourgeois reason to its limits, so that its speculative foundations stand out starkly in the contradiction between the universal and the particular, which Hegel could only resolve speculatively in the dialectical development of Reason. In exactly the same way, Smith, and later Ricardo, recognised the real contradictions between universal human needs and aspirations and the particular social relations of the capitalist system of production, but again resolved these contradictions speculatively, in the dialectical development of Nature. Whether the supra-human force which makes history is called Reason or Nature is neither here nor there. Thus, Marx's critique of Hegelian idealism can be translated immediately into a critique of the idealism of political economy – however 'materialist' political economy might appear at first sight – because it is a critique of their common ideological foundations. Marx no more 'continued the work' of political economy, than he completed that of Feuerbach.[34] The ideological foundations of Hegelian philosophy and political economy lie in their attempt to present bourgeois social relations as the culmination of the history of the synthesis of Reason and Nature, and it is precisely this that characterises them as bourgeois. Consequently, Marx's critique of Hegel is a critique of the ideological foundations of all forms of bourgeois social thought, both idealist and materialist.

Marx could apply the method developed in the critique of Hegel's abstract spiritualism to the critique of political economy because the

---

[33] Marx 1975b, p. 422.
[34] Lenin b.

theories were two sides of the same coin. Like Hegel, political economy is content to describe the alienated forms of social existence, attributing their social character not to their human origins but to an alien power: on the one hand, the Idea, on the other, Nature.

Excursus: Marx, Engels and the inversion of Hegel

The principal authority for Lenin and Plekhanov's characterisation of Marxism as a philosophical materialism is the famous passage in the Afterword to the Second German Edition of *Capital*, in which Marx wrote: 'My dialectical method is not only different from the Hegelian, but is its direct opposite ... With me ... the ideal is but the material transposed and translated in man's head'. With Hegel the dialectic 'is standing on its head. It must be turned right side up again, if you would discover the rational kernel within the mystical shell'.[35]

The orthodox interpretation of this passage regards the inversion as *philosophical*, Marx setting the dialectical method on a rational foundation by replacing Hegel's idealist monism with a symmetrical materialist monism. Thus Plekhanov argued that

> Materialism is the direct opposite of *idealism*. Idealism strives to explain all the phenomena of Nature, all the qualities of matter, by these or those qualities of the *spirit*. Materialism acts in the exactly opposite way. It tries to explain psychic phenomena by these or those qualities of *matter*, by this or that organisation of the human, or, in more general terms, of the animal *body*.[36]

Thus Hegel's dialectical method is valid, once it is appreciated that the dialectical laws are not laws of thought but laws of matter. For Lenin, Hegel's 'transition of the logical idea to *nature*' at the end of the *Logic* 'brings one within a hand's grasp of materialism'. Indeed

> the whole chapter on the 'Absolute Idea' ... contains almost nothing that is specifically *idealism*, but has for its main subject the *dialectical method*. The sum-total, the last word and essence of Hegel's logic is the *dialectical method* – this is extremely noteworthy. And one thing more: in this *most idealistic* of Hegel's works there is the *least* idealism and the *most materialism*.[37]

Against this interpretation, it should be noted that Marx defined his inversion not as an inversion of Hegel's *ontology*, but precisely of his *method*, which the orthodox interpretation regards as being untouched by Marx's critique. As noted above, Marx did not characterise his

---

[35] Marx 1976, p. 103
[36] Plekhanov 1940, pp. 13–14.
[37] Lenin 1961, p. 234.

philosophy as a 'materialism', but as a 'humanistic naturalism' or a 'naturalistic humanism'. When he used the term 'materialism' positively, he used it as a synonym for 'science'. Marx's extensive discussion of his method, in contrast to that of Hegel, in the 1857 Introduction to the *Grundrisse*, contrasts the laborious development of scientific knowledge with the re-presentation of such knowledge by speculative philosophy. Thus Marx's dialectical method is the method of scientific labour, while that of Hegel is the method of speculative philosophy. Marx's inversion of the Hegelian dialectic is not a matter of a *philosophical* inversion which replaces a monistic idealism with a monistic materialism, but of inverting the idealist relation between science and philosophy.

Where does Engels stand between Marx and Plekhanov? The answer, appropriately enough, is somewhere in the middle. In *Ludwig Feuerbach* Engels referred to the Hegelian system as 'a materialism idealistically turned upside down in *method and content*'.[38]

Engels espoused, as Marx arguably did not, a philosophical materialism. Thus he argues that 'it is self-evident that the products of the human brain, being in the last analysis also products of nature, do not contradict the rest of nature's interconnections but are in correspondence with them',[39] and he characterises dialectics – 'the science of the general laws of motion and development of nature, human society and thought'[40] – as 'nothing more than the mere reflection' of the flux of reality 'in the thinking brain'.[41] These arguments come directly from Feuerbach, who believed that he had overcome the dichotomy of thought and matter, not by reducing thought to matter, but by integrating the two, thought being not an effect of matter but one of its properties. As a natural being, I am not a subject contemplating an object, but a part of the object reflecting on itself, so there can be no contradiction between thought and being. However, Engels was dismissive of Feuerbach's materialism, which he regarded as being as metaphysical as Hegel's idealism in resting on abstract concepts of 'Man' and 'Nature', rather than on the real historical relations between men and nature. For Engels the 'nature' on which his materialism rests is not a philosophical category but a scientific one, different forms of materialism corresponding to different conceptions of nature emerging from science. Historical materialism is made possible by the development of a new conception of nature, which sees the world as constructed not of things mechanically related to one another, but as processes in change. Thus his Feuerbachian argument is not used as a metaphysical prop, but turns into his pragmatic epistemology, for which the relation between thought and being is an historical and practical relationship of 'experiment and industry'. But this argument is not used by Engels, as it came to be used by 'dialectical

---

[38] Engels 1962b, p. 372. My emphasis.
[39] Engels 1962a, p. 55.
[40] Engels 1962a, p. 194.
[41] Engels 1962b, p. 363. And many more such formulae are to be found, particularly in *The Dialectics of Nature*.

materialism', as an ontological guarantee of the truth of the laws of the materialist dialectic.

Engels's use of the word 'reflection' does not imply either the reflectionist theory of knowledge or the correspondence theory of truth which Lenin attributed to him. Engels repeatedly stresses that 'human history ... cannot find its intellectual final term in the discovery of any so-called absolute truth',[42] and insists on the hypothetical and limited character of all knowledge, a principle which he applies to his and Marx's work.[43] In contrast to Lenin's argument against the neo-Kantians that such relative truths constitute successive approximations to an absolute truth, marked by the correspondence of the connections established in 'thought' with those existing in 'matter', Engels has a pragmatic view of truth, dismissing the scepticism of Hume and Kant as a product of the chimerical pursuit of 'absolute truth', which has no significance once it is recognised that one can only pursue 'attainable relative truths along the path of the positive sciences', whose methods of 'experiment and industry' make the 'thing-in-itself' into a 'thing-for-us'.[44] Engels's dismissal of Kant may be naïve, but far from serving as an irrationalist critique of science, his materialism serves as a defence of science against philosophy, to support his pragmatism against a Kantian epistemological dualism which sees 'consciousness' as 'something given, something opposed from the outset to being, to nature',[45] establishing a gap between thought and reality which can only be bridged by metaphysics, whether metaphysical materialism or speculative idealism.[46]

Although Engels regards Marx's inversion of Hegel as both philosophical and methodological, it is the latter aspect which he constantly stresses, and to which he subordinates Marx's supposed philosophical revolution. He describes Marx's theoretical innovation as a scientific revolution, in contrast to that of Feuerbach, which remained firmly within the antinomies of philosophy. In Marx's case

> the separation from Hegelian philosophy was here also the result of a return to the materialist standpoint. That means it was resolved to comprehend the real world — nature and history — just as it presents itself to everyone who approaches it free from preconceived idealist crochets. It was decided mercilessly to sacrifice every idealist crochet which could not be brought into harmony with the facts conceived in their

---

[42] Engels 1962a, p. 38.
[43] Cf. Engels 1962a, p. 57, p. 83, p. 92, p. 125, p. 129, pp. 207–9; Engels 1962b, pp. 362–3, pp. 377–8.
[44] Engels 1962b, p. 363, p. 371.
[45] Engels 1962a, p. 55.
[46] Engels's *Dialectics of Nature* may be equally naïve but it does not set out to revolutionise the natural sciences by applying the laws of the dialectic, but rather to assimilate Marxism to modern science by demonstrating the universality of those laws through a comprehensive survey of the achieved results of the modern natural sciences. Engels claims no scientific advances, but merely wraps scientific findings in the bizarre rhetoric of the dialectic.

own and not in a fantastic interconnection. And materialism
means nothing more than this.[47]

Thus Engels follows Marx in seeing the inversion of the Hegelian
dialectic as an inversion of the relation between science and philosophy,
which becomes possible when science incorporates the principle of the
dialectic as its own method.

Modern materialism is essentially dialectic, and no longer needs any
philosophy standing above the other sciences. As soon as each special
science is bound to make clear its position in the great totality of things
and of our knowledge of things, a special science dealing with this
totality is superfluous. That which still survives, independently, of all
earlier philosophy is the science of thought and its laws – formal logic
and dialectics. Everything else is subsumed in the positive science of
nature and history.

Consequently the materialist dialectic does not *invert* the idealist
relationship between reason and nature, it overcomes that opposition as
science becomes aware in its own practice of the dialectical principles of
flux and interconnectedness. The dialectical method does not define an
irrationalist critique of science, but confirms a scientistic positivism.

A materialist conception of history?

Plekhanov's resurrection of bourgeois materialism as the principle of
Marxism faces the same dilemma that he identified at the heart of
hitherto existing materialism. If the development of the manners, morals
and constitution of society are determined by the development of the
forces of production, how are we to explain the active role of human
agency in historical development? It would seem that a monistic
materialism has once again condemned us to the populist oscillation
between fatalism and voluntarism.

Plekhanov sought to overcome this dilemma by drawing, as we have
seen, on the Hegelian analysis of the relation between freedom and
necessity, to argue that *knowledge* gives us the freedom to overcome
necessity. However, this does not offer a solution. If knowledge is a
mere knowledge of necessity, it remains purely contemplative and
retrospective. But if knowledge is to be the means of changing the
direction of history, then we have returned to the dualism with which
Plekhanov charges bourgeois materialism, and the question arises once
more of the demarcation of the realms of freedom and necessity.
Plekhanov answers this question by distinguishing between the *direction*
and the *pace* of historical development, and between the *content* and the
form of legal, political and ideological superstructures. The direction of
historical development is determined by necessity, but its pace is subject
to human intervention. The content of superstructures is ultimately

---

[47] Engels 1962b, p. 608.

determined by the needs of production, mediated by class interests, but the same content may be expressed in a variety of forms.

While the development of the forces of production unequivocally determines the *direction* of historical development, the *pace* of development of the productive forces is by no means independent of the form of the social relations of production. Thus, for example, 'slave labour is not very favourable to the development of the productive forces; in conditions of slavery it advances extremely slowly, but still it does advance',[48] while, under capitalism, the forces of production develop at an historically unprecedented rate.

The legal and political superstructure can also play a part in determining the pace, but not the direction, of historical development. The law and the constitution are determined functionally by the needs of society, which are in turn determined by the '*modes of production and on those mutual relations between people which are created by those modes*'.[49] Particular legal and constitutional systems express particular ideas, but ideas emerge on the basis of needs, and those ideas which prevail are those which meet society's needs. 'In reality, only that is "ideal" which is useful to men, and every society in working out its *ideals* is guided only by its needs. The seeming exceptions to this incontestably general rule are explained by the fact that, *in consequence of the development of society*, its *ideals* frequently lag behind its *new needs*'.[50] It is this lag which enables the law and politics to have an impact on the pace of social development, if not on its direction.

> Political institutions influence economic life. They *either facilitate* its development *or impede* it. The first case is in no way surprising from the point of view of Marx, because the given political system has been created for the very purpose of *promoting the further development of the productive forces* (whether it is consciously or unconsciously created is in this case all one to us). The second case does not in any way contradict Marx's point of view, because historical experience shows that once a given political system ceases to correspond to the state of the productive forces, once it is transformed into an obstacle to their further development, it begins to decline and finally is eliminated.[51]

The social needs which give rise to particular legal, political and ideological superstructures are expressed in particular, and conflicting, class interests. The productive forces determine the economic relations of society. 'These relations naturally give rise to definite interests, which are expressed in *law*', and which give rise to '*state* organisation, the

---

[48] Plekhanov 1956, pp. 165–6.
[49] Plekhanov 1956, p. 187.
[50] Plekhanov 1956, p. 188. In the same way 'the psychology of society is always expedient in relation to its economy, always corresponds to it, is always determined by it'. Plekhanov 1956, p. 206.
[51] Plekhanov 1956, p. 203; cf. p. 272.

purpose of which is to protect the dominant interests'.[52] The pace of historical development is therefore determined by the outcome of the class struggle which expresses the balance of class forces: 'the further development of every given society always depends on the relationships of social forces within it'.[53] It is therefore only the concrete study of the relations of social forces which 'can show what is "inevitable" and what is not "inevitable" for the given society'.[54] Thus, for example, the inevitability of capitalism in Russia was dictated 'not because there exists some external force, some mysterious law pushing it along that path, but because there is no effective internal force capable of pushing it from that path'.[55]

The struggle over the forms of law and the constitution does not appear immediately as a struggle between conflicting class forces, but as a struggle between different ideas, which express conflicting class interests. The *content* of these interests is determined by economic relations, but the economic relations do not determine the ideological *forms* in which those interests are expressed. Thus 'the state of social consciousness ... does determine *the form which the reflection of the given interest takes in the mind of man*'.[56]

The relation of ideas to social needs and to class interests is not a simple one. The world of ideas is an autonomous world, subject to its own laws, so that ideas are not the direct expression of class interests. Intellectuals cannot be reduced to the sycophantic spokespeople of particular interests, but their ideas are nevertheless circumscribed by their historical environment, including their particular intellectual milieu, which in turn is related to those of previous epochs, of other countries and of other classes with which they interact. Through these complex interdependencies 'ideas, feelings and beliefs are co-ordinated according to their own particular laws' corresponding to the intellectual forms in which they appear. But, at the same time, 'these laws are brought into play by external circumstances which have nothing in common with these laws'.[57]

The relationship between interests and ideas is not, therefore, a genetic relationship, but is rather one of a Spinozist correspondence between the material world of interests and the intellectual world of ideas. This conception obviously corresponds very closely to the reality of Russian political and ideological conflicts, which were fought out amongst intellectuals who had very limited contact with any organised class forces, so that the dividing lines of political conflict were drawn

---

[52] Plekhanov 1940, p. 23.
[53] Plekhanov 1956, p. 298.
[54] Plekhanov 1956, p. 298.
[55] Plekhanov 1956, p. 302. This account of history is, once again, indistinguishable from that of Adam Smith and the Scottish Enlightenment, whose development of a theory of class, on the basis of the new science of political economy, was designed precisely to identify the contending class interests which determined the course of history.
[56] Plekhanov 1940, p. 40.
[57] Plekhanov 1956, p. 236.

not so much in terms of the social forces in struggle, as in terms of the interests which particular ideas supposedly *represented*.[58]

It should not be surprising to find that Plekhanov ultimately overcomes this Spinozist dualism in classically Hegelian terms. Ideas obey their own laws, but, at the same time, are subject to the laws of material necessity, and the laws of material necessity determine that humanity will transcend the rule of necessity to realise its freedom. '[W]ith the development of the productive forces the mutual relations of men in the social process of production become more complex, the course of that process completely slips from under their control, the producer proves to be the slave of his own creation (as an example the capitalist anarchy of production)'. But,

> the relations of production, social relations, by the very logic of their development bring man to realisation of the causes of his enslavement by economic necessity. This provides the opportunity for a new and final triumph of consciousness over necessity, of reason over blind law.
>
> Having realised that the cause of his enslavement by his own creation lies in the anarchy of production, the producer ('social man') organises that production and thereby subjects it to his will. Then terminates the kingdom of necessity and there begins the reign of freedom, which itself proves to be necessity.[59]

The coming revolution is a matter not so much of the realisation of the material interests of the working class or the liberation of the working class from capitalist exploitation, as of the realisation of human reason. The working class appears as the agent of this realisation:

> Modern dialectical materialism strives for the elimination of classes. It appeared, in fact, when that elimination became an historical necessity. Therefore it turns to the producers, who are to become the heroes of the historical period lying immediately ahead. Therefore, for the first time since our world has existed and the earth has been revolving around the sun, there is taking place the coming together of science and workers: science hastens to the aid of the toiling mass, and the toiling mass relies on the conclusions of science in its conscious movement.[60]

---

[58] This dislocation appeared most starkly in Lenin's critique of economism in *What Is To Be Done?*, which reached the bizarre conclusion that proletarian consciousness is bourgeois, while that of the radical bourgeois intelligentsia is proletarian. Plekhanov, retaining some link between interests, ideas, and the social forces they represent, looked to an *alliance* between the radical bourgeoisie and the proletariat, which was the point at which Lenin broke with him politically. There can be no doubt that in this division it was Plekhanov who remained closer to Marxism, while Lenin reverted to populism, as indicated by the very title of his text, assimilating Marx to Chernyshevsky.
[59] Plekhanov 1956, pp. 273–4.
[60] Plekhanov 1956, p. 279.

Plekhanov offers an extremely powerful critique of voluntarism, but he certainly does not offer a Marxist critique. His standpoint is not the *'human sensuous activity*, practice ... practical-critical activity ... human society or socialised humanity'[61] which Marx took as his starting point, but an anonymous 'dialectic' which is no less idealist for being attributed to natural geographical, technological, biological and psychological processes.

Plekhanov's philosophy makes no sense at all as an interpretation of Marx. But it makes a great deal of sense as a critique of the first generation of populists, who proved unable to connect their revolutionary ambitions to the material base of the aspirations of the peasantry, and so tempered their philosophical materialism with a voluntaristic romanticism, and it is from this that Plekhanov's work derived its power and its influence in Russia. But it is a critique from within populism, the contrast between materialism and idealism corresponding to the emerging division within the populist movement, and not a critique from the position of Marxism, which would have led Plekhanov to oppose both the 'materialist' and the 'idealist' wings of the populist movement, on the basis of the aspirations of the emerging working class movement. However, such a critique was obviously impossible in Russia in the late 19th century, just as it had been impossible in Germany in the early 19th century, for such a movement did not yet exist. In Russia socialism remained the preserve of the intelligentsia, and so remained in the realm of ideas. Whereas German Social Democrats could look for the necessity of the revolution to the concrete historical development of the working class movement, as anticipated by Marx and Engels in the *Communist Manifesto*, in Russia the necessity of revolution could only be defined philosophically, through the principles of 'dialectical materialism' and the mystical laws of 'the transformation of quantity into quality' and the 'negation of the negation'.

Lenin's populist interpretation of Marxism

The dilemma faced by Russian Marxists was that their revolutionary ideas ran far ahead of the degree of development of the workers movement. This inevitably gave the intelligentsia a leading role in the revolutionary movement, a role which Plekhanov's 'dialectical materialism' served to justify philosophically. It was the intellectuals who could transmit the lessons learnt in the more advanced countries, and embodied in the scientific laws of historical materialism, to the Russian proletariat. These laws enabled revolutionary intellectuals to grasp scientifically the connection between the interests of the working class and the ideals of socialism, even where this connection was not yet

---

[61] Marx 1975b, p. 421–3.

apparent to the workers themselves. However this brings us back to the political dilemma of populism. What is the political imperative of a revolutionary movement in which the mass of the population has not yet become aware of the ideas which express their objective interests? Will revolutionary ideas inevitably emerge from the agitation of the working class as the workers come to self-consciousness through struggle, as Bakunin had believed, and as was argued by the 'economists' and 'ultra-leftists' against whom Lenin fought so vigorously? Or should revolutionary ideas be disseminated by a patient process of propaganda, education and evangelising, as the 'subjective sociologists' had believed, and as the 'Legal Marxists' came to argue? Or should the revolution be taken in hand by a small group of dedicated revolutionaries, armed with a vision of a just society, as Chernyshevsky had argued, and as the terroristic wing of populism, from which Lenin emerged, believed?

The orthodox Marxist answer to this question was a combination of the first and second answers: social democracy developed the class-conscious workers' movement through agitation, organisation and education. In the case of Russia, this would necessarily be a long-drawn out historical process, for the working class remained a small minority of the population. The latter also implied that the working class would have to look elsewhere for allies in its struggle, for without allies it would be crushed by the autocratic state. The peasantry could not provide such an ally, for it was a doomed class which sought to resist the development of capitalism. Instead, the social-democratic movement had to look abroad, to the international workers movement and the prospect of a world revolution, and had to forge a tactical alliance with the liberal bourgeoisie, with which it shared an interest in democratic reform against the tyrannical rule of the autocracy. Although Plekhanov legitimated the role of the intelligentsia in the revolutionary movement in terms of a philosophy of history which had nothing in common with Marxism, politically he remained attached to Marxist orthodoxy in assigning the leading role in the revolution to the organised working class movement.

Nevertheless, Plekhanov's philosophy of history could be given an altogether different interpretation. If the intelligentsia has a privileged access to the scientific understanding of reality, and if the role of ideas in history is to accelerate the necessary development of the historical process, why should the intelligentsia wait on the historical development of the working-class movement? Should not the revolutionary intelligentsia itself play the leading role in history, seizing power by whatever means might be necessary, looking to whatever social classes and strata might be mobilised in its support, and taking whatever measures might be necessary to pursue its historic role? This was precisely the logic which drove the first generation of radical populists into terrorism, and it was the logic which led Lenin to transform Plekhanov's 'dialectical and historical materialism' into the ideology of Bolshevism. The privileged status of the intelligentsia, which was established by Plekhanov's philosophy, is realised in the Leninist conception of the party, which represents the working class not because it is the political form through which the mass of the working class represents its interests, but because it is the institutional form in which the revolutionary ideology is mobilised as an historical force. Lenin could justly criticise Plekhanov for not following the logic of his own philosophy through to its political conclusions. This was why Lenin could vigorously criticise Plekhanov politically, while remaining slavishly faithful to Plekhanov's philosophy. But Lenin's transformation of Plekhanov's political theory was not in the direction of Marxism, but rather assimilated Plekhanov's Marxism back into the populist traditions from which Lenin had emerged. While Plekhanov used the populist philosophy to bridge the gap from populist to Marxist politics, Lenin used it to reverse the movement, and to put the revolution back on the Russian agenda.

The populist roots of Lenin's political thought are obvious and well-known. Revolutionary populism had four distinctive features which Lenin brought into the centre of his Marxism and which formed the core of 'Marxism-Leninism'.

First, it stressed the active role of revolutionary ideas in determining the course of history, and so gave the intellectuals a prominent political role. This was the element which was developed by Plekhanov and adopted from him by Lenin. The orthodox Marxism of the Second International certainly did not underestimate the role of ideas in historical development, but revolutionary ideas emerged out of the revolutionary movement, however much intellectuals might play a role in their formulation. Although Kautsky's theory gave the intellectuals a special position in the struggle for socialism, it did not give them any special authority. For Lenin, the spontaneous struggle of the working class is inevitably a sectional struggle for economic aims. It is only the scientific theory of Marxism which can reveal the wider class perspective which is necessary to advance beyond trades union demands to a political struggle. This perspective is provided by the intellectuals, and institutionalised in the party, which expresses the political interests of the class as a whole against the sectional interests of its component parts. For Kautsky, by contrast, there is no such divorce of economic from political struggles and the revolution depends not on the leading role of the vanguard party, representing the class as a whole, but on the *fusion* of socialist ideas with working class struggle. 'The socialist movement is nothing more than the part of this militant proletariat which has become conscious of its goal'.[62] With the integration of socialism and the labour movement the socialist party is able to transcend the limits of any sectional representation, and to express the aspirations of all the non-capitalist classes and strata, so that the 'ways

---

[62] Kautsky 1910, p. 183

of feeling' of the proletariat 'are becoming standard for the whole mass of non-capitalists, no matter what their status may be'.[63]

Second, populism stressed the power of the revolutionary will, expressed through a disciplined organisation of dedicated revolutionaries, in realising the revolutionary ideal. This was the idea which Lenin took from his revolutionary mentor, Chernyshevsky, but one which had been rejected by orthodox Marxists, who stressed the mass democratic character of the proletarian movement.

Third, it was marked by a radical rejection of the state, and opposition to any involvement in constitutional politics, on the grounds that the state was essentially the agent of capitalist development, while the basis of the new society lay outside the state, in the commune and in co-operative production. It accordingly had an insurrectionary view of the revolution, the task of which was to destroy the economic and political forces of capitalism to set free the elements of socialism. This idea was also rejected by orthodox Marxists, who certainly did not believe that socialism could be achieved by electoral means, but who regarded the democratisation of the state and the achievement of civil liberties as a primary condition for the development of the workers' movement, and political agitation as a primary form of propaganda. Orthodox Marxists also rejected the populist belief that the material base of socialism lay in the commune and co-operative production, believing instead that it was necessary to take control of the state in order to nationalise the means of production, to provide the material base of socialism. Lenin's revolutionary party, by contrast, provided a means of organising which did not require democracy or civil liberties, while his conception of the leading role of the party dispensed with the need to develop the self-consciousness of the working class. On the question of the material base of socialism Lenin was more ambivalent. He rejected the populist faith in the commune, and the revisionist faith in co-operative production, but before the revolution he wavered between a commitment to the soviet as providing the material and political base of the new society, with the state serving only a transitional role as the instrument of the 'dictatorship of the proletariat', and an orthodox belief in the state as providing a more permanent basis of the new society. In the event, he combined the worst of both viewpoints, soon institutionalising a dictatorial state as the permanent basis of the new society.

Fourth, populism was most fundamentally characterised by its faith in the revolutionary role of the peasantry. This was the point at which orthodox Marxism broke most decisively with populism, on the grounds that the peasantry was a doomed class, which could therefore play only a reactionary role, and that its conditions of life were such that it could never unite as a self-conscious class force. For this reason Plekhanov and the Mensheviks looked to the liberal bourgeoisie for a political

---

[63] Kautsky 1910, p. 210

alliance against the autocratic state. On the other hand, in the most advanced capitalist countries, like Germany, the proletarianisation of the rural population meant that the latter could play a positive role in the revolutionary movement not as peasants, but as workers. Lenin, in *The Development of Capitalism in Russia*, proposed a critique of populism which paradoxically maintained the role attributed by the populists to the peasantry, in arguing that the extent of the capitalist development of Russian agriculture was such that the Russian peasantry was already well on the way to destruction. While this meant that it was no longer possible to look to the rural commune as the basis of socialism, it also meant that the rural population could still play a revolutionary role. Lenin's conception of revolutionary politics meant that it did not matter that the rural population was not organised as a part of the proletariat, and did not express proletarian or socialist aspirations, for the operative interests and aspirations of the peasantry were not those expressed by the peasants themselves, but those expressed on their behalf by the revolutionary party. Unfortunately for the peasantry, Lenin's characterisation of their condition was quite wrong. The mass of the Russian peasantry had not been proletarianised by 1917, any more than they had been in 1899, as Lenin had to recognise when he introduced the NEP; or than they were in 1929, when Stalin decided to take matters into his own hands and accelerate the necessary course of history by proletarianising the peasantry by force.

References

Engels, Frederick 1962a [1878], *Anti-Dühring*, Moscow: Foreign Languages Publishing House.

Engels, Frederick 1962b [1888], *Ludwig Feuerbach and the End of Classical German Philosophy* in *Selected Works* Volume II, Moscow: Foreign Languages Publishing House.

Kautsky, Karl 1910, *The Class Struggle*, Chicago: Charles H. Kerr and Company.

Lenin, V.I. a (n.d.) [1908], *Materialism and Empirio-Criticism*, Moscow: Progress Publishers.

Lenin, V.I. b (n.d.) [1913], *Three Sources and Three Component Parts of Marxism* in *Selected Works* Volume 1, Moscow: Foreign Languages Publishing House.

Lenin, V.I. 1961 [1914], *Philosophical Notebooks* in *Collected Works* Volume 38, Moscow: Progress Publishers.

Marx, Karl and Frederick Engels 1964 [1846], *The German Ideology*, Moscow: Progress Pulishers.

Marx, Karl 1975a [1844], 'Economic and Philosophical Manuscripts' in *Marx and Engels Collected Works*, Volume 3, Moscow: Progress Publishers.

Marx, Karl 1975b [1845], 'Theses on Feuerbach' in *Marx: Early Writings* edited by Lucio Colletti, London: Pelican.

Marx, Karl 1976 [1873], 'Afterword to the Second German Edition of *Capital*' in *Capital* Volume 1, London: Penguin.

Plekhanov, Georgi 1929 [1908], *Fundamental Problems of Marxism*, London: Lawrence and Wishart.

Plekhanov, Georgi 1940 [1897], *The Materialist Conception of History*, New York: International Publishers.

Plekhanov, Georgi 1956 [1895], *The Development of the Monist View of History*, Moscow: Foreign Languages Publishing House.

So The Party's Over? Marxism and Political Strategy After 'the Fall'

Howard Chodos & Colin Hay

It hardly needs saying that the Left in the advanced capitalist economies is in a state of severe disarray. Inspired, or perhaps more accurately, dis-inspired, by the dull conflation of globalisation and welfare retrenchment that marks the neoliberal orthodoxy of the times, the former social-democratic Left has abandoned all socialist advocacy. It marches instead towards a 'Centre' that itself continues to drift rightwards. Meanwhile, at least in the industrially developed world, serious movements and parties to the left of social democracy have become harder and harder to find.

For example, in Britain (a country that in recent years has so often been the initiator of regressive tendencies), the Labour Party has been busily conjuring a Faustian pact with the neoliberal devil, intoxicated as it became with the mere whiff of governmental power. Setting out its stall for government in terms of its ability to manage the contradictions of the Thatcherite legacy better than the Tories themselves, New Labour restricted itself in opposition to that set of policies and strategic resources compatible with the dominant neoliberal economic paradigm that is at the heart of the problem. Thus far, its term in office has only served to confirm the full extent of the party's capitulation to neoliberalism and to the Thatcherite legacy.[1]

A quick glance around the globe suggests that similar scenarios are being played out by almost all social democratic parties. The degree of capitulation to the neoliberal tide no doubt varies from situation to situation, but it is hard to resist the conclusion that the 'golden epoch' of social democracy, in which its aim was to (re-)construct the welfare state in its own image, has been swept away by the juggernaut of jobless growth in an era of global competition.

The immediate prospects for more radical variants of the socialist tradition are, if anything, bleaker still. Whatever one's assessment of the former Soviet Union, it is clear that its collapse has further compressed the space necessary for the flourishing of alternatives of all kinds. The seeming inability of the radical Left to respond to the two great challenges it faces – that of producing a cogent analysis of the developments cascading through contemporary capitalism and of generating a transformative programme that incorporates a compelling balance sheet of its own past – can only continue to ensure its marginal

---

[1] For an attempt to gauge the full extent of this capitulation to neoliberalism see Hay 1998a. See also Panitch and Leys 1997 and Hay 1997.

status. And all this regardless of the extent of spontaneous resistance to the imposition of the neoliberal agenda by its victims across the globe.

As always, we must attempt to define our political tasks in terms of the monumental challenges that confront us. While the demise of former orthodoxies leaves us bereft of easy and immediate answers, it allows and entreats us to consider new alternatives. At the same time, novelty itself offers no guarantee against ephemerality. In this regard, we would simply note that much of the lustre has come off the 'new' social movements which had seemed to offer hope only a few years ago. Now they seem to be suffering from many of the same defects as the old social movements some thought they were destined to replace, arguably because they too are unable to articulate a broader politics of societal transformation.

In such a context it might at first appear bizarre, or at the very least groupuscularian, to want to inquire into the organisational conditions that are necessary to the radical transformation of capitalism, but this is what we propose to do. It seems to us that the question of the party is in many ways at the centre of our contemporary dilemmas. We need a party not only in order to participate in, and, in so doing, to reconstitute, the political process, but also to provide an indispensable context in which we can define who we are and what we stand for. Our programmatic ineptitude cannot be dissociated from our organisational deficiencies. We will argue that to postpone posing the question of the party until after we have clarified the basics of our political programme is both to consign its creation to political 'never-never-land' and also to deny ourselves the necessary tools actually to elaborate a transformative agenda.

Our argument proceeds in three parts. In the first section we outline a general theoretical framework for understanding organisational questions, while in the second we present a few critical comments on the two most important traditional models, Leninism and social democracy. This will allow us to sketch, by way of conclusion, an approach to organisational matters with features which, in our opinion, distinguish it from other significant theoretical positions.

Rethinking Marxist strategy, rethinking strategy

Put simply, our central contention in what is to follow is that there is a distinctively creative component to politics. This, in itself, is not a new idea, but we think that following it through in a certain fashion can help us interrogate the question of transformative agency in a genuinely original way. Political activity for us is one kind of collective agency, where agency simply refers to the ability of people to act intentionally, purposively. Two core principles are relevant here.

First, purposive activity always takes place in a social context. Any attempt to understand how social action – of which political activity is a subset – comes about must therefore take into account two key facts. Roy Bhaskar captures this in the idea that individuals and social structures constitute ontologically distinct but existentially intertwined entities.[2] This means that the way we act is driven by ineliminable causal factors which emanate from our makeup as individual, living, thinking, beings, and that these are never reducible without remainder to the circumstances in which we act. At the same time, there are also causal factors which are rooted in those circumstances, and these are independent of our will as individuals. This produces two dualities: a duality of structure; and a duality of agency.[3]

The duality of structure can be expressed as the idea that social structures only exist in and through (that is, they are reproduced or transformed by) the activity of living human beings. At the same time they simultaneously constitute a constraining and enabling environment for that activity. The complementary duality of agency points to the existence of an irreducible individual dimension to human action (captured roughly as our free will, or our capacity to act intentionally) but also notices that this individuality is always constituted in a definite and irremediably social context. *Contra* methodological individualism, then, there is no human action that does not contain both social and individual components. There is no social structure that is not both the product of human action while also being the context in which human action occurs. There is no individual outside of specific social contexts. Thus structure and agency, society and individual, each refer to distinct ontological realities. There are elements of each that can be analysed separately, and aspects of their respective dynamics and particularities which can be understood individually. But they always come into being simultaneously. In Bhaskar's terms, they are ontologically distinct but existentially intertwined.

Second, when considered from the point of view of the participants this points to the need to think in terms of strategic action. The notion of strategy or strategic action implies the orientation of an agent to a (structured) context. Such contexts are strategically selective in that they circumscribe, or differentially enable and constrain, the range of strategic possibilities.[4] Within such a perspective, the formulation and reformulation of political strategy is understood as a practice, an accomplishment on the part of strategic actors. As such, it takes place within a strategic context that is itself constantly evolving through the consequences of strategic action. Strategies, once formulated, are operationalised in action. Such action yields effects, both intended and unintended. And since individuals are knowledgeable and reflexive, they

---

[2] Bhaskar 1979 and 1989, in particular Chapter 5.
[3] It is worth noting that although Bhaskar himself employs the term 'duality of structure' in his writings, he has recently suggested that he agrees with Margaret Archer's critique of the term (in Archer 1995). Archer insists instead on the importance of 'analytical dualism' and criticises Bhaskar for conciliating with the 'elisionism' of Anthony Giddens. For a critique of both Archer and Bhaskar see Chodos 1997.
[4] Jessop 1990.

routinely monitor the consequences of their action, assessing the impact of previous strategies, and their success or failure in securing prior objectives.

Strategic action thus yields: 1) direct effects upon the structured contexts within which it takes place and within which future action occurs, producing a partial (however minimal) transformation of the structured context (though not necessarily as anticipated); and, 2) strategic learning on the part of the actor(s) involved, enhancing awareness of structures and the constraints/opportunities they impose, providing the basis from which subsequent strategy might be formulated and perhaps prove more successful.[5]

Yet this does not exhaust the selectivity of the context. For the strategically selective context is also discursively selective, in that it can only be accessed through perceptions, misperceptions and representations. Such perceptions may or may not enhance the ability of actors to realise their intentions, and, in certain contexts, may militate severely against their realisation. Moreover, strategic action is also informed by anticipated future scenarios. Strategic actors simply cannot assume some unchanging and immutable context within which cumulative strategic learning can occur. They are instead consigned to gauge, assess and project the strategic conduct of others and the impact this is likely to have on the context itself.[6]

One of the necessary filters through which strategic political opportunities must therefore be processed is the vision of the long-term goal towards which we are striving (a vision which is by no means set in concrete, and which may – indeed must – itself evolve). The strategic horizon is thus circumscribed by one's beliefs about how one's present interests (projected over a fairly limited time-horizon) are best served, as well as by beliefs about what constitutes the 'good' society (in the longer term).

One way of putting this is that collective strategic action involves what we would call the actualisation of 'belief-dependent emergent capacities'. What we mean is that people's beliefs themselves, as well as their awareness of the strength of those beliefs, can contribute to generating new, or emergent, capacities. This is because the calculations people customarily perform before undertaking any activity involve an assessment of the extent to which the participants in the activity being considered are aware of, and have confidence in, their own capacities – including those emergent capacities which *arise only as a result of* the willingness to engage in the collective undertaking.

Let us give an example. A factor in assessing the risks involved in going on strike would be an evaluation of the degree of determination on the part of the potential strikers to overcome the inevitable hardships the struggle entails. The fact that each is convinced that the others are prepared to shoulder their part of the burden contributes to the

[5] Hay 1995.
[6] Hay 1998b and 1998c.

emergent collective capacity to engage in the struggle and have a chance of winning. It is part of a belief in the collective capacity to accomplish something, and the scope of that capacity is a function of the strength of the belief.

Belief in the capacity is not a mere reflection of a pre-existing capacity that was somehow dormant, but is constitutive of that capacity. It helps create a capacity that would not exist without the belief. This is not a crude voluntarism, because it is not the assertion that the capacity will necessarily be realised in the way in which those who believe in it would hope or expect. In fact, it says nothing about an eventual outcome, and only asserts that certain outcomes become possible as a result of belief-dependent emergent capacities. Because they are emergent they cannot be turned on and off like a light switch, but require an appropriate confluence of conditions, including the contingent presence of individuals with the requisite talents and abilities.

This is largely what we meant when we stated at the outset that politics is a creative, and not merely a representative, activity. Parties of all kinds do not simply 'represent' the interests of a pre-existing class (or other social/political aggregate), but are necessary instruments in the process of creating interests; they are integral to the very constitution of classes (and other social categories) as actors on an historical stage. We would argue that there is an interactive relationship between interests, the organisations to which a recognition of such interests give rise, and the strategic action this enables. Parties function to make possible certain things that would not otherwise be achievable, and contribute to creating both a vision and a capacity to act that would not and could not otherwise exist. This applies as much to parties dedicated to the preservation of the status quo as well as to those which strive to bring about radical change. We could say, to paraphrase a celebrated dictum, that we create ourselves, but not under conditions of our own choosing.

Political organisations, on this view, provide contexts within which belief-dependent emergent capacities can be actualised. This, in turn, means that they serve a multi-dimensional mediating function. The party bridges the gap between the future and the present, translating long-term goals into concrete action today, and ascribing meaning to more immediate political action in terms of such goals. It takes our personal, private experience and translates it into public proposals. It allows an evolving theoretical perspective to find expression in practical politics. It enables individuals who share common experiences, circumstances, expectations and/or aspirations to bond together and act collectively for (what they perceive to be) their mutual benefit (or that of others).

As it mediates between future and present, private and public, theory and practice, individual and collective, the party simultaneously generates new capacities and new identities. It gives us the ability to do

33

new things, providing us with a context in which to discuss the best ways in which to use our new-found abilities. It is not merely the coming together of people who already share a similar outlook, but it is an indispensable locus for defining those commonalities in such a way that strategic action based on them can be undertaken.

We now turn to a brief critical evaluation of two traditional views of the party – Leninism and social democracy – in the light of the above discussion. We will then conclude with some tentative thoughts on what all this means for people interested in furthering the cause of radical social change today.

Leninism

Controversy has always surrounded Lenin's theory of the party. It was born in the struggle against the Russian 'economist' tendency, as a defense of the orthodoxy of the Second International. It immediately had to weather sharp criticisms from luminaries such as Rosa Luxemburg and Leon Trotsky. Lenin himself said, somewhat cryptically, that in the *locus classicus* of his theory of the party, his 1902 pamphlet *What Is To Be Done?*, he had 'bent the stick' too far the other way in his polemic against economism, although he never specified precisely which aspects had been distorted.[7]

In order, then, to work out a provisional balance sheet of the Leninist legacy 90 years on, it is first necessary to try to define as clearly as possible what is meant by Leninism. This is not an entirely straightforward matter, as the competing characterisations of what is central to Leninism testify.[8] In our view, it is the very complexity of the Leninist formula that contributes to the wide range of possible interpretations of its merits and defects. We cannot, in the context of this article, undertake even a cursory review of the literature. Instead, we will begin by outlining what we see as the core Leninist propositions. We will then examine their strengths and weaknesses before exploring some of the reasons that the analysis of Leninism is so contested.

We would offer the following as a capsule summary of the Leninist view of the role of the party. In virtue of its mastery of Marxism, its consistent advocacy of the rights of the oppressed, and its rigorous application of democratic centralism, the Leninist party is uniquely positioned to foster a genuine class consciousness within the working class and to lead it in the complex struggle to replace capitalism with socialism.

---

[7] See Kolakowski 1981. p. 392

[8] For example, Kolakowski states that 'the theoretical source, or rather justification, of that machine [ie. the party] was Lenin's conviction that the party, by virtue of its scientific knowledge of society, is the one legitimate source of political initiative' (Kolakowski 1981, p. 391). Geras, for his part, argues that the 'central proposition in Lenin's theory of the party, ... in a nutshell, is that the party is necessarily an instrument of political centralization'. Geras 1986, p. 183.

This definition allows us to see that the Leninist party is poised in the midst of a tangled web of relations. It is a commonplace among commentators to highlight the centrality of the party in Lenin's thinking and in his revolutionary practice. We would suggest that the best way to grasp this centrality is to triangulate the role of the party in relation to three related components. These are Marxism, the working class and the political struggle. The flexibility of Leninism, as well as its vulnerability to a wide range of criticisms, stems from the fact that these elements are not linked in a stable, unchanging fashion either to the theoretical understanding of the party, or to its actual practice. Rather, depending on the circumstances or on the point to be made, it is possible to stress one or the other aspect of these complex relationships.

The first thing to note, however, is that it is impossible theoretically to establish the universal primacy of any one of these elements in determining the course of a revolutionary struggle. Even if one grants, for the sake of argument, the universal truth and complete limpidity of Marxian analyses of capitalism, they alone could not ensure the defeat of capitalism. Theory has to be seized by real people in order to become a transformative force. Similarly, even if we accept the Marxist proposition that it is only the working class that is the truly revolutionary class under capitalism, this is not enough to ensure that its revolutionary potential be realised. Objective circumstances and the skill of the working class in the political arena have a necessary bearing on the eventual outcome. It is also clear that no matter how revolutionary one's politics, and no matter how radiant and auspicious the prospects at a given time, there is much about any complex struggle in the political arena that is subject to contingent events beyond anyone's control.

The matter becomes more complicated still once one recognises that each of these constitutive elements is itself open to many competing interpretations. Can anyone today provide a definition of Marxism that would be able to unite all those who claim to be Marxists? On the contrary, every one of what Lenin would have taken to be the incontrovertible truths of Marxism, from the labour theory of value to the dictatorship of the proletariat,[9] has been challenged, not only by non-Marxists, but by many claiming to trace a direct lineage to the spirit of the tradition. Similarly, Marxists themselves have never been able to make good the absence of a definition of the working class in Marx

---

[9] Lenin's classic statement regarding the importance of the dictatorship of the proletariat is to be found in *The State and Revolution,* written from August to September 1917. In Chapter 2, Section 3, he writes: 'He who recognizes *only* the class struggle is not yet a Marxist; it may turn out that he has not yet gone beyond the bounds of bourgeois thinking and bourgeois politics. To confine Marxism to the doctrine of the class struggle means curtailing Marxism, distorting it, reducing it to something acceptable to the bourgeoisie. Only he is a Marxist who *extends* the recognition of the class struggle to the recognition of the dictatorship of the proletariat. This is what constitutes the most profound difference between the Marxist and the ordinary petty (as well as big) bourgeois. This is the touchstone on which the *real* understanding and recognition of Marxism is to be tested.' (All emphases in the original). See Lenin 1978.

himself.[10] And the relationship between politics, economics, identity and consciousness remain as difficult to specify today as they were when Lenin railed against economism.

Accordingly, we can say that, whilst it is in relation to these elements that one must construct a revolutionary theory of the party, there are nonetheless many ways to do so. In this regard, we highlight four key issues relating to the nature and role of a revolutionary party that arise out of the theory and practice of Leninism: the relationship between spontaneity and consciousness in the formation of a social agent capable of transforming social relations; the class nature of the party; the vanguard character of the party; democratic centralism as the key to the internal practice of the party.

The question of the relationship between spontaneity and consciousness is the starting point for Lenin's theorisation of the nature of the revolutionary party. Sympathetic accounts of Lenin's approach rightly stress that it is wrong simply to translate the distinction between spontaneity and consciousness into an opposition between workers and intellectuals.[11] Similarly, Lenin's understanding does not map neatly onto the distinction between economic and political struggle.[12]

Others, less favourably inclined towards the Leninist perspective, and going back as far Rosa Luxemburg, have argued that Lenin overemphasises the conscious dimension, ultimately substituting the activity of the party for that of the class. While this line of criticism was prescient, and rightly castigated the anti-democratic proclivities of the Bolsheviks, it could be argued that the alternative to which it gave rise was itself marred by economic determinism. Thus, Luxemburg's insistence on the ultimate success of the spontaneous mass movement relied on the inevitability of the collapse of the capitalist system through the workings of its own internal contradictions.[13]

We want to suggest that there is an underlying difficulty in the way in which the problem is framed both by Lenin and many of his contemporary opponents. A theory of the party that responds primarily to the tensions posed by the binary opposition between spontaneity and consciousness cannot avoid overemphasising one of the other of the two poles. The key theoretical error in all positions that try to negotiate their way between spontaneity and consciousness consists in ignoring the fact that all human action is in fact both. Spontaneity in this context can only mean placing the emphasis on unintended consequences. It is action that comes about as a result of the interaction of forces that no one controls and no one directs. However, such forces are an irreducible aspect of the context of human social interaction. Similarly, there is always a conscious dimension. Human action is always in some sense willed. What we will and what we do may not be congruent, but in

---

[10] The manuscript for the third volume of *Capital* concludes with an aborted chapter on class after only 5 paragraphs.
[11] See Shandro 1995, pp. 275–6, and LeBlanc 1990, p. 44.
[12] Shandro 1995, pp. 277–8.
[13] See Chodos 1992, pp. 40–3.

analysing any outcome, the influence of a conscious will is one datum that must be assessed.

Ascertaining whether the conscious will of an individual or of an aggregated group is the determining factor in shaping a particular outcome or whether it is the impact of forces beyond anyone's control is something that can only be done after the fact. It is an historical and empirical question. There can therefore be no *a priori* primacy of one element over the other, no determination in advance that certain kinds of activity are primarily spontaneous and others primarily conscious. This is why framing the question of the party as a function of the tension between spontaneity and consciousness cannot yield a satisfactory response.

In our view, there are two interrelated binaries that can better define the nature of the revolutionary party. The first situates the party in terms of the consequences of social action, while the second poses its character in temporal terms. All social action contributes either to the reproduction or to the transformation of existing social relations. Political parties are collective organisms that bring together people concerned to influence the direction of social life. Their intervention either reinforces the prevailing pattern of social relations or modifies them in a given direction. A revolutionary party is one that attempts in all contexts to pose the transformative question, to inquire into the strategic and tactical measures that will bring about a change in the dominant structure of social relations. The temporal dimension means that posing this question must take the form of imagining the future and attempting to direct our intervention in the present so that a particular vision of the future can someday be realised. This vision must itself be revised as lessons are learnt in the course of attempting its implementation.

This is a form of conscious action, but there are many such forms. One cannot therefore simply assert that the party is the embodiment of either the objective or the subjective interests of the working class. In order to define the party as an instrument of a given class it is necessary either to supply an *a priori* definition of the consciousness particular to that class (as with Lenin), or to envisage a necessary sequence of events that enables the realisation of the class project (as with Luxemburg). The alternative to defining the party as the party of the working class is to accept that the social composition of the party, as well as both its short- and long-term goals, will vary according to its particular circumstances. It will be a revolutionary socialist party to the extent that it seeks to replace existing capitalism with a version of socialism. But what this version of socialism will be, and how one will get there cannot be decided in advance, any more than the exact class nature of the party can be defined for all circumstances.

It is striking that, in the 20th century, Marxist-inspired revolutions that have relied on indigenous forces have only occurred in countries in which the working class has been a small minority. In both Russia and

China, it was by skilfully negotiating their way through a complex set of class alliances that Marxist parties were able to overthrow the old regime and begin a transition towards post-capitalism. The vanguard character of such a party did not reside in its embodiment of a predefined set of class interests, but in its having been able to pose the transformational question: what is it that will enable us to break with capitalism? What kind of socialism can be brought about that is appropriate to the conditions that we actually face? In this sense, the vanguard character of the party is dispositional rather than substantive. It fulfils its leadership role by providing answers that are contextually appropriate to these questions, and not in any rigid adherence to a predefined dogma.

Thus, with regard to the first three issues we earlier identified, it is fair to say that by defining the terrain of party formation in terms of the tension between spontaneity and consciousness, the Leninist tradition leaned heavily in the direction of what could be called an 'objectivist' orientation.[14] It was Marxism that provided the 'scientific' foundation for the critique of capitalism, and for the identification of the working class as the only truly revolutionary agent. It was the acceptance of this critique that was the measure of class consciousness. The party, as repository of this knowledge, had to bring it to the working class by applying it relentlessly to every instance of oppression and exploitation, by being at the forefront of all political struggles. What was contingent in all this was simply the fidelity of the party to its Marxist roots and its skill and determination in executing the Marxist strategy.

It is here that the final issue we noted is relevant. Democratic centralism was to be the guarantor of the unity of action of the party, providing the organisational cement that would enable the successful translation of the Marxist strategy into political practice. It can be tempting to dismiss democratic centralism as a Leninist aberration which must be eliminated from our organisational toolkit. But matters are not so simple. We would argue that, with regard to its prohibition of dissent once a decision has been reached, the practice of democratic centralism is pretty well identical to the practice of cabinet solidarity that prevails in many parliamentary democracies, such as both Britain and Canada. There the cabinet debates matters behind closed doors, reaches a decision, and subsequently all members of the cabinet are expected to defend and implement the decision in unison.

The difference between the practice of these, non-Leninist, parties and the Leninist tradition is not in the nature of the approach to achieving unity in action, but in its scope. In a Leninist party the limits to free expression associated with democratic centralism applied to the whole party. When combined with the additional stricture that lower

---

[14] For more thorough discussions of the links between philosophy and politics in Lenin's thought, in particular with regard to his philosophical treatise *Materialism and Empiriocritism*, see Bakhurst 1991, Pannekoek 1975, and Chodos 1992.

bodies and individual members had to submit to the decisions made by higher bodies, it is clear that the restrictions to democratic life were unnecessarily broad. But it is the scope of the application of democratic centralism rather than its core content that made it undemocratic.

We would argue that a similar type of assessment of other aspects of the Leninist tradition is also possible. The problems Leninism sought to confront were real ones, ones that will confront any viable transformative movement, but there was a constant tension in the Leninist tradition between two strands of thought. The first was what we termed its 'objectivist' cast, while the second might be termed its properly political emphasis. The centrality of politics to Leninism, both in its recognition that it is only through the political struggle that one can acquire a sufficient knowledge of the workings of the system so as to be able to transform it, and in its emphasis on the need for an organisation up to this task, are lessons that need to be carried forward. Similarly, Leninism's ability to engage in cross-class alliances and its tactical flexibility provide important examples of how actual transformative movements can be built. Unfortunately, by investing these achievements with a sense of infallibility drawn from its self-proclaimed access to the absolute truth provided by 'scientific socialism', Leninism simultaneously closed the door on the possibility of collectively *discovering* the road to revolution, thereby opening wide the door to party diktat.

Social democracy

Turning our attention to social democracy, it is fairly uncontroversial to suggest that its perspective on the party and political strategy is the very antithesis of the Leninist conception. Where the Leninist party is a revolutionary vanguard seeking to smash the state apparatus, the social democratic party is ostensibly a reformist, parliamentary and a liberal democratic entity seeking to operate, at least in the first instance, within the confines of the existing (capitalist) state apparatus. Where Leninism denies and rejects the idea that the capitalist state (as the repressive arm of the bourgeoisie) can be taken over to serve the interests of the proletariat, the social-democratic party relies precisely upon such a notion. Where Leninism envisages a singular, decisive and revolutionary overthrow of the capitalist system symbolically associated with the smashing of the state itself, social democracy projects a gradual, evolutionary and iterative road to socialism paved with good democratic intentions. Where the Leninist party is an overwhelmingly proletarian political organisation, the social democratic party courts other social groups beyond the working class and, where appropriate, engages in electoral pacts to further its pursuit of governmental power.

If Leninism is characterised by a tendency to subordinate (democratic) means to (socialist) ends, (representative) practice to (revolutionary) principle, then social democracy tends to the converse: ends are subordinated to (parliamentary political) means, socialist principle to the practice of electoral expediency. Classic social democracy is essentially animated by a vision of the democratic road to socialism. Its strategy is electoral, to take power of a state (conceived of as a neutral instrument) by liberal parliamentary means; its goal to steer the 'ship of state' inexorably onwards towards a socialism whose initiation will not be marked by any sharp break. Social democracy is, above all, a gradualist strategy premised upon the pursuit of power by a parliamentary party.

If this serves to establish the principal differences between social democratic incrementalism on the one hand, and Leninist vanguardism on the other, this should not be taken to imply that social democracy has been, or remains, an uncontested notion. Quite the contrary. Even the most fleeting of glimpses at the voluminous literature on the subject (theoretical, analytical and practical) can scarcely fail to notice the bewildering variety of senses to which the concept has been attached.[15] Thus, for some, social democracy is synonymous with Marxist reformism, whilst for others with an at best fairly trivial attempt to ameliorate some of capitalism's worst excesses in an effort to promote social harmony and hence the expanded reproduction of capital over time. Whilst such apparent conceptual confusion might well be taken as evidence of the term's 'essential contestability', it is perhaps more useful to see it as a consequence of some of the antinomies of revisionism itself.[16]

Social democracy at its inception was indeed Marxist in its inspiration and in its commitment to socialism, but it believed that the cause could most successfully be advanced through the politics of parliamentarism and gradual reform. For Bernstein, in particular, the conditions for socialist transformation had first to be created. They could not, as in the more deterministic versions of Marxist theory prevalent at the time, simply be assumed to exist. In contrast to the assurances that came with determinism and a teleological conception of history, for Bernstein there could simply be no guarantees. History would have to be made, and be made in perhaps rather inauspicious circumstances. The best, then, that could be achieved was a long and potentially rather winding road to socialism, punctuated frequently by social reforms.

The subsequent history of social democracy, from Marxist revisionism to social reformism and, more recently, from Keynesian social reformism to post-Keynesian neoliberalism in all but name is, in the search for a revivified and revitalised Marxist political party, a cautionary tale. It indicates above all the dangers of losing sight of the goal of socialism itself and the need to maintain a constant dialogue within the party as to the nature and purpose of the struggle in process.

---

[15] See Hay forthcoming, chapter 2.
[16] On 'essential contestability' see Gallie 1956.

Nonetheless, there are certain theoretical strengths even to Bernstein's revisionism. There is something refreshingly sanguine, for instance, about his refusal to accept the inevitability of capitalist crisis, class polarisation and attendant socialist revolution. Even Bernstein's famous, and much vilified, formula that 'the movement is everything, the final goal nothing' contains an important grain of truth. Reforms are not in and of themselves reformist. Whether given reforms contribute to the consolidation of the system or to its eventual undermining does indeed depend on the direction of the movement in which they are inserted.

At the same time, however, the history of social-democratic practice from 1914 onwards has, with the benefit of hindsight, a certain air of inevitability. As Luxemburg noted in her critique of Bernstein at the time, far from being more 'realistic', the idea of a stable, non-confrontational path to socialism is in fact inherently utopian.[17] A movement that cannot see beyond the limits of existing social relations will thus necessarily confine any reforms it does succeed in implementing to the prevailing framework. This not only circumscribes their scope but renders them vulnerable to the vicissitudes of the dominant ideology as to what constitutes a legitimate sphere for government intervention. In this sense, under capitalism, there are no permanent, unassailable reforms. With the withering, not of the state, but of Keynesianism since the mid-1970s, the conditions of capitalist reformism on post-war social-democratic terms would seem, for now, to have been exhausted.[18] Arguably, this merely serves to re-establish the pressing need for a genuinely revolutionary, yet at the same time a genuinely democratic and self-radicalising Marxist political practice.

That social democracy failed in practice to pave a democratic and parliamentary road to socialism should be traced not so much to the initial incrementalism of its vision of social transformation, but to its inability (practical and theoretical) to develop a self-radicalising critique both of its own practices and of capitalism itself. This, it should be noted, is no easy task, especially when viewed from our current vantage point, marked as it is by a paucity of theoretical innovation. Without an ever more concrete and complex conception of a viable socialism based on an ever more concrete and complex critique of the contours of contemporary capitalism, no self-radicalising – far less revolutionary – political momentum can be generated.

This presents a considerable challenge for the party itself. For it is here that such a self-animating and self-radicalising critique must be developed. Indeed, it is *only* here that such a critique and the always-developing vision of socialism that it might sustain *can* develop. The party must, in this sense, serve as the key locus for the very synthesis of theory and praxis. What distinguishes the radical from the incremental

---

[17] Luxemburg 1971.
[18] The argument of, for instance, Wood, 1995. pp. 284-93.

in the end is not the content of a particular reform, but the process in which it is inserted.

The role of the party, then, must be to ensure that the process within which such reforms (however seemingly insignificant their initial content) are integrated is a genuinely revolutionary one. We cannot know in advance what socialism will look like, but, at some point, we need to be able to identify what kind of break will separate us from capitalism. And even before we are in a position to identify concretely the content of this break, we need to remain committed to its possibility. In the end, the belief that a radical break with capitalism is needed is what separates reformists from revolutionaries.

In the current context, gradualism may appear enticing. Indeed, arguably, there is little chance of Marxists 'making a difference' without first establishing (governmental) credibility by demonstrating themselves capable of realising immediate, not necessarily radical goals. Incremental reformism would then seem an appropriate – perhaps even a necessary – starting point. Yet we must be extremely wary of the incrementalist inertia to which social democracy seems inevitably prone, and to the reactionary politics of retrenchment to which its progenitors now seem magnetically drawn. Social democratic practice has, as yet, never got beyond the initial incrementals. That this is so, we argue, can be attributed to its failure to integrate each and every reform into a self-radicalising and self-sustaining revolutionary process. However difficult the task, this is the role of the party.

Conclusions: once more on the party

So this, then, is the dilemma: is there a 'third way'? Can we envisage a form of political organisation which is both democratic and revolutionary? Is it possible to avoid the debilitating rigidity and anti-democratism bound up with the Leninist tradition without committing ourselves to an incrementalism that has no end and that can never take us beyond capitalism?

At best, we can only sketch the beginnings of what an affirmative response to these questions would look like. The key, we believe, lies in the way we think about socialism. As we noted earlier, the party is the one location where ongoing debate about the nature of socialism can be given a strategic outlet. Its role is thus to allow us to consider the strategic implications of current policy. In the first instance, any party which hopes to acquire a mass audience and membership must identify and set itself relatively parochial, realistic yet desirable goals which it is capable of realising in the short term. It is only by establishing perceptions of competence and credibility in this way that we might hope to extend the realms of what is considered possible and desirable.

At the same time, the party must be able to locate these initial steps on the path towards a longer-term goal, but one which is not predefined. In a sense, whatever the circumstances and the concrete limits on policy and action imposed by a particular conjuncture, it remains the party's job to interrogate the present in the name of the future.

To be revolutionary, the party must openly and decisively embrace the goal of working towards a post-capitalist future, but for its commitment to democracy to have any meaning it cannot arrogate unto itself the right to specify what that future will look like. We know enough about capitalism to know that we must do better. But what 'better' means in this context can only be decided in the course of real historical evolution. To be able to give organisational form to both these principles simultaneously requires that Marxists radically rethink their notion of socialism.

Most, if not all, Marxist accounts of the transition to socialism and then on to communism suffer from the defect of stageism. The very idea that socialism leads to communism is both stageist and teleological. There is a temporal sequence inherent in this conception that places the transition to mature communism within an epochal trajectory of social systems, which in some orthodox accounts goes back all the way to primitive communism. To talk in terms of 'higher' and 'lower' stages of socialism, as Marx himself did in the *Critique of the Gotha Programme*, merely provides illustration of this.

Our hypothesis is instead to try to think of communism and socialism as co-evolving, as temporally simultaneous processes which do not describe different stages of human social evolution, but rather constitute necessary responses to different kinds of problem that human history has bequeathed to us.[19] This would allow us to retrieve Marx's distinction between the lower and higher stages of socialism without the inherent teleology of Marx's own formulation.

Socialism, on this view, defines how to remunerate people equally and fairly based on their contribution to social life; communism regulates the meeting of individual needs. Insofar as people contribute what they can to social life ('from each according to their ability') socialism requires an egalitarian distribution; communism, however, will always entail a nominally inegalitarian one, so that each person's individual particularities can in fact be accommodated ('to each according to their needs').

Socialism is a system which can be instituted by majority rule; communism is something which can only be voluntarily enacted. It is

---

[19] The distinction we are trying to explore has a definite affinity with A. K. Sen's notions of 'shortfall' and 'attainment' equality. He writes: "Equality between persons can be defined either in terms of *attainments*, or in terms of the *shortfalls* from the maximal values that each can respectively attain. For "attainment equality" of achievements, we compare the actual levels of achievement. For "shortfall equality", what are compared are the shortfalls of actual achievements from the respective maximal achievements. Each of the two views has some considerable interest of its own. Shortfall equality takes us in the direction of equal use of the *respective potentials*, whereas attainment equality is concerned with equal absolute levels of achievement (no matter what the maximal potentials are)." Sen 1992, pp. 90–91.

not a system which can be implemented, but rather is an attitude, a way of life, a philosophy, a moral code which revolves around the idea of taking individual responsibility for our common social life. Working to implement socialism is a necessary precondition for creating propitious conditions for the voluntary adoption of communism, in the same way that a progressive and voluntary adoption of communism is a condition for the fullest possible efflorescence of socialism. Communism is a possibility which emerges alongside socialism, just as socialism is a possibility that emerges from capitalism.

This gives us a framework in which to reconceptualise the process of cumulative radicalisation that will be necessary to any transition *from* capitalism. In fact, we would argue that we need to rethink what it means radically to transform social relations. The perspective developed here posits a cumulative raising in the extent, scope and scale of political, social and economic reform as expectations, aspirations and desires are raised on the basis of past successes, and as the boundaries of what is perceived to be politically and economically possible are peeled back to reveal genuinely socialist possibilities. For without such a cumulative radicalisation and the transition from incremental to radical reformism that it entails nationally and internationally, there can surely be no transition to socialism in the context of a global capitalist world system.

But this process must itself be understood to be path-dependent. Outcomes cannot be predicted in advance; neither can the form of the socialism towards which it builds. Similarly, within such a framework neither socialism nor communism can ever be fully realised. They can only be in a process of realisation that entails a constant balancing between their irreducible and potentially competing imperatives. There is then no socialist *telos*, no end-point, only a constant interrogation of the present in the name of a yet-to-be-created future.

In this way, what we would call revolutionary gradualism becomes a feasible strategic orientation, without implying that we know in advance the exact meaning of the term 'revolutionary', yet still ensuring a never-ending commitment to transcend 'gradualism'. Such a strategic orientation also highlights the importance of distinguishing those features inherited from capitalism that, while being given a new meaning in a transformed context, may retain many of their outward characteristics, from those that will require a radical overhaul. Nor is it only institutions that will be so transformed. Revolutionary gradualism suggests that, over time, people will have the opportunity to refashion themselves and their ongoing social interaction.

It has been the argument of this paper that it is the party itself that is, or must become, the principal agent of such an interrogation – the critical core of a self-renewing socialist project that can never be finalised, but always only in a constant process of finalisation. The party, like socialism itself, can never be 'over'.

References

Archer, Margaret 1995, *Realist Social Theory: The Morphogenetic Approach*, Cambridge: Cambridge University Press.

Bakhurst, David 1991, *Consciousness and Revolution in Soviet Philosophy*, Cambridge: Cambridge University Press.

Bhaskar, Roy 1979, *The Possibility of Naturalism: A Philosophical Critique of the Contemporary Human Sciences*, London: Harvester Wheatsheaf.

Bhaskar, Roy 1989, *Reclaiming Reality: A Critical Introduction to Contemporary Philosophy*, London: Verso.

Chodos, Howard 1992, 'Epistemology, Politics and the Notion of Class Interest in Lenin, Luxemburg and Gramsci', *Journal of History and Politics*, 10: 35-60

Chodos, Howard 1997, 'Critical Realism, Collective Agency and the Crisis of Marxism', paper presented at the inaugural conference of the Centre for Critical Realism, University of Warwick.

Gallie, William 1956, 'Essentially Contested Concepts', *Proceedings of the Aristotelian Society*, 56: 167–98.

Geras, Norman 1986, *Literature of Revolution*, London: Verso

Hay, Colin, 1995, 'Structure and Agency', in *Theory and Methods in Political Science* edited by David Marsh and Gerry Stoker, London: Macmillan.

Hay, Colin 1997, 'Blaijorism: Towards a One-Vision Polity', *Political Quarterly*, 68, 4: 372–9.

Hay, Colin 1998a, 'That Was Then, This Now: The Revision of Policy in the Modernisation of the British Labour Party, 1992–97', *New Political Science*, 20, 1: 7–33.

Hay, Colin 1998b, 'The Tangled Webs We Weave: The Discourse, Strategy and Practice of Networking', in *Comparing Policy Networks* edited by David Marsh, Buckingham: Open University Press.

Hay, Colin 1998c, 'Political Time and the Temporality of Crisis: On Institutional Change as "Punctuated Evolution"', paper presented at the 11th Conference of Europeanists, Baltimore.

Hay, Colin forthcoming, *Labouring Under False Pretences? Modernisation for an Era of Globalisation*, Manchester: Manchester University Press.

Jessop, Bob 1990, *State Theory: Putting Capitalist States in their Place*, Cambridge: Polity.

Kolakowski, Leszek 1981, *Main Currents of Marxism*, volume 2, Oxford: Oxford University Press

LeBlanc, Paul 1990, *Lenin and the Revolutionary Party*, Atlantic Highlands, N.J.: Humanities Press.

Lenin, V.I. 1978, *The State and Revolution*, in Lenin, *Marx, Engels, Marxism*, Peking: Foreign Languages Press.

Luxemburg, Rosa 1971, 'Social Reform or Revolution', in *Selected Political Writings of Rosa Luxemburg* edited by Dick Howard, New York: Monthly Review Press.

Panitch, Leo and Leys, Colin 1997, *The End of Parliamentary Socialism: From New Left to New Labour*, Cambridge: Polity.

Pannekoek, Anton 1975, *Lenin as Philosopher*, London: Merlin Press.

Sen, A.K., 1992, *Inequality Reexamined*, Oxford: Clarendon Press.

Shandro, Alan 1995, '"Consciousness from Without": Marxism, Lenin and the Proletariat', *Science and Society*, 59: 268–97.

Wood, Ellen Meiksins 1995, *Democracy Against Capitalism: Renewing Historical Materialism*, Cambridge: Cambridge University Press.

How Not To Write About Lenin

John Molyneux

Eighty one years on, the Russian Revolution remains an event of unique significance for socialists, Marxists and historical materialists. It is the only occasion to date of which it can plausibly be claimed that the working class itself overthrew the capitalist state, established its own power and maintained it on a national scale for a significant period of time. Discount the Russian Revolution and we are left only with heroic but local and short-lived attempts and near-misses such as the Paris Commune, the Hungarian Revolution of 1919, the Munich Soviet and Barcelona 1936, or the long list of seizures of power, usually by armed forces of one sort or another, in the name of the working class or Marxism (Eastern Europe 1945–47, China 1949, Cuba 1959, etc.).

Of course, this claim for Russia 1917 has always been contested. A lot rides on the argument. If the claim is valid it follows: 1) that we have at least some empirical confirmation of the proletariat's capacity to fulfil the role assigned to it in *The Communist Manifesto* and in classical Marxism; 2) that, while not expecting any mechanical repetition, we have some idea of the form and institutions of workers' power (Soviets/workers' councils based in workplace delegates, etc.); 3) that, in the shape of Bolshevik organisation and practice and Leninist theory, we have some idea of the kind of political leadership necessary for proletarian victory.

If, however, the claim is not valid, all of this goes out of the window. The argument that working class self-emancipation is a utopian fantasy and that the whole project should be abandoned is greatly strengthened. Even if the goal is somehow retained, the idea that there exists a viable political strategy for achieving it – if only in outline – is thoroughly discredited. It becomes necessary to rethink everything from the beginning.[1]

With so much at stake, the debate on the Russian Revolution has never been innocent. From the outset, the bourgeoisie and its academic representatives have waged intellectual war on the October Revolution in general and on Leninism in particular. In this campaign they have

---

[1] Of course the idea of 'rethinking everything from the beginning' is music to the ears of many academics – think of all those conferences, papers, articles, books – but for activists in the working-class movement and active revolutionary socialists having to 'start from scratch' is a huge step backwards. Imagine the position of a shop steward or union rep who on Monday decides that all the accumulated experience and principles of trade unionism are worthless and should be thrown on the scrap heap, pending 'rethinking', on Tuesday dissolves her trade-union branch and resigns her union position, and on Wednesday is sacked for alleged bad time-keeping.

been ably assisted by social democracy, beginning with Karl Kautsky,[2] with a special contribution being made by former Mensheviks such as Boris Nicolaevsky. By the 1950s and 1960s the academic mainstream was almost totally dominated by an anti-Bolshevik interpretation of twentieth century Russian history.

According to this view, the Soviet Union under Stalin and his successors was an evil totalitarian dictatorship which had its origins in, and grew organically out of, the totalitarian dictatorship established by Lenin and the Bolsheviks more or less immediately after the October Revolution. This, in turn, was the more or less inevitable product of the fact that the October insurrection was not in any sense a genuine workers' revolution but was merely an opportunistic *coup d'état* executed by the minority Bolshevik Party on the insistence of Lenin. That Lenin and the Bolsheviks behaved in this way in 1917 was the logical outcome of the fact that they were, from the outset, a totalitarian conspiracy whose main aim was to win power for themselves. The driving force in all this was the personal power-hunger of Lenin, which characterised all his dealings with his comrades in the pre-revolutionary social-democratic movements.

The key documentary evidence of Lenin's personal power-hunger and totalitarian aspirations was to be found in *What Is To Be Done?*, with its call for a party of professional revolutionaries and its doctrine that socialism would have to be introduced into the working class 'from without'. This, with only minor variations, was the line to be found in the work, of Leonard Schapiro, Bertram D. Wolfe, Alfred Meyer, Merle Fainsod, Zbigniew Brzezinski, Carl Friedrich, R. Carew Hunt, Robert Conquest, and innumerable other 'scholars' of the cold war period.

When I was an undergraduate in the late 1960s, almost the only alternative voices on Leninism which were in any way academically acceptable were E.H. Carr and Isaac Deutscher.[3] The radicalisation of 1968 and after changed this somewhat, with the emergence of 'history from below' and the academic 'age of Althusser', but the shift to the right in the 1980s, the epidemic of postmodernism and, above all, the 'collapse of Communism' in 1989–91 more or less completely restored the hegemony of the right-wing argument. Witness the success of Orlando Figes's *A People's Tragedy*.

Logically, the fall of the Stalinist regimes in Eastern Europe and the Russian Empire had few implications for the evaluation of the Revolution or Leninism. The major crimes of Stalinism were well known even to supporters of these regimes, and almost nothing of substance emerged from the opening of the archives.[4] Those in Britain and Western Europe who maintained some public solidarity with the rulers of 'the socialist countries' (members of the Communist parties,

---

[2] See Kautsky 1918 and 1919.
[3] There was, of course, a non-academic literature – Trotsky, Dunayevskaya, Cliff, etc.
[4] See Haynes 1998, pp. 63–4.

left Labour fellow travellers, etc.) had, almost without exception, long ago renounced insurrection and Leninism as out-of-date and inappropriate under advanced capitalism. Conversely, those who proclaimed their fidelity to Leninism almost all declared their hostility to the bureaucratic régimes of the East.

But, of course, neither the history of ideas nor the history of academic fashion develop according to logical rules, and 'the fall' produced all manner of 'revaluations' and 'repudiations'.[5] As a result, a climate has arisen in the media and in wide swathes of academia where it is open season on Lenin and Leninism. It is so taken for granted that Leninism is discredited that it becomes possible to write any nonsense about Lenin, apparently without fear of contradiction. Which brings me to Simon Clarke's 'Was Lenin a Marxist? The Populist Roots of Marxism-Leninism'.

Clarke makes a startling claim, namely that 'Lenin never broke from the theoretical and political traditions of Russian populism'.[6] It would be nice, as well as polite, to say that he advances a serious – even if not convincing – case for it. Unfortunately this is not the case. Instead, Clarke's whole argument fails to get off the ground because of its deeply flawed method. This method is best described as 'philosophical determinism', a sub-variant of rampant idealism. By this I mean that Clarke seems to believe that Lenin's politics – both his political practice and his political theory – were to all intents and purposes determined by his philosophy, specifically his epistemology, and that therefore only his philosophy needs to be examined, his actual politics requiring almost no independent consideration at all.

Moreover, Clarke applies the same method to Marx and Marxism, to Engels, to Russian Populism and to Plekhanov. In each case, he seems to believe that the subject's entire political character is determined by and reducible to their philosophy/epistemology; and that if he can show, therefore, that Lenin shared certain philosophical premises with Plekhanov, and that Plekhanov shared those premises with the populists, this makes Lenin essentially a populist, not a Marxist.

Now, of course, an individual's philosophy influences their political ideas and practices. To see it as determining in this way, however, is to abolish politics and history; to leave out of the story all real conditions, economic circumstances, class forces and political organisations.

Not surprisingly, I am in strong disagreement with the account of Marxist philosophy which dominates Clarke's article and underpins his argument about Lenin. Clarke asserts that '[a]gainst the common interpretation of Marx as a "materialist" it is essential to be clear that Marx did not oppose materialism to idealism'.[7] This he supports with a

---

[5] See, for example, the various responses to Rees 1991 in *International Socialism* 55, especially Service 1992 and Blackburn 1992.
[6] Clarke, 'Was Lenin a Marxist?', this issue. p. 3.
[7] Clarke p. 11.

quotation from the 1844 *Manuscripts*: 'Consistent naturalism or humanism is distinct from both idealism and materialism, and constitutes at the same time the unifying truth of both'.[8] Clarke also cites a part-quotation from the Theses on Feuerbach:

> Thus in his early works Marx criticised materialism and idealism alike from the standpoint of *'human sensuous activity, practice* ... "practical-critical activity"', 'human society or socialised humanity'.[9]

In my opinion, Clarke misinterprets Marx here. I think the 'materialism' referred to in the quote from the 1844 *Manuscripts* is shorthand for the mechanical, undialectical and bourgeois materialism of the 18th century and of Feuerbach. In other words, it is short for what in the First Thesis on Feuerbach Marx calls 'all hitherto existing materialism – that of Feuerbach included'.[10] I would claim that Marx's dialectical critique of this materialism was on a materialist basis and from within the materialist camp.[11]

This is, of course, the conventional view, shared by – amongst many others – Plekhanov and Lenin. It seems to me clearly to be the thrust of Marx and Engels' main works – *The German Ideology, The Poverty of Philosophy, The Communist Manifesto*, the *1859 Preface, Capital, Anti-Dühring*, etc. Apart from anything else, the attempt to deny Marx's materialism involves asserting: a) a fundamental philosophical divergence between Marx and Engels; b) a failure to notice this divergence by Engels; c) a failure to notice it by Marx. This is just not credible.[12]

Clarke is also mistaken in his presentation of Lenin's philosophical relationship to Plekhanov. 'Lenin could vigorously criticise Plekhanov politically,' he writes, 'while remaining slavishly faithful to Plekhanov's philosophy'.[13] Certainly Lenin was massively influenced by Plekhanov, especially in the early years, and certainly he continued to pay generous tribute to Plekhanov's pioneering role and to his philosophical work. But to describe this as slavish faithfulness is gross caricature. This is to ignore, among much else, Lenin's sharply critical remarks about Plekhanov in his *Philosophical Notebooks*. For example:

---

[8] Clarke p. 12.
[9] Clarke p. 12.
[10] Marx 1962, p. 403.
[11] By materialism I mean: a) the belief that the material world exists independently of and prior to human consciousness; b) the belief that social being determines consciousness rather than vice versa; c) the belief that historical analysis must proceed from the material forces and social relations of production to the realms of religion, philosophy, politics and psychology, rather than the other way round.
[12] For a much fuller refutation of the claim of a split between Marx and Engels, see Rees 1994.
[13] Clarke p. 24.

Plekhanov criticises Kantianism (and agnosticism in general) more from a vulgar-materialistic standpoint than from a dialectical materialistic standpoint.[14]

To be elaborated:
Plekhanov wrote on philosophy (dialectics) probably about 1,000 pages ... Among them, about the large *Logic*, in connection with it, its thought (i.e. dialectics proper, as philosophical science) nil!![15]

I have dealt very summarily with these philosophical differences because, although in one sense they are fundamental, they are of secondary importance to my critique of Clarke's argument about Lenin. The most shocking feature of that argument is not what it contains but what it omits.

In the first place, it fails to discuss the real history of Lenin's relationship to and break with the Narodniks. As is well known, Lenin's elder brother, Alexander, was a Narodnik and was hanged in 1887 for plotting to assassinate the Tsar. In addition to this, the populists were, during Lenin's formative years, the overwhelmingly dominant tendency in the Russian revolutionary movement and viewed as exemplary heroes by the younger radicals. In these circumstances Lenin's organizational/political break with Narodism could not fail to have involved a deep inner struggle over a period of time. Given that Clarke is arguing that this break was somehow illusory or 'unreal', one might have expected him to pay some attention to what occurred. Not a bit of it.

Then again, to expound and strengthen his case that Lenin was essentially a populist, one might have expected Clarke to consider some of the major texts in which Lenin developed his criticism of Narodism. These might include 'What the "Friends of the People" Are and How They Fight Against the Social Democrats' (1894); 'The Economic Content of Narodism and the Criticism of it in Mr Struve's Book' (1894); and *The Development of Capitalism in Russia* (1896).

Given Clarke's argument, one would have thought that an article such as 'Why the Social Democrats Must Declare Determined and Relentless War on the Socialist-Revolutionaries' (1902) might have caught his eye as requiring comment or explanation. Of course, it would still be open to Clarke to argue, even in the face of these overtly hostile works, that at a deeper level Lenin retained certain key populist assumptions or failed to sever all his intellectual ties with the populist movement (in the same way that one could argue that many vaunted 'anti-Stalinists' remained at bottom ideologically dependent on Stalinism, as was shown in 1989).

---

[14] Lenin 1963, p. 179.
[15] Lenin 1963, p. 277. For other critical comments on Plekhanov see Lenin 1963, p. 359 and p. 362.

To pursue this tactic, however, it would have been necessary actually to argue the point, to engage with the texts and reveal their ambiguities, equivocations, aporias etc. In fact, none of these works receives any consideration whatsoever. But if it was too much trouble or too space-consuming to attend to these admittedly rather long-winded texts, then surely Clarke could at least have outlined and discussed the central issues which divided the Marxists from the Narodniks.

Three issues were key: 1) the extent to which capitalism was developing in Russia (and therefore whether Russia might be able to sidestep or avoid capitalism and leap straight to socialism on the basis of the peasant commune); 2) the admissibility of terrorism as a method of struggle; 3) the question of whether the proletariat or the peasantry (or the undifferentiated 'people') should be seen as the principal revolutionary class. In Clarke's piece, there is no systematic discussion of any of these issues. The first is alluded to, but no more. The second – which was politically the most immediate and sharpest point of division and on which Lenin took a characteristically uncomprising stand – is not mentioned at all. The third – which from the standpoint of Marxist theory is the most fundamental of all – is discussed but only briefly and in an appallingly cavalier fashion.

Clarke writes:

> Marx's 'political economy' established the possibility of the advance of capitalism, against the populist belief that the lack of markets made capitalist development impossible in Russia, while also showing the limitations of capitalism, and identifying in the proletariat the sound force which could overthrow it. Ultimately, however, the Marxists of the 1890s were as little concerned with the conditions of the proletariat as had the populists of the 1870s been concerned with the conditions of the peasants. The turn from peasantry to the proletariat did not come about because the suffering of the proletariat was greater than that of the peasantry, and still less because the proletariat constituted a majority of the population, but because the proletariat was identified as the new vehicle for the old populist hopes, the 'material base' for the realisation of socialist values.[16]

That this is a highly unsatisfactory treatment of this question would, I hope, be evident to readers of *Historical Materialism* without comment. I have chosen to discuss it, however, because it is so similar to so much right-wing and bourgeois writing about Lenin (and Marxists in general) with its half-stated insinuations of bad faith and a manipulative attitude to the working masses.

The first point to make is that, of course, the Russian Marxists did not come from the peasantry to the proletariat because of the proletariat's greater suffering, or because it was a majority of the

---

[16] Clarke pp. 4–5.

population (no one, so far as I know, has advanced either such proposition). The reasons, simply, were that the proletariat did not suffer more than the peasantry and was not, at the time, anything remotely approaching a majority. But it does not at all follow from this that either Lenin or any of the other Russian Marxists were not 'concerned' or not genuinely concerned with proletarian conditions.

In political debate the accusation that one's opponents do not 'really care' about the peasants/the workers/the ordinary people is rather common coin, and it is always difficult to measure sincerity. However, I would challenge Simon Clarke to find another political leader or theoretician of any stripe[17] who paid such close attention to the conditions of the working class as did Lenin during those years.

Krupskaya records:

> I remember, for example, how the material about the Thornton factory was collected. It was decided that I should send for a pupil of mine named Krolikov, a sorter in that factory ... Krolikov ... brought a whole exercise book full of information, which he further supplemented verbally. The data was very valuable. In fact Vladimir Ilyich fairly pounced on it ... It was solely on the basis of material gathered in this manner that Vladimir Ilyich wrote his letters and leaflets. Examine his leaflets addressed to the working men and women of the Thornton factory. The detailed knowledge of the subject they deal with is at once apparent.[18]

As for the motive behind the turn to the proletariat, it was not 'because the proletariat was identified as the new vehicle for the old populist hopes', except in so far as those hopes were the hopes of all revolutionaries, rebels and radicals for a society of freedom and equality. Karl Marx made his reasons for orientating on the proletariat absolutely clear in *The Communist Manifesto*.

> Society as a whole is more and more splitting up into two great hostile camps, into two great classes directly freeing each other: Bourgeoisie and Proletariat ...[19]

> In proportion as the bourgeoisie, ie. capital, is developed, in the same proportion is the proletariat, the modern working, developed ...[20]

---

[17] With the exception of Engels when writing *The Condition of the Working Class In England* in 1844 and Marx when researching for *Capital*.

[18] Krupskaya 1970, p. 26. Lenin, it should be said, made an equally detailed investigation of the conditions of the peasantry. For *The Development of Capitalism in Russia* Lenin made use of 299 works in Russian and 38 studies in German, French and English, which makes Clarke's dismissive (but unsubstantiated) assertion that Lenin's 'characterisation of their condition was quite wrong' particularly light-minded and irritating.

[19] Marx and Engels 1973, p. 68.

[20] Marx and Engels 1973, p. 73.

> Of all the classes that stand face to face with the bourgeoisie
> today, the proletariat alone is a really revolutionary class. The
> other classes decay and finally disappear in the face of
> modern industry; the proletariat is its special and essential
> product ...[21]

> All the preceding classes that got the upper hand, sought to
> fortify their already acquired status by subjecting society at
> large to their conditions of appropriation. The proletariat
> cannot become masters of the productive forces of society,
> except by abolishing their own previous mode of
> appropriation, and thereby also every other previous mode of
> appropriation ...[22]

> All previous historical movements were movements of
> minorities, or in the interests of minorities. The proletarian
> movement is the self-conscious, independent movement of
> the immense majority, in the interest of the immense
> majority.[23]

> [I]f, by means of a revolution, it makes itself the ruling class
> and, as such, sweeps away by force the old conditions of
> production, then it will, along with these condition, have
> swept away the conditions for the existence of class
> antagonisms and of classes generally and will thereby have
> abolished its own supremacy as a class.
> In place of the old bourgeois society, with its classes and class
> antagonisms, we shall on association, in which the free
> development of each is the condition for the free development
> of all.[24]

Why should we suppose that Lenin's reasons for focusing on the
proletariat were any different?

There is another aspect of this question which is extremely
important for Lenin's alleged populism, an aspect Clarke partly
travesties and partly ignores. That is, the actual relationship between
Bolshevism and the working class. Clarke tells us of 'the reality of
Russian political and ideological conflicts, which were fought out
amongst intellectuals who had very limited contact with any organised
class forces'.[25]

> However, such a critique [of populism, on the basis of the
> aspirations of the emerging working class movement] was
> obviously impossible in Russia in the late 19th century, just as
> it had been impossible in Germany in the early 19th century,
> for such a movement did not yet exist. In Russia socialism

---

[21] Marx and Engels 1973, p. 77.
[22] Marx and Engels 1973, p. 78.
[23] Marx and Engels 1973, p. 78.
[24] Marx and Engels 1973, p. 87.
[25] Clarke p. 20.

remained the preserve of the intelligentsia, and so remained in
the realm of ideas.[26]

As a description of Russia in the late nineteenth century this is by no
means accurate. The workers' movement was very small but not
completely non-existent. For example, there were the Chaikovists in St.
Petersburg, Moscow and elsewhere between 1870 and 1874. In Odessa
there was the Union of Workers of South Russia, while between 1877
and 1879, there was a strike wave in St. Petersburg involving twenty-six
strikes which led to the formation of the Union of Workers of North
Russia. The movement fell back in the 1880s but revived in the 1890s.
It culminated in May 1896 in a mass strike of textile workers in St.
Petersburg in which members of the St. Petersburg League of Struggle
for the Emancipation of the Working Class (Lenin's organization)
played a leading role.[27]

But whatever the adequacy of Clarke's observations about the late
nineteenth century they are completely awry when it comes to the years
1903–17. These were the years of Bolshevism's emergence,
development and maturation. Of these years, which include the great
mass strikes and attempted uprising of 1905, the bitter reaction of
1907–11 and the resurgent strike wave of 1912–14, it is absurd to say
that 'socialism remained the preserve of the intelligentsia and so
remained in the sphere of ideas' or that 'Russian political and
ideological conflicts were fought out amongst intellectuals who had very
limited contact with any organised class forces'. Trotsky writes:

> In order to understand the two chief tendencies in the
> Russian working class, it is important to have in mind that
> Menshevism finally took shape in the years of ebb and
> reaction. It relied chiefly upon a thin layer of workers who
> had broken with the revolution. Whereas Bolshevism, cruelly
> shattered in the period of the reaction began to rise swiftly on
> the crest of new revolutionary tide in the years before the war.
> 'The most energetic and audacious element, ready for tireless
> struggle, for resistance and continual organisation, is that
> element, those organisations, and those people who are
> concentrated around Lenin.' In these words the Police
> Department estimated the works of the Bolsheviks during the
> years preceding the war.[28]

Nor is it a question of the word of Clarke versus the word of Trotsky
and of the Police Department. There is plenty of hard evidence. In the
elections to the fourth Duma in 1912, six Bolshevik deputies were
elected. They were all in the workers' curias and the six constituencies
which elected them contained 1,144,000 industrial workers. Moreover,
the six deputies were themselves workers – four metal and two textile

---

[26] Clarke p. 22.
[27] Cliff 1975, pp. 62–78.
[28] Trotsky 1977, pp. 57–8.

workers.[29] Also in 1912, the Bolshevik daily paper *Pravda* received contributions from 620 workers groups (in contrast to 89 groups donating to the Menshevik paper) and by May 1914 this had risen to 2873 workers groups (with 671 for the Mensheviks).

Pravda was almost completely financially dependent on workers, not intellectuals, with 87 per cent of its 1914 donations coming from workers' collections and only 13 per cent from non-workers. What is more, *Pravda* was not just a paper for workers but one to which workers themselves actively contributed. The paper published an average of 35 items per day sent in by workers.[30] To all this must be added the experience of 1917 itself, when Bolshevism clearly won a large majority among the Russian proletariat, as even Martov was obliged to recognise.[31]

This historical evidence – which can easily be multiplied many times over – to which Clarke pays not the slightest attention, refutes his whole thesis about Lenin's supposed populism. For it was precisely in close contact with the practical activity of the rising Russian workers movement that Lenin's political thought developed and acquired its characteristic features. Throughout his article, Clarke writes as if 'Leninism' was a unified and more or less unchanging system of thought which arrived fully formed in Lenin's head somewhere in the 1890s, the essence of which is expressed in *What Is To Be Done?* and *Materialism and Empirio-Criticism*. Nothing could be further from the truth.

The practical proposals of *What Is To Be Done?* were a concrete response to the concrete situation facing the movement at that time. Its theoretical arguments in support of those proposals were partly drawn from Kautsky and partly developed in opposition to the trend known as 'Economism'. The experience of the mass revolutionary movement of 1905 modified both the practical proposals and the theoretical arguments.[32] The years of reaction deepened Lenin's opposition to

---

[29] Cliff 1977, p. 351.

[30] All those figures are taken from Cliff 1977, pp. 338–52. Cliff gives a detailed description of *Pravda's* production, distribution and content which provides an illuminating picture of the intimate interaction between Lenin's politics and the Russian working class movement.

[31] 'Understand, please, that before us after is a victorious uprising of the proletariat – almost the entire proletariat supports Lenin and expects its social liberation from the uprising.' Martov to Axelrod, 19 November 1917 cited in Getzler 1967, p. 172.

[32] For a more detailed and contextualised account of *What Is To Be Done?* and the origins of Bolshevism, as well as how Lenin's views changed under the impact of 1905, see Molyneux 1978, pp. 36–55 and pp. 57–63. Clarke, in particular, seems totally unaware of the fact that after 1905 Lenin modified the formulations of *What Is To Be Done?* calling it 'a controversial correction of "economist" distortions...[which] it would be wrong to regard...in any other light.' (Lenin, 1962b, p. 108). Lenin also claimed that 'The working class is instinctively, spontaneously social democratic' (Lenin, 1962a, p. 32) and noting 'how the elementary instinct of the working class movement is able to correct the conceptions of the greatest minds.' (Lenin 1965, p. 155). Of course it is possible that Clarke does know about this but chooses not to mention it, in which case it seems less than honest to present *What Is To Be Done?* as a defining text of Leninism and Bolshevism.

Menshevism and clarified his ideas on the revolutionary use of elections, the combination of legal and illegal work and the right of nations to self-determination in the Russian Empire.

The outbreak of World War I and the collapse of the Second International produced a whole raft of new developments in 'Leninism': a complete break with social democracy; a retrospective understanding that Bolshevism had been 'a party of a new type' all along; a clarification of the Marxist attitude to war in general and the specific response of revolutionary defeatism to imperialist war; the development of the general theory of imperialism as the latest stage of capitalism; the beginning of the restoration and development of the Marxist theory of the state; a reconsideration of Hegel and the dialectic. To this, the year 1917 adds a new understanding of the significance of the Soviet, a further development of theory of the state and a substantial revision of his previous theory of the class nature of the Russian Revolution.

In all of this, Lenin influenced the Russian workers but the Russian workers also influenced Lenin. Just as Marx got his first concrete ideas on the form of the dictatorship of the proletariat from the Paris Commune, so Lenin drew the concept of soviet power from the deeds of the Petrograd workers in October 1905 and February 1917. If Lenin were 'essentially' or 'fundamentally' a 'populist', none of this would have been possible.

If Lenin's response to the war in 1914 — his refusal to defend the fatherland, his call to transform the imperialist war into a civil war, and his call for the formation of a new workers' international — is the response of a 'populist' then political terms have no meaning. Moreover, the following question must be asked: how is it that none of the numerous real populists in Russia responded in any similar way to Lenin, whereas those few who did take a broadly similar internationalist stand — Luxemburg and Liebknecht, John MacLean, Trotsky, et al. — were all revolutionary socialists and Marxists? Or were they all populists too?

Of course, for Clarke, none of this real history matters and none of these vulgar political questions arise, for everything is reducible to and apparently determined by abstract theory and philosophy. The result, it has to be said, is an account of Lenin and of Bolshevism which is not only false, and profoundly idealist, but also incredibly similar in structure and content to the standard bourgeois critique of Lenin outlined at the beginning of this article. Whereas for Leonard Schapiro and his ilk, the original sin of Bolshevism lay in Lenin's personal totalitarianism as manifested in *What Is To Be Done?*, for Clarke '[t]he philosophical roots of Bolshevik politics can be traced directly back to Plekhanov's fundamental misunderstanding of the significance of Marx's critique of political economy'.[33] The one thing this kind of analysis is most certainly not is historical materialist.

---

[33] Clarke p. 14.

There is one further feature of Clarke's article on which I want to comment. This is its persistent tendency to theoretical and historical carelessness or sloppiness – there is no way of putting this politely – in its formulations and assertions. The result is numerous claims, statements and allegations about or against Marx, Plekhanov, Lenin et al., which either make little sense, are serious distortions, or are completely unsubstantiated. To deal with all these dubious claims and statements would require a polemic out of all proportion to the significance of its object and the patience of the reader. I shall therefore restrict myself to a few examples.

First the article's opening lines:

> Lenin's name has been coupled with that of Marx as the co-founder of the theory of 'Marxism-Leninism'. However, despite his emphasis on the role of revolutionary theory, Lenin's original theoretical contributions to the development of Marxism were very limited. His talents were those of a determined revolutionary, in the populist tradition of Chernyshevsky, and a brilliantly effective propagandist and political organiser.[34]

Almost every phrase of this passage requires criticism. 'Lenin's name has been coupled with ...'. The use of the passive tense here hides the fact that the people who performed the coupling and invented the term 'Marxism-Leninism' were the Stalinists (followed by the Maoists), and that they did so as part of the cult of Lenin which was used to reinforce the cult of Stalin (and Mao). Lenin himself would never have countenanced the term had it arisen in his lifetime, which it did not.

Clearly the co-founders of Marxism were Marx and Engels, and in so far as we can speak of 'Leninism', it is as a term for Lenin's specific contribution to the development of Marxism. Clarke tells us this contribution was 'very limited' and that Lenin was primarily a 'brilliantly effective propagandist and political organiser'. This is palpably false. Lenin was not especially distinguished as a propagandist – which books, pamphlets etc. does Clarke have in mind? Most of Lenin's writings were for the party cadres and others, such as Trotsky, were much more 'brilliant' writers and speakers – but his theoretical contributions (on the development of capitalism, on the party, on the national question, on war, on imperialism, on the state, on revolutionary strategy and tactics) were enormous.

But, in any case, this is not Clarke's argument. His argument is that Lenin's theoretical contribution (large or small) was not to the development of Marxism but to its transformation or distortion. Even this is not expressed clearly, for in the next sentence we are told that Lenin's

---

[34] Clarke p. 3.

contribution to 'Marxism-Leninism' was to modify Marxist orthodoxy in such a way as to integrate the political and organisational principles of revolutionary populism into Marxism ...[35]

In the sentence after that, Clarke claims that Lenin 'completed Plekhanov's project by assimilating Marxism to the very different theoretical framework of populism'.[36] Did Lenin integrate populist politics and organisation into Marxism or did he assimilate Marxism to the populists' theoretical framework? Clarke is simply not bothering to think what he is saying from sentence to sentence.

A second example:

> Marxism had been influential in Russia from an early stage in the development of populism, for Marx provided the most powerful critique of modern capitalism, and the strongest of arguments for resisting its advance. But the greatest importance of Marxism was that it provided the ideological bridge from romantic populism to modern socialism, providing a scientific theory which could both explain the failures of populism, and point a new way forward. Marx's 'political economy' established the possibility of the advance of capitalism, against the populist belief that the lack of markets made capitalist development impossible in Russia, while also showing the limitations of capitalism, and identifying in the proletariat the social force which would overthrow it.[37]

What does it mean to describe Marxism as the 'bridge' from populism to modern socialism? What was modern socialism in Russia if not Marxism? Was Marxism a bridge to itself, to nothing, to something unspecified, or is the sentence simply careless? We are then told how Marx's political economy established various positions against populism. But, if we ask who actually showed that Marx's political economy demonstrated the possibility of capitalist development in Russia, and who identified the Russian proletariat as the force that would overthrow Russian Tsarism and capitalism, it turns out to be Plekhanov and Lenin – the same people identified in the rest of the article as essentially populists.

A third and final example.

> On the question of the material base of socialism Lenin was more ambivalent. He rejected the populist faith in the commune, and the revisionist faith in cooperative production, but before the revolution he wavered between a commitment to the soviet as providing the material and political base of the new society, with the state serving only a transitional role as

---

[35] Clarke p. 3.
[36] Clarke p. 3.
[37] Clarke pp. 4–5.

> the instrument of the 'dictatorship of the proletariat', and an
> orthodox belief in the state as providing a more permanent
> basis of the new society. In the event, he combined the worst
> of both viewpoints, soon institutionalising a dictatorial state as
> the permanent basis of the new society.[38]

It is very hard to make sense of this at all. How could Soviets provide the 'material base' of the new society, and can one speak of a 'material and political base' when politics – including Soviets – is part of the superstructure not the base? And how can one attribute this muddle to Lenin? And where and when did Lenin 'waver' between a commitment to the soviet and 'an orthodox belief in the state' (as so often, Clarke does not trouble to quote or cite texts)? What does 'orthodox' mean in this context, orthodox Marxist(?), orthodox bourgeois, or what? Surely, for Lenin, it was not Soviets *or* state: the Soviets were the newly discovered form *of* the workers' state. In the end, all this whole passage amounts to is the ever so familiar charge that the terrible Lenin set up a permanent dictatorial state as a kind of personal choice with, once again, no reference to material circumstances, class forces, concrete conditions etc. I suspect that this is all the whole article amounts to as well.

My reason for dwelling on these contradictions, errors and clumsy formulations is not pedantry nor polemical zeal but my suspicion that they are symptomatic of the climate I referred to earlier, where anything goes as far as Lenin and Leninism are concerned. About 20 years ago Simon Clarke, greatly to his credit, produced a major critique of Althusser.[39] The difference in quality between the work on Althusser and the present piece is striking, even in such matters as conscientious referencing. If today Clarke were producing a critique of, say, Stuart Hall, Anthony Giddens or even Theodor Adorno, I think he would feel obliged to display more care and meticulousness than he does with Lenin. This seems to me deplorable and worth protesting about.

In this context I must say a word about Howard Chodos' and Colin Hays's 'So The Party's Over? Marxism and Political Strategy After "the Fall"'. This study has the merit of at least posing the question of socialist organisation – rare enough these days. Nevertheless, its treatment of Leninism can hardly be considered serious.

Chodos and Hay claim that, '[I]n order … to work out a provisional balance sheet of the Leninist legacy 90 years on, it is first necessary to try to define as clearly as possible what is meant by Leninism'.[40]

Yet this 'capsule summary' discusses a timeless abstract model of 'Leninism' which is set up by Chodos and Hay without reference to any of Lenin's writing or (similarly to Clarke) any actual history. The most catastrophic effect of this is the eradication of any distinction between Leninist and Stalinist forms of organisation. It is not that Chodos and

---

[38] Clarke p. 25.
[39] Clarke 1980.
[40] Chodos and Hay, p. 32.

Hay argue that Leninism and Stalinism are the same, they simply fail even to consider the question. But the question *must* be considered.

If there is no difference between Leninism and Stalinism, then Leninism is not a model of radical organising: it is a model of oppression and counter-revolution. The Communist parties of the Soviet Union (from Stalin to Gorbachev), of China, of Eastern Europe etc., were not somewhat deficient in democracy or somewhat over zealous in their centralism. They were undemocratic and anti-democratic full stop. If, on the other hand, a distinction is made between Leninism and Stalinism, then the assessment of Leninism as so 'influential and successful' must be revised, since it is clear that, after 1923, the Stalinist 'model' has been far more widespread and 'successful' than anything remotely resembling original Leninism.[41]

The failure to distinguish Leninism and Stalinism may be the most serious consequence of this historical approach, but it is by no means the only one. In fact, the Leninist theory of the party is more or less reduced to 'democratic centralism', which is presented in terms of a few formulae ('unity on action', 'free discussion', 'minority submitting to the majority, lower level bodies to higher level bodies') which could be drawn from any Stalinist textbook. This completely misses the essence of Leninism, which lies not in any organisational formulae or 'model' but, for good or ill, in a view of the relationship of the party to the working class, its struggle and its consciousness. Furthermore, Chodos and Hay tell us that

> democratic centralism was to be the guarantor of the unity of the party... [but] [i]n a Leninist party the limits to free expression associated with democratic centralism apply to the whole party. When combined with the additional stricture that lower bodies and individual members had to submit to the decisions made by higher bodies, it is clear that the restrictions to democratic life were unnecessarily broad. ... [T]he scope of the application of democratic centralism ... made it undemocratic.[42]

Once again, assertions are made about 'Leninism' without any reference to Lenin's writings, any actual examples of his political practice, any supporting facts or evidence at all. But, then, the claim that '[T]he scope of the application of democratic centralism ... made it undemocratic' could not be supported by quotations from Lenin. It is

---

[41] Chodos' and Hay's confusion on this question is graphically illustrated by their phrase 'the Leninist tradition of the Third International'. Do they mean the Third International which debated centrism and ultra-leftism, revolutionary participation in elections and the united front, or the Third International which switched from the theory of social fascism to the popular front without a word of dissent? Do they mean the Third International of John Reed, Victor Serge and Alfred Rosmer or of Dimitrov, Thälman and Thorez? The Third International can reasonably be described as Leninist for about four years: it was Stalinist for 20.

[42] Chodos and Hay, pp. 36–7.

refuted by numerous episodes in the history of Bolshevism,which was marked by vigorous internal discussion, debate and controversy, beginning with the original split with the Mensheviks and ending with the 21 conditions of admission to the Comintern (designed explicitly to exclude left social democrats and centrists). For Lenin, for example, considerations of unity in action and democratic centralism were always subordinate to questions of fundamental politics.

What I am advocating and counterposing to the articles by Clarke and by Chodos and Hay is an historical materialist approach to Lenin. This means, first and foremost, starting out from the real historical facts of Lenin's political life and work (which include Lenin's voluminous writings).[43] Secondly, it means understanding Lenin and Leninism in the context of Russian and world capitalism and the Russian and international class struggle of the time.

Naturally, this advocacy is not and cannot be innocent. I believe that an historical materialist account of Lenin[44] will conclude: a) that Leninism was quite distinct from and did not (in other than the chronological sense) 'lead to' Stalinism; b) that Leninism in the shape of the Bolshevik Party achieved an historically unique fusion with the politically advanced layers of the Russian working class and this played a crucial role in enabling that class to take power; c) that, although some features of Leninism were specific to Russia at the turn of the century or Russia in 1917, its most important characteristics and principles (especially those concerning the necessity of building an independent revolutionary party based in the working class) were valid internationally and remain valid today.

In left-wing journals these days, articles proclaiming the necessity of rethinking socialist principles, Marxist theory and radical strategy are ten-a-penny. I take the unfashionable opposite view, namely that socialist theory can only be kept up and developed if it builds on the rich and fertile foundation of classical Marxism, of which Leninism is an important part. In other words, I share with Isaac Newton the view that if we can see far it is because we stand on the shoulders of giants. I am also all too familiar with the sight of those who boldly declare they have dispensed with all foundations, and that giants' shoulders are certainly not needed in this brave new world, falling flat on their faces.

---

[43] Marx and Engels repeatedly insisted that their philosophical and historical method could not be a substitute for serious study of historical facts. See for example, Engels to C. Schmidt, 5 August 1890 in Marx and Engels 1962, pp. 486–7. See also Trotsky's comment: 'Dialectics cannot be imposed on the facts; it has to be deduced from the facts, from their nature and development', Trotsky 1973, p. 233.

[44] For my own attempt at a historical materialist account of Lenin's theory of the party, see Molyneux 1978, Chapters 2 and 3. For more comprehensive and substantial Marxist analyses of Lenin and Leninism, see Lukács 1970, and Cliff 1975–9. And, for an interesting account of Lenin's philosophy, including its relation with Plekhanov, see Rees 1998.

References

Blackburn, Robin 1992, 'Reply to John Rees', *International Socialism* 55: 107–12.

Clarke, Simon 1980, 'Althusserian Marxism' in *One-Dimensional Marxism: Althusser and the Politics of Culture*, edited by Simon Clarke et al, London: Macmillan.

Cliff, Tony 1975–9, *Lenin* (4 volumes), London: Bookmarks.

Cliff, Tony 1975, *Lenin Volume 1: Building the Party*, London: Bookmarks.

Getzler, Israel 1967, *Martov*, Cambridge: Cambridge University Press.

Haynes, Mike 1998, 'Social History and the Russian Revolution' in *Essays on Historical Materialism*, edited by John Rees, London: Bookmarks.

Kautsky, Karl 1981, *The Dictatorship of the Proletariat*, Westport, Conn.: Greenwood Press.

Kautsky, Karl 1920 [1918], *Terrorism and Communism*, London: National Labour Press.

Krupskaya, Nadezhda 1970, *Memories of Lenin*, London: Lawrence and Wishart.

Lenin, V.I. 1962, *Collected Works* Volume 10, Moscow: Foreign Languages Publishing House.

Lenin, V.I. 1962, *Collected Works* Volume 13, Moscow: Foreign Languages Publishing House.

Lenin, V.I. 1961, *Collected Works* Volume 38, Moscow: Foreign Languages Publishing House.

Lenin, V.I. 1965, *Two Tactics of Social Democracy in the Democratic Revolution*, Peking: Foreign Languages Press.

Lukacs, Georg 1970, *Lenin: A Study on the Unity of his Thought*, London: New Left Books.

Marx, Karl and Engels, Friedrich 1962, *Marx Engels Selected Works* Volume 2, Moscow: Progress Publishers.

Marx, Karl and Engels, Friedrich 1973, *The Communist Manifesto* in *The Revolutions of 1848*, Harmondsworth: Penguin.

Molyneux, John 1978, *Marxism and the Party*, London: Bookmarks.

Rees, John, 1998, *The Algebra of Revolution*, London: Routledge.

Rees, John 1991, 'In Defence of October', *International Socialism* 52. 3–79.

Rees, John 1994, 'Engels' Marxism', *International Socialism* 65. 47–82.

Service, Robert 1992, 'Did Lenin Lead to Stalin?', *International Socialism* 55. 77–84.

Trotsky, Leon 1973, *Problems of Everyday Life*, New York: Pathfinder.

Trotsky, Leon 1977, *The History of the Russian Revolution*, London: Pluto Press.

DOXA
Cuadernos de Ciencias Sociales
A Quarterly Review of Social and Political Theory and Criticism
from BUENOS AIRES

Articles, papers, interviews, books reviews, conference reports on Sociology, History, Philosophy, Economy, Politics, and Cultural Studies
(in Spanish)

Issue No 19, Primavera - Verano 1998
Coming soon!

Dossier : *Marx (ism) in the year of celebrations*:

E. HOBSBAWN: The 150 Anniversary of the *Communist Manifesto* ❑ S. CLARKE: The *Communist Manifesto* (The Political Problem of Globalisation of Capital) ❑ A. DINERSTEIN y M. NEARY : Class Struggle and the *Communist Manifesto* (The (De)constructive Capacity of the *Manifesto*) ❑ E. LOGIUDICE : Insights into Ideology and the State ❑ P. GILABERT : Marx and Democracy. Notes for a further Investigation

and L. FERREYRA: Comments on Gianfranco Lagrassa's "Capitalismo Lavorativo" ❑ E. MAGNANI: Argentine Cinema under the New Cinema Act ❑ A. CIRIZA: Insights into the Crisis of Politics ❑ Eduardo GRUNER: The Other Mirror ❑ A.G. QUINTERO RIVERA *Salsa* of the Great Escape ❑ Fabián BOSOER: Rediscovering Kelsen

SUBSCRIPTIONS AND BACK ISSUES

Annual Subscription Rates for 3 issues (includes postage)
Individual: £ 24
Libraries and Institutions: £ 40
Back issues (includes postage)
Single issues: £ 6
Back issues: nos. 13-16: £ 5

Name:	
Address:	
City:	Country:
Postcode:	Sub-amount:
Back issues:	Tot. Amount

Please start my subscription with No 17 ❑ 18 ❑ 19 ❑

Postal Orders or cheques to Tesis 11. Grupo Editor SRL
Send to: Av. de Mayo 1370 - Piso 14 - Of 355/56
(c.p.1362) Capital Federal Buenos Aires - Argentina

Problems of Leninism

John Ehrenberg

We live in strange, frustrating and paradoxical times.[1] Like other trends on the left, Marxism is immobilised by theoretical confusion and practical ineffectiveness just when a relentless state-led war against the working class is nearing the end of its second decade, the greatest transfer of wealth from the poor to the rich in human history has reasserted the centrality of class with a vengeance, the international capitalist financial system teeters on the edge of collapse, whole countries are bankrupt, and hundreds of millions of people are undergoing absolute immiseration and devastating attacks on their standard of living. The gap between what the objective situation demands and what the Left has to offer is so profound that public affairs has become little more than a debate between a powerful right and an eviscerated 'centre' – all this at a time of unprecedented crisis and opportunity. Indeed, we do not even seem to know *what* to talk about. Reminders of how theoretical blind alleys and historic openings have often gone hand in hand may help us orient ourselves to broad trends, but they only underline how essential it is that we begin addressing the profoundly important questions of contemporary life. Until we do, we should not be surprised that people put their trust in angels, consult soothsayers, and are not interested in what we have to say.

But if we are to articulate a credible alternative to the present, we have to come to terms with some of the ghosts from our past. Marxism has always been a theory of communism as much as a critique of capitalism, and a sober accounting is indispensable for consolidation and advance. A wholesale rejection of our theoretical and organisational traditions is clearly not in order, but neither is a ritualistic adherence to past analyses. It is never easy to blend innovation with fundamental principles. Flexibility need not come at the expense of orthodoxy, but we are victimised by a contemporary history which limits our political development because we do not know what sense to make of it. Part of our political project needs to be the articulation of plausible alternatives to prosperous and democratic capitalist social orders. But, for the most part, Marxists have stopped short of a comprehensive assessment of the Russian Revolution and of Soviet-style socialism because a strategy of state-led industrialisation has long seemed uniquely applicable to backward societies.

---

[1] The foundations of much of the following can be examined in more detail in Ehrenberg 1992.

It is particularly important that we consider Lenin, all the more so because he began his critically important work in similar circumstances of a radical disjuncture between an objective situation which was full of opportunities and a theoretically impoverished and organisationally confused Left. The most important figure in twentieth-century Marxism, he was far more than an organisational leader pure and simple. But the Left is often scared of dealing with him. It has become fashionable to focus almost exclusively on his theory of the party and then dismiss it by describing it as a uniquely Russian phenomenon – an understandable, if unfortunate, combination of political autocracy, conspiratorial traditions and numbing backwardness, which has no relevance to the more open environment of the West. Such a position is, of course, not new. The old saw that Lenin was a voluntarist terrorist conspirator is rooted in Menshevik attacks on his organisational projections and has stood at the centre of all bourgeois attacks on him for three quarters of a century. But these attempts to sever Lenin the communist from Marx the humanist critic were always conditioned by a certain reluctant admiration. Even at the height of the Cold War, the most anti-communist analysts were willing to grant his extraordinary tactical mind even as they derided his contributions to the *corpus* of Marxist theory.

This dilemma afflicts the Left all over the world, but a particularly clear example of how it can paralyse fruitful debate can be found in the pages of this journal. Simon Clarke deals with Lenin by simply denying that he needs to. His approach is interesting only in its strategy; seeking to sever the link between Marx and Lenin, he traces the latter's populist roots to Plekhanov. Marx can be saved by denying Lenin.

But this argument simply flies in the face of the early history of Russian Marxism. The turn of the century was characterised by years of acute theoretical struggle about Russia's future, a debate which engulfed the nascent Left for years. Russian Marxism arose out of these struggles, and it did so by sharply distinguishing itself from the populists. Indeed, Plekhanov became famous because of his work against populism, and his central claim – that Russia was already being transformed by markets, that capitalist social relations had already become dominant in the country, and hence that the proletariat, in alliance with the peasantry and led by the socialist intelligentsia, would be the decisive agent of political and social transformation – rested on eminently Marxist foundations. The most important intellectual leader of the first generation of Russian Marxists, Plekhanov established an indispensable link between Lenin and the body of orthodox theory, which he was the first to popularise. The claim that Plekhanov was a populist flies in the face of what he and those around him – Narodnik *as well as* Marxist – knew to be the case. It also trivialises the importance of the theoretical and political debate which was absorbing the energy of many talented and principled Russian leftists.

Like many other young men of his generation, Lenin was absorbed in the theoretical, economic and political struggle against Russian populism. It was during these years – years which culminated with *The Development of Capitalism in Russia* – that his criticism of Russian populism brought him to the centre of Russia's rapidly-growing Marxist movement. Neil Harding's important analysis of this struggle rightly focuses on its impact on the history of Russian Marxism and the course of the Russian Revolution.[2] This is not the place to recapitulate his excellent analysis. Suffice it to say that Lenin's documentation of the differentiation of the peasantry, the appearance of regional and national markets, the growth of cities, and the appearance of a combative proletariat continued Plekhanov's work and laid the groundwork for a distinctively Marxist analysis of Russian conditions. If capitalism was the future – as Plekhanov, Lenin and a whole generation demonstrated – then the proletariat was the class toward which Russian revolutionaries should be directing their attention and Marxism provided the theoretical grounding with which to assess accurately the possibilities of broad political action. The relationship between the proletariat and the peasantry, and between the bourgeois and socialist revolutions, the role of the socialist intelligentsia, even Lenin's celebrated theory of the party cannot be understood apart from his early struggles against both the legacy of Russian populism and the related orientation of 'legal Marxism' and 'economism'.

Clarke's tortuous attempt to link Plekhanov to Feuerbach and populism, and thereby to demonstrate that Lenin can be dissociated from Marxism, leads to some serious misinterpretations which only make it more difficult to navigate the serious questions which confront us. If the populists rested their hopes on the revolutionary potential of the peasantry, the Marxist turn toward the proletariat signified considerably more than simply identifying a new agent to accomplish a revolution whose main outlines were shared by both strands of the Russian Left. A peasant revolution is qualitatively different from a proletarian transformation, and one does not get any closer to the truth by pretending that the only difference between the populists and the Marxists was who was going to lead. The proletariat was much more than Clarke's 'new vehicle for the old populist hopes',[3] and everyone involved in the debate knew that the issue was the *kind* of revolution which would come to Russia. In this context, it is simply not the case that Marxists resisted the advance of capitalism in Russia. They knew that it was not up to them to begin with, and, in any event, they were all clear that it was important to support the further development of capitalist social relations and bourgeois democracy *in the interests of a proletarian revolution*. It was the *populists* who were the reactionaries on this score, and Clarke continues their mistake by mistakenly attributing it to Marx.

---

[2] See Harding, 1983.
[3] Clarke, p. 5.

Clarke's convoluted attempt to sever Plekhanov from Marx by locating the roots of 'dialectical materialism' in Feuerbach and populism makes it impossible to understand Marx's critique of Hegel. Marx certainly saw himself as a materialist and was always a sharp critic of plans for social reform by would-be saviours of Humanity. Such an attitude was rooted in his early critique of Hegelian idealism, and having him defend 'social science' over 'philosophy' is to ignore the critical importance of the *Preface to a Critique of Political Economy*. Marx's famous description of his own intellectual development quite clearly establishes how he defined himself in this matter, and it would have been useful if Clarke had engaged with that particular text.

In any event, Clarke wants to identify Plekhanov's explication of 'dialectical materialism' as a distortion of Marxism which enabled the populist Plekhanov to clothe himself in orthodox Marxist terminology. But Clarke's main target here is Lenin. If Plekhanov can be severed from Marxism through an analysis of method, then so can Lenin. Clarke's critique of Plekhanov is incidental to his main project.

But even if he is right about Plekhanov – which he is not – Clarke fails to do justice to 'the Lenin problem' because Plekhanov was never as important to Lenin as Clarke maintains. Lenin inherited and used a great deal of material in his formative years. As important as he was, Plekhanov was only one influence.

Clarke attempts to demonstrate Lenin's roots in populism's voluntaristic, conspiratorial and terroristic tradition by saying that he faced the same dilemma as his populist forebears and responded to it in the same way. Confronted, says Clarke, by a situation in which their theoretical projections ran far ahead of the proletariat's political capacity, Marxists had to choose between waiting for the spontaneous appearance of revolutionary consciousness, engaging in legal propaganda and political education, and organising a conspiratorial revolutionary vanguard. True to his roots in Chernyshevsky's populism, Lenin chose the latter course and then provided theoretical justification for his position by using Plekhanov's version of 'dialectical and historical materialism' to argue that the organised revolutionary intelligentsia should substitute itself for the recalcitrant proletariat. For Clarke, '[t]he privileged status of the intelligentsia, which was established by Plekhanov's philosophy, is realised in the Leninist conception of the Party'[4] which expressed the leading role of Marxist ideology. Lenin's party-led Bolshevism was born as a voluntaristic populist perversion of Marxism.

This is an old claim, but our current dilemma requires that we take it seriously. Clarke claims that four distinctive characteristics of Russian populism found their way into Bolshevism via Plekhanov and Lenin and constitute the latter's break with what he calls 'orthodox' Marxism: the importance of theory and the leading role of revolutionary intellectuals;

---

[4] Clarke, pp. 23–4.

the power of revolutionary will and the leading role of the party; the hostility to the state, a commitment to insurrection and inattention to the content of socialist democracy; and a faith in the revolutionary potential of the peasantry. But it was always Marx and Engels who made it clear that party-led comprehensive mass political activity represents the fullest development of the class struggle and who placed particular emphasis on the role of theory. All of Lenin's early work, culminating as it did in *What Is To Be Done?*, leads in the same direction, and he enthusiastically, explicitly and repeatedly supported Kautsky's eminently orthodox observation that Social Democracy was the fusion of socialist theory with the spontaneous working-class struggle – something which Clarke neglects to mention. This is not to suggest that Russian Marxists were not seriously divided on the nature of the revolutionary party – a question which is highly relevant to contemporary discussions. But it is not sufficient to ignore the importance of the problem by denying that Lenin was working within the Marxist tradition. Like Clarke's 'orthodox' Marxists, Lenin also rejected populist nostalgia for peasant communes and co-operatives and looked to organise the already-active proletariat into a sustained political campaign for the fullest measure of bourgeois democracy and land reform – a campaign which, he repeatedly observed, would inevitably take the workers, peasants and revolutionary intelligentsia beyond the boundaries of Russian capitalism and bourgeois democracy.

Marx had drawn exactly the same lessons from the failed revolutions of 1848, and Lenin carefully studied his rejection of the liberal and republican bourgeoisie as he turned his attention to Russia's vast peasantry. Indeed, for Clarke to say that Lenin was a populist because he took theory and party organisation seriously, tried to orient the Russian Left to comprehensive political struggle and the seizure of state power, and addressed himself to rural affairs is to make exactly the same mistake which relegated the Narodniks to well-deserved obscurity: denying that Marxism provides the way to understand capitalism. Whether Lenin's political and organisational projections make any sense for socialists in advanced democratic bourgeois social orders is another – and very important – matter.

But if we are to move forward we have to take seriously the questions posed by the *real* history of twentieth-century communism, and we cannot begin until we recognise Lenin as a Marxist. In an age of fragmentation, identity politics and self-indulgent postmodernism, it might be wise to consider Lenin's words in *What Is To Be Done?*

> Working-class consciousness cannot be genuine political consciousness unless the workers are trained to respond to *all* cases of tyranny, violence, and abuse, no matter *what* class is affected – unless they are trained, moreover, to respond from a Social-Democratic point of view and no other. The consciousness of the working masses cannot be genuine class-consciousness, unless the workers learn, from concrete,

and above all from topical, political facts and events to observe *every* other social class in *all* the manifestations of its intellectual, ethical, and political life, unless they learn to apply in practice the materialist analysis and the materialist estimate of *all* aspects of the life and activity of *all* classes, strata, and groups of the population. Those who concentrate the attention, observation, and consciousness of the working class exclusively, or even mainly, upon itself are not Social-Democrats, for the self-knowledge of the working class is indissolubly bound up, not only with a fully clear theoretical understanding – or rather not so much with the theoretical, as with the practical, understanding – of the relationships between *all* the various classes of modern society, acquired through the experience of political life.[5]

To their credit, Howard Chodos and Colin Hay take Lenin seriously, recognise how destructive the logic of spontaneity and fragmentation has been, and understand the importance of broad party-led political activity. Their discussion of Lenin's theory of the party suggests that posing the problem as one between spontaneity and consciousness is too restricted a formulation which misses important elements of individual and group activity and makes it difficult to appreciate Lenin's achievements and his limitations. Lenin certainly posed the question of party organisation because he wanted to safeguard the political independence of the increasingly powerful Russian workers' movement, and he was convinced that only a certain kind of political organisation was adequate to the tasks at hand. But his assessment of the overall situation facing the Russian workers was critical.

The pull of the spontaneous movement toward reformism and compromise was particularly dangerous, he repeatedly asserted, precisely because the labour movement was becoming such a powerful force. Everyone – police spies, Christian socialists, Social Democrats, liberals and populists alike – was trying to understand how to orient themselves to a labour movement whose spontaneous motion drew it into incessant conflict with Tsarism but whose ability to pose a credible alternative to the autocracy was limited by lack of effective *political* leadership. Providing such leadership was the task of communists, and Lenin considered the situation so desperate because the Left did not know what to do. It was the weakness and disorientation of the *Social-Democrats*, and not his alleged contempt for the workers, which drove Lenin's theory of the vanguard party.

But Lenin stands accused of a certain theoretical dogmatism with respect to Marxist fundamentals. Chodos and Hay are right that the political program of a putative party cannot be determined beforehand and that in many respects it can take shape only in the actual course of the class struggle. They value Lenin's orientation toward the state, his determination to phrase the issues facing the workers in political terms,

---

[5] Lenin 1960, pp. 412–13.

and his tactical flexibility. Predefined positions are certainly to be avoided, but it is by no means clear that Lenin was the dogmatist that Chodos and Hay suggest. If Leninist vanguardism stemmed from theoretical rigidity and rigid adherence to first principles – and not, *à la* Clarke, to Lenin's populist roots – then Chodos and Hay should substantiate this claim with solid analysis. They may be right that Lenin's politics need to be moderated with Social Democracy's commitment to internal party democracy and a heightened willingness to let situations define themselves. The project of a self-critical and self-radicalising socialism which does not impose predetermined ideological categories on a fluid political situation is certainly vital to a rejuvenated Left. Chodos and Hay are right to begin to articulate a vision of party organisation and activity which might make the important strengths of Lenin's approach more appropriate to those of us who are working in advanced democratic societies.

But socialism is considerably more than the moment of rupture, and Marxists must be able to articulate more than the necessity of a break with capitalism. It is certainly true that we cannot know what the future will look like with certainty – something which Marx, Engels and Lenin knew, by the way. But if the future lies within the present, it also follows that the present can be evaluated only with respect to its future. Where integral political theory ends and dangerous teleology begins is often difficult to determine, but an understandable desire to avoid dogmatism should not blind us to the necessity of posing alternatives. Chodos and Hay are right that '[w]e know enough about capitalism to know that we must do better'.[6] But that is not enough, and my students – Brooklyn-born, largely African-American, female and overwhelmingly proletarian – always temper their enthusiasm for Marxism's analysis of capitalism with understandable questions about its vision of the future. They are right to be careful. Theory is certainly not a crystal ball, but it can do more than Chodos and Hay are willing to admit. Progressives, socialists and communists have become far too frightened of talking about the future in a way that makes sense. We all dismiss The Baroness's crude claim that there is no alternative, but we often act as though she is right.

From Richard Rorty to Cornel West, American leftists avoid theory like the plague and increasingly content themselves with the most modest suggestions for improvement. But we do not have to. Modifying Lenin does not require an embrace of the very spontaneism against which his theory of the party took shape. Socialism, like everything else, is surely a work in progress. But classes still produce leaders, and the workers expect their leaders to lead. If the history of twentieth-century communism tells us anything, it is that no conceivable coalition of organisations, movements and grouplets can contest the bourgeoisie and its state unless it is animated by a political vision and led by a political party. It will be enormously difficult to give this elementary

[6] Chodos and Hay, p. 41.

principle a practical expression, but it is all the more important that we begin. Chodos and Hay have made some important initial suggestions about how to proceed. Let's move the discussion forward.

References

Ehrenberg, John 1992, *The Dictatorship of the Proletariat: Marxism's Theory of Socialist Democracy*, New York and London: Routledge.

Harding,Neil 1983, *Lenin's Political Thought*, London: Macmillan.

Lenin, V.I., 1961, *What Is to be Done?* in *Collected Works* Volume 5, Moscow: Foreign Languages Publishing House.

Political Action, Context and Conjuncture

Alan Shandro

Concerned to remedy the 'state of severe disarray' that immobilises the left in advanced capitalist countries, Howard Chodos and Colin Hay set out to inquire into 'the organisational conditions that are necessary to the radical transformation of capitalism'.[1] This disarray is expressed in the drift of social-democratic parties in the wake of the neoliberal mainstream, the inability of a fragmented and disappearing radical Left to orient either itself or spontaneous resistance to the global neoliberal agenda, and the failure of the 'new' social movements as a vehicle of 'broader social transformation'. Against this background of fragmentation, dispersal and division, the authors spell out their central contention: the idea that 'there is a distinctively creative component to politics',[2] as the claim that organisation in general and the political party in particular provide the necessary context for the actualisation of 'belief-dependent emergent capacities'. Fulfilling a 'multi-dimensional mediating function', the party provides 'an indispensable context in which we can define who we are and what we stand for',[3] a locus for the definition of commonalities, and hence it constitutes a basis for strategic action.

This line of thought is presented as an invitation to rethink the terms in which Marxists have conceived political action and its relation to forms of political organisation. The appropriate organisational vehicle is not to be found in the traditional models of the Left, neither in the democratic centralism of the Leninist vanguard nor in the parliamentary electoral apparatus of social-democratic reformism. To actualise the emergent capacities requisite to 'a self-radicalising and self-sustaining revolutionary process', the form of party organisation must eschew the undemocratic rigidity of Leninism and overcome the incrementalist inertia of social democracy. Providing the context in which a process of 'revolutionary gradualism' might emerge, such a form would overcome the fragmentation and traditional division of the Left.

The invitation to reflect upon the assumptions of revolutionary political organisation is welcome, but it seems to me that at the heart of Chodos and Hay's argument is some confusion as to the logical character of the categories with which they operate. This confusion results in persistent equivocation. The authors set forth a framework of

[1] Chodos and Hay, p. 28.
[2] Chodos and Hay, p. 28.
[3] Chodos and Hay, p. 28.

analysis in terms that suggest the need for a party as a determinate organisational response to the current situation of the Left. Yet one of the principal virtues of that framework, they argue, is the promise it bears of openness to a creative process of political self-definition. But this promise suggests a form of organisation that can be all things to all people, at least to all people on the Left. The kind of openness they promise is bought by deferring any application of their framework to a determinate conjuncture of struggle and, I will argue, the framework lends itself to such reticence. Whatever plausibility their approach possesses derives from its very indeterminacy and it is likely, therefore, to help to perpetuate the very disarray the authors decry.

The authors develop their claim that politics can be a creative, and not a merely representative, activity through an account of the nature of human agency. Agency, the ability of individual humans to act purposively, intentionally, is always exercised in a social context. An understanding of it must therefore reckon both with individuals and with social structures; entities which, though existentially intertwined, are ontologically distinct. Although social structures cannot exist apart from the activity of individual human beings, they provide the effective context, at once constraining and enabling, for that activity; although the individual exercise of agency is thus constituted in and through the concrete context of social structures, it is irreducible to its context. That individual agency is exercised only in context (in society) suggests a need on the part of individual agents to think strategically, that is, to calculate courses of action taking account of the actions and likely reactions of other agents. The social-structural context of action opens up some strategic possibilities and effectively excludes others, but, through strategic action and strategic learning, agents are, conversely, capable not only of reproducing, but also of transforming their context of action.

Since strategic action cannot assume an unchanging context, not only the immediate aims but also the long-term goals of the actors enter into the strategic calculation. The capacity to pursue collective aims is dependent in part upon the beliefs of the individual actors; for example, upon the confidence of each in the commitment and solidarity of the others. And since the formation and consolidation of such beliefs requires the context of organisation, emergent capacities are dependent upon the context of political party organisation.

But this argument is a *non sequitur*. It relies upon a conflation between two distinct types of issue: the ontological issue of the relation between individual action and social structures; and the political issue of the appropriate form of organisation for revolutionaries. If it is true, as the authors assert, that individual action cannot be understood in abstraction from its social context, then even 'the disarray of the Left' must be understood as a social context. Thus understood, it would, like any other context, differentially enable and constrain actions, beliefs and strategies, and so give rise to belief-dependent emergent capacities of one sort or another. In this context, the claim that a party is necessary to overcome 'the disarray of the Left' must be spelled out as a claim that a party is needed to foster the emergence of some particularly valuable belief-dependent capacities. And making such a claim requires specific analysis of the constraints imposed and opportunities afforded by the present social context of strategic action and of the transformations these are likely to undergo with the formation of a new party. But nothing like such an analysis is even attempted by Chodos and Hay.

In the absence of such an analysis, the need for a party follows only if it is equated, not with a particular context of action, but with the very possibility of contextualised action. If the party is the site of emergent capacities *simply in virtue of providing a social context for action*, this must be because the present state of disarray finds the Left without belief-dependent emergent capacities. But this disarray would then be tantamount to a state of nature, an absence of the very possibility of mutual understanding, an a-contextual anomaly out of which independent individuals must somehow establish a social convention as the precondition of any common action. The conflation of social ontology and politics permits the authors to evade the commitment entailed by analysis of a specific social context and thereby generates persistent equivocations in their argument.

Marx developed a related point in his *Grundrisse* in connection with the eighteenth-century 'Robinsonades' that underpinned the social contract of Rousseau and the classical political economy of Smith and Ricardo. The myth of the natural individual standing outside society as an ideal to be achieved and, projected into the past, as the appropriate point of departure for the analysis of material production and moral-political action represented not only an illusory yearning for simplicity but also, and more profoundly, the self-expression of a specific set of social relations, the nascent bourgeois society of free competition, that emerges only through a process of social evolution. 'The human being is in the most literal sense a *Zoon politikon*, not merely a gregarious animal but an animal which can individuate itself only in the midst of society.'[4] That the productive activity of individuals must be conceived in the context of their social relations implies, therefore, not only that the analysis of material production must begin with individuals producing in society, but also that it must always be an analysis of 'production at a definite stage of social development'.[5] That production is inherently social implies not only that 'there is no production in general',[6] but also that there is no *social* production in general.

The activity of material production is always activity in a determinate mode of production, either capitalist, communist, feudal or some other specific mode. What is true of material production is true of political action: just because the actions and inaction, beliefs and

---

[4] Marx 1973, p. 84.
[5] Marx 1973, p. 85.
[6] Marx 1973, p. 86.

delusions, capacities and failings of individual political actors must be conceived in social context, they must always be understood in relation to some determinate context of social relations and political institutions and practices. An insight into the irreducibly social character of production (and action) can yield determinate conclusions only when it functions as the conceptual scaffolding for analyses of specific social relations of production, of specific social contexts of action. When it functions, we might say, as the framework for 'concrete analyses of concrete situations'.

Now, I do not claim that Chodos and Hay adhere to the eighteenth-century myth of the natural individual. But their acknowledgement that individual human beings are existentially intertwined, through the exercise of their agency, with social structures, does not lead them to an analysis of any determinate social context of political action. And I do claim that their inability to generate such an analysis prevents them from escaping the theoretical opposition between the individual in general and society in general; that is, the theoretical orbit of the eighteenth-century 'Robinsonades'. They do pass the most influential traditions of leftist political organisation and political activity, Leninism and social democracy, in review. But this review does not serve to contextualise 'the disarray of the Left'. For these traditions are themselves treated in abstraction from the contexts of their emergence and development. There is no indication that Leninism and social democracy were constituted in struggle with each other – for example, that Lenin wrote *What Is To Be Done?* as a critique of 'Russian Bernsteinians'.

The traditions are assessed, then, not as elements constitutive of the social, political and ideological context in which contemporary political action must unfold, but as a selection of items in a smorgasbord which 'we' may mix and match – lots of democracy, some gradualism, just a dash of centralism, a little parliament, but not too much – to create our own platter. And the authors are careful to avoid any specification of who 'we' are. It would seem that any definition, that is, any context, might pre-judge the results of the very process of self-definition, the 'self-radicalising and self-sustaining revolutionary process', for which the party is necessary. 'We' seems to signify an undefined, inchoate aspiration to revolution in search of a context (a party) in and through which to express, concretise and thereby realise itself. 'We' must, it would seem, find ourselves a context before we can act.

Marx remarks, in the *Critique of the Gotha Programme*, that the bourgeois have good reason to attribute 'supernatural creative power' to labour.[7] Just as one cannot simply produce oneself, neither can one simply define oneself. One always finds oneself already in context, even if the terms in which the context is to be understood are contested. And so one is always already defined, even if the terms in which one is

---

[7] Marx 1974, p. 341.

understood/understands oneself are contested. In order to transform one's context and, in so doing, redefine oneself politically, some understanding of that context is requisite. The material available for the arduous work of transforming contexts and redefining political projects, aspirations and identities is supplied by the historical movement of the class struggle and by its current conjuncture. The uses to which this material can be put are both enabled and constrained by the co-ordinates of one's location within the conjuncture.

The struggle through which Leninist and social-democratic traditions were constituted is properly understood as a struggle, in part, over how social contexts of action are to be understood and how 'we' are to be defined. It was Lenin more than anyone who insisted upon this question of self-definition: 'Before we can unite, and in order that we may unite, we must first of all draw firm and definite lines of demarcation'.[8] And once this struggle is grasped as partially constitutive of the present context of political action, then the problem of how 'we' are to be defined is inescapably inscribed in that context. The terms in which Marxists and their adversaries have understood the movement of the class struggle and debated the appropriate strategies and institutions demand careful and critical re-examination, because, in shaping the debates and divisions in the working class and popular movements, they have entered into the present context of political action. But I would suggest that such re-examination is indispensable for another reason. For the very reason that earlier Marxists had to grapple with the difficulties and uncertainties of situating themselves politically and theoretically in determinate contexts of the class struggle, it may be possible to derive from their example analytical tools that can be brought to bear upon contemporary conjunctures. His almost dogged insistence that concrete situations be analysed concretely, and that the problem of political self-definition be addressed, makes Lenin exemplary in this respect.

Chodos and Hay insist upon the alleged fact that 'all human action' is both conscious (willed) and spontaneous (a consequence of the unconscious, undirected interaction of forces) and criticise Lenin's 'self-proclaimed access to the absolute truth provided by "scientific socialism"'.[9] This suggests that they have mistakenly identified his distinction between spontaneity and consciousness with their own distinction between individual action and social-structural context, ontologically distinct but existentially entwined. There is no need to read Lenin sympathetically, only to give his texts the care and patience that other writers are accorded as a matter of course, in order to appreciate that such profundity provides no grip at all upon the argument of *What Is To Be Done?*. That work was an intervention in a determinate political conjuncture shaped by the emergence of the nascent Russian working-class movement into political life, by the

---

[8] Lenin 1972, p. 354.
[9] Chodos and Hay, p. 37.

struggle between the proletariat and the liberal bourgeoisie for hegemony in Russia's bourgeois-democratic revolution, and by a tendency, on the part of some social democrats – the 'Russian Bernsteinians' – to subordinate revolutionary strategy to events as they unfolded and hence to risk playing into the hegemonic strategy of the liberal bourgeoisie.[10] Effective intervention in and beyond this conjuncture, Lenin argued, necessitated a form of organisation capable of sustaining an independent politico-strategic conception, while responding to the shifting currents of class struggle, and thus of directing the proletarian struggle for hegemony.

Read in this context, spontaneity and consciousness function as politico-strategic or, more precisely, as meta-strategic terms. They enabled Lenin to distinguish the conscious political project and activity of more or less organised Marxists from the spontaneous tendencies of the working-class movement – that is, tendencies beyond the grasp and the control of those Marxists, which shape the political situation in which they find themselves, and upon which they must intervene in order to act as a vanguard of the proletariat. The distinction drawn here is not one between Marxist intellectuals and non-Marxist workers, or even between Marxist workers and intellectuals and non-Marxist workers. By 'the spontaneous movement', Lenin designates the struggles and aspirations, including socialist aspirations, that arise among the workers apart from the conscious influence of a Marxist vanguard but subject, crucially, to the intervention of bourgeois strategy and bourgeois ideology in shaping their context and redefining their significance.

The social, political and ideological relations of capital are not merely a fixed backdrop against which workers and revolutionary intellectuals strive to define a socialist project: just as the workers spontaneously innovate in the course of their struggles, the ruling class innovates, through its political and ideological representatives, in response to working-class struggles. The process of working out a socialist project, of elaborating the political self-definition of the working-class movement, is one in which the adversary is inevitably and actively present. The distinction between spontaneity and consciousness is therefore not a simple one – it presupposes further distinctions among the complex, uneven and contradictory movements and tendencies that shape the field of political struggle. Thus, it equips Marxist political actors conceptually to grasp successive conjunctures of struggle and to orient (and reorient) their own action within them.

In 'A Talk with Defenders of Economism',[11] a brief article he described as a 'synopsis' of *What Is To Be Done?*, Lenin was concerned to disentangle a confusion he detected in his opponents' position between two different distinctions: between the socioeconomic base and the ideological superstructure on the one hand, and between

---

[10] See Shandro, 1995.
[11] Lenin 1961.

spontaneity and consciousness, on the other. While the former may serve the political analyst who seeks to grasp the movement of the social totality 'from the outside', as it were, the latter is an indispensable tool for the political strategist who, confronted with a determinate alignment of forces, must act upon it from within the totality. Conflating these two distinctions, the Russian Bernsteinians drew from the historical materialist primacy of the economic base the illegitimate conclusion that consciousness must reflect spontaneity. That is, they made their own revolutionary action conditional upon the prior actions of others, a mode of thought which, if generalised, would preclude revolutionary action. Not only does this procedure spirit away the ubiquitous influence of bourgeois ideology and the ever-renewed play of bourgeois strategy upon the spontaneous movement; by the same stroke it occludes the conceptual space within which consciously Marxist political actors might try to situate their own political action. Thus, in the course of recommending a particular form of party organisation as peculiarly suited to the concrete conditions of struggle in Tsarist Russia, Lenin would come to see himself as defending the very possibility of organised Marxist political action and hence as making explicit, in the notion of a contradiction between socialist consciousness and the spontaneous working-class movement, the conditions of this possibility.

Marxist political action does not stand to the spontaneous working-class movement in a simple relation of representation – while it implies an effort to diagnose and to align with the interests of the working class, it cannot take the place of the working-class struggle. But neither does the Marxist vanguard simply work through the spontaneous working-class movement – while it tries to educate and persuade the workers, its activity does not assume an implicit consensus. The struggle for proletarian hegemony is neither the act of the conscious vanguard nor that of the spontaneous mass movement; it assumes the active conjunction of both and it assumes that each, differently situated in the context of the struggle, exhibits distinct, indeed contradictory, modes of action. And it is precisely the assertion of a contradiction between spontaneity and consciousness that allowed Lenin to grasp the innovative character, not only of the conscious vanguard, but also of the spontaneous movements of the masses. Thus, it was not despite his thesis of 'consciousness from without', but just because of it, that he was able to assess the emergence of the Soviets in 1905 out of the spontaneous working-class movement as an exercise of proletarian hegemony

> We have been speaking ... of the need for a militant alliance of social democrats and revolutionary bourgeois democrats. We have been speaking of it and the workers have actually done it.[12]

---

[12] Lenin 1962c, p. 22.

That is, out of institutional arrangements and ideological themes imposed/bequeathed by the state and the employers,[13] the workers spontaneously constructed an arena of political activity open to the masses of workers, peasants, and petty bourgeois, a terrain of political struggle hospitable to the party's project of proletarian hegemony.

Farther afield, Lenin diagnosed in the scope and tempo of the peasant movement in 1905 the need to revise his estimate of the development of capitalism in the Russian countryside and, consequently, his assessment of just what was at stake in the bourgeois-democratic revolution and of the likely configuration of class alliances. And this led him to the project – misunderstood when it is not studiously ignored in the voluminous literature on Lenin, but pursued by him nonetheless through the years after the 1905 revolution – of fostering the development of an independent political party of the peasantry; that is, of extracting the kernel of peasant democracy from 'the husk of Narodnik utopias'.[14] It is instructive, in this regard, to compare his formulations concerning the potential of the petty-bourgeois democratic intelligentsia as a vehicle of political education for the peasantry and the petty bourgeoisie, and hence as a kind of hinge for the proletarian-peasant alliance, with Gramsci's later treatment of the Southern question.[15]

The concept of the vanguard party elaborated by Lenin is dependent upon the ability to make good cognitive claims about the context in which consciously Marxist political action takes place; claims both about the general coordinates of the field of struggle in which such action is situated (the contradictions of spontaneity and consciousness) and claims about the capacity to generate practical knowledge of the alignment of forces in determinate and shifting conjunctures. Consciousness is thus not simply an understanding of socialism as the aim of working-class struggle, nor even a specific kind of political analysis of class forces, but, in addition, the theoretical and political practice of revising and rectifying political analyses across successive conjunctures and redefining the aim of the struggle (and thereby, one supposes, the political identity of the movement) accordingly. This requires a theory sophisticated enough to signal shifts in the logic of the class struggle and open enough to accept amendment when it does not; and, in order that those shifts can be felt and registered, it requires an organisation in touch with the movements of the masses. Democratic centralism is not appropriately grasped as a particular organisational scheme; in the course of the class struggle, it has assumed a number of different organisational forms and will doubtless take on still others. Its import is to be sought in the movement of the class struggle and the struggle for hegemony, as the construction of a forum in which the

---

[13] See Anweiler 1974, p. 24f.
[14] Lenin 1973, p. 359.
[15] See Lenin 1962b, p. 215; Gramsci 1978.

contradiction between spontaneity and consciousness can be consciously, and dynamically, played out.

The kinds of claims to political knowledge that are found in Lenin are to be to be found equally in the words and actions of any other Marxist political actor/analyst; what distinguishes Lenin in this regard is merely his lack of demagogy. Such claims are indispensable to political action and especially to the exercise of political leadership. They require no additional claim to infallibility, to exclusive 'access to the absolute truth'.[16] It is unclear what Chodos and Hay have in mind in imputing such a claim, which in fact he never made, to Lenin. But it may be worthwhile exploring the possibility that the imputation responds to a certain tendency in Lenin's discourse, a commonplace among the Marxists of his time and still current and even predominant, to cast the unity of the working-class movement in terms of the development of consciousness. This kind of usage provides a conduit through which two quite different sorts of question may be confused: 1) a philosophical question as to the appropriate criteria to assess claims to knowledge in the class struggle; and 2) a political question as to the appropriate criteria to assess the unity of the working-class movement.

This confusion sustains the illusion that the working-class movement might be unified through a clarification of consciousness, and to this corresponds the treatment of the working class as a homogeneous subject of knowledge and the identification of politics with education. Now Lenin, alone to my knowledge among his contemporaries, would do much to diagnose and to try to remedy the more blatant forms of this confusion.[17] But, especially where the imperatives of civil war seemed to identify class solidarity with an awareness of the overriding task of the moment – All out for the fight against Denikin! All out for the fight against Kolchak! – or when the first groping attempts to establish some order among the unprecedented demands of socialist construction came to be haunted by the notion of a socialist economy transparent to the gaze of the planners,[18] something like this confusion does indeed figure in Lenin's discourse. And something like it would serve to short-circuit political argument in some later variants of Leninism.

But the confusion attendant upon this mode of discourse is by no means restricted to Lenin or to Leninism. The conceptualisation of working-class unity in terms of socialist consciousness was built into the conceptual foundations of Second International Marxist orthodoxy and provided the theoretical pendant for a political practice that, in essaying an educational reformation of the backward working masses in the image of the class-conscious social-democratic workers, unconsciously repressed the diversity of working-class struggles.[19] Something similar

---

[16] Chodos and Hay, p. 37.
[17] See, for example, Lenin 1962a.
[18] See Linhart 1976.
[19] See Shandro, 1997–8.

to this same confusion enters unquestioned into much so-called 'critical Marxism'. Thus, as an assumption of primordial harmony, or perhaps identity, between Marxism (properly understood) and the working-class movement, it shapes Simon Clarke's contribution to the present discussion. Indeed, the same sort of confusion is at work in the deferral/evasion by Chodos and Hay of the question of political identity, of who 'we' are. It is implicit in their claim that the emergence of belief-dependent capacities will enable us to elaborate a common vision, a vision around which we can unite; it is hidden only by their refusal to anticipate the terms of the vision. The 'disarray of the Left' is thus, in the final analysis, the result of a lack of vision rather than the result of determinate conjunctures of the class struggle. But when socialism is understood as a vision in which diverse popular priorities are permanently reconciled in a harmonious social order, it is transformed into a utopian goal distant from the immediate reality of the class struggle.

In reality, the contradictions of working-class and popular movements are to be understood in the context of the material diversity of popular circumstance, experience and aspiration, and the practical deployment of bourgeois ideology and strategy. But however constituted, these contradictions are not simply illusory. They could not be dissipated or resolved simply in being recognised. Socialism must accordingly be understood, in conformity with the character of working-class and popular struggle, as a complex, uneven, contradictory process of the realisation of diverse struggles in varying balances of consonance and cacophony. The politics of socialist leadership can only be understood as the effort to orchestrate the diverse fractions of the working class and the various strata of the people, through the arts of audacity, organisation, persuasion, negotiation and compromise, in working out the forms of the economic emancipation of labour and in revising them in accord with changing needs, capacities and circumstances. If this is understood as a vision, it is not one that all the participants will, or even should, share.

Paradoxical as it may appear, I want to suggest that Lenin's mode of political analysis constitutes an indispensable resource in coming to grips with the 'disarray of the Left', that is, with the inevitable circumstantial diversity and multifaceted character of working-class experience and interests and with the hegemonic inventiveness of bourgeois ideology and strategy. This mode of analysis is grounded in the postulate of a contradiction between spontaneity and consciousness which enables him to situate himself as a Marxist political actor amidst the conjunction of diverse and contradictory political currents, within and without the working-class movement. But its applicability to contemporary conjunctures is perhaps more readily apparent in Lenin's recognition that differently situated actors can sometimes reach a common destination only in adopting different – even contradictory – courses of action. This recognition is most memorably articulated in his

defence of the right of nations to self-determination, where he argues
that the question of national self-determination must be approached on
very different terms by revolutionaries in oppressed and in oppressor
nations: proletarian internationalism would require that the former
place a critique of nationalist illusions at the forefront of the struggle,
while the latter accord priority to the right of the oppressed nation to
self-determination, including the right to secession. Thus, in order that
their own belief-dependent capacities as well as those of the masses may
emerge, even 'conscious' Marxist political actors, differently situated in
the conjuncture of class struggle, may have to act, and to organise,
independently and, indeed, along contradictory lines. Lenin would
suggest in a related connection that the 'variegated and discordant,
motley and outwardly fragmented' character of mass struggles was
essential to socialist revolution

> Capitalism is not so harmoniously built that the various
> sources of rebellion can immediately merge of their own
> accord ... [T]he very fact that revolts do break out at different
> times, in different places, and are of different kinds,
> guarantees wide scope and depth to the general movement.[20]

There is no reason why such an analysis of the inevitable concrete
complexity of the class struggle, set to work here by Lenin in relation to
the national question, cannot be deployed by contemporary Marxists to
situate themselves, and the masses, in relation to other modes of
proletarian and popular diversity.

The terms in which Chodos and Hay pose the problem of
organisation carry the suggestion that, in order to endow oneself with
the belief-dependent emergent capacities requisite to effective analysis
and action, one must first organise with others a context for action, a
party. This represents a latter-day variant of the equivocation of the
Russian Bernsteinians before the tasks of leadership. Without analysis of
existing contexts of action, there is no way to determine whether, for
example, the requisite capacities should be brought to bear upon, and
the relevant others be sought in, say, the United Kingdom, England, or
the European Union; in Canada, Quebec/the 'rest of Canada', or the
NAFTA area. Without such analysis, the question of the appropriate
modes of organisation could not even be addressed. These and similar
questions are necessarily controversial and the analyses necessary to
address them will inevitably be controverted. But the only way of
transcending them is to work through them. The unity of the working-
class and popular movements is always a particular pattern of unity-
and-division. Rather than assuming an imaginary unity as a condition of
action, one can follow the example and the mode of analysis of Lenin
and try to grasp one's concrete circumstances and to act where one
finds oneself. New and more effective forms of popular and

---

[20] Lenin 1964, p. 356, p. 358.

revolutionary unity are certainly worth seeking. But if they really are to be effective, they cannot emerge without concrete analyses of concrete situations.

References

Anweiler, Oskar 1974, *The Soviets: The Russian Workers, Peasants, and Soldiers Councils, 1905–1921*, New York: Pantheon Books.

Gramsci, Antonio 1978 [1926], 'Some Aspects of the Southern Question' in *Selections from Political Writings, 1921–1926*, London: Lawrence and Wishart.

Lenin, V. I. 1961 [1901], 'A Talk with Defenders of Economism' in *Collected Works*, Volume V, Moscow: Progress Publishers.

Lenin, V. I. 1962a [1905], 'On Confounding Politics with Pedagogics' in *Collected Works*, Volume VIII, Moscow: Progress Publishers.

Lenin, V. I. 1962b [1905], 'In the Wake of the Monarchist Bourgeoisie or in the Van of the Revolutionary Proletariat and Peasantry?' in *Collected Works*, Volume IX, Moscow: Progress Publishers.

Lenin, V. I. 1962c [1905], 'Our Tasks and the Soviet of Workers' Deputies' in *Collected Works*, Volume X, Moscow: Progress Publishers.

Lenin, V. I. 1964 [1916], 'The Discussion of Self-Determination Summed Up' in *Collected Works*, Volume XXII, Moscow: Progress Publishers.

Lenin, V. I. 1972 [1900], 'Declaration of the Editorial Board of *Iskra*' in *Collected Works*, Volume IV, Moscow: Progress Publishers.

Lenin, V. I. 1973 [1912], 'Two Utopias' in *Collected Works*, Volume XVIII, Moscow: Progress Publishers.

Linhart, Robert 1976, *Lénine, les paysans, Taylor: essai d'analyse matérialiste historique de la naissance du système productif sovietique*, Paris: Éditions du Seuil.

Marx, Karl 1973 [1859], *Grundrisse*, Harmondsworth: Penguin Books.

Marx, Karl 1974 [1875], *Critique of the Gotha Programme* in *The First International and After*, Harmondsworth: Penguin Books.

Shandro, Alan 1995, '"Consciousness from Without": Marxism, Lenin and the Proletariat', *Science & Society*, 59, 3: 268–297.

Shandro, Alan 1997–8, 'Karl Kautsky: On the Relation of Theory and Practice', *Science & Society*, 61, 4: 474–501.

Realistic Organisation?

Jonathan Joseph

These are difficult times for the Marxist Left and many tough questions are being asked. Unfortunately two extremes often come to the fore. One position takes an ultra-revisionist course, questioning the very foundations of Marxism. Another takes a profoundly dogmatic approach, defending orthodoxy in knee-jerk fashion.

It is necessary to distinguish between conducting a genuine reassessment of Marxist ideas and practice, and a wholesale abandonment of fundamental tenets. In all this we need to be very conscious of the pernicious influence of the period and its ability to play havoc with our critical sensibilities.

In this short piece I want to defend what is probably the most unfashionable of all the Marxist 'principles', the Leninist theory of organisation. At the same time it is important to recognise the dangers of 'Leninism' as a fetishised cult with an unthinking method and practice. 'Leninism' has been abused, not only by the Stalinist caricatures who are an obvious target, but also by much of the 'anti-Stalinist' and 'Trotskyist' Left.

If it is to have any usefulness, we need a more open and self-critical understanding of Leninism. For this reason I welcome the opportunity to discuss the paper by Howard Chodos and Colin Hay in this issue, not least because organisational theories are rarely talked about in academic journals. I am also interested – though not entirely convinced – by their engagement with critical realist ideas. The philosophical insights of critical realism can add a lot to our understanding of Marxism – but not necessarily in this area, where I believe these arguments are over-extended. I therefore do not agree with their conclusions, and wish to defend critically a form of Leninist organisation. But in times like these this is an interesting and important dialogue to have.

Critical realism: a reply to Chodos and Hay

In 'So the Party's Over?[1]' Chodos and Hay argue the not uncommon view that traditional Leninist-style forms of organisation are unable adequately to represent left forces. However, they do this through an ambitious usage of critical realist arguments and it is this that I want to examine briefly.

---

[1] See Chodos and Hay in this issue.

I too would count myself a supporter of critical realism, albeit a critical one. In fact this criticism would be directed against critical realism's evolution, which has seen it develop away from its original role as an under-labourer for the sciences into a more ambitious role as a branch of social science itself. The early form of critical realism could be used to help clarify key aspects of Marxist theory, a role that the so-called 'Marxist philosophy' seemed incapable of doing.

Therefore, as a second-order critique, critical realism can help clarify the Marxist understanding of such things as materialism, dialectics, causality, ontology, structurality and the relation between theory and practice. It reasserts some of the fundamental philosophical positions while adding a new degree of precision and rigour. One aspect, for example, long forgotten by the Hegelian tradition of Lukács, Korsch, Sartre, Marcuse and the rest is the primacy of social being, structure and ontology over consciousness, practice and epistemology. Instead of the epistemological concern – given that social practice and consciousness exist what is their meaning? – critical realism asks, given that social practice and consciousness exist and are intelligible, what does this say about the structure of the world itself? If human knowledge and action, for example, are intelligible, this surely presupposes that the social world is structured in a certain way and that this is open to analysis.

However, as Roy Bhaskar's project became increasingly ambitious, the transcendental arguments and philosophical claims turned into bold statements of social scientific theory. This is an inevitable consequence of the close interrelation between philosophy and social science. But Bhaskar's attempts to systematise and politicise his philosophy have taken this to a new level. In short, rather than acting as Marxism's helpful companion, the new, 'dialectical critical realism' has become its competitive rival. It is therefore probably correct to say that there are two types of critical realism. The earlier form plays the role of a philosophical under-labourer for the sciences[2] and is therefore important as a source of second-order knowledge and as a tool capable of analysing Marxist claims. However, Bhaskar's later version sees itself as contributing directly to social science itself.

While critical realism still has a positive role to play, and works like *Dialectic* still have a vast importance, I am increasingly sceptical about critical realism's encroachment into Marxist debates. Chodos and Hay's critical realist contribution to the debate on political organisation is one such example. Despite this, however, I shall try to reply through critical realist concerns.

Chodos and Hay base their approach on the transformational model of social activity and the duality of structure and agency. This is outlined by Bhaskar so that:

---

[2] Bhaskar 1989b, p. 182.

> Society is both the ever-present *condition* (material cause) and the continually reproduced *outcome* of human agency. And praxis is both work, that is conscious *production*, and (normally unconscious) *reproduction* of the conditions of production, that is society. One could refer to the former as the *duality of structure* and the latter as the *duality of praxis*.[3]

Such a formulation is important since traditional Marxist accounts of the relation between structure and agency often stress agential factors to the point of voluntarism, or else stress structural factors to the point of reification.

However, Chodos and Hay introduce the realist model in too individualistic a manner, arguing that individuals and social structures constitute 'ontologically distinct but existentially intertwined' entities.[4] Strategic action is then talked about in terms of the orientation of an agent to a structured context. The trouble with taking this as the starting point of the discussion is that individual strategic action and the 'irreducibly individual dimension to human action' (free will and intentionality) are very limited in their effects.

The important relation in critical realism's transformational model is not that between social structures and individual agents, but between structures and *collective* agents. It is true that individual agents act upon intentions. It is also true that social structures are (unconsciously) reproduced and (consciously) transformed through intentional activity. But these should not be reduced to one another.

To give a well-known example from Bhaskar, people do not marry to reproduce the nuclear family; however, it is the unintended consequence of their actions.[5] It would be ludicrous to suggest that this relation can be broken down to the intentional actions of one agent. It is only because millions of people act on their intentions and marry that the relation gets unconsciously reproduced.

It is the fact that these actions collectively occur that gives rise to our understanding of social *practice* – something distinct from individual agency but organising of it, and something distinct from social structures, but related to their reproduction. Margaret Archer rightly criticises Anthony Giddens's elisionism and his effective reduction of social structures to human practices. We might extend this to distinguish between agents and practices. The reproduction of the nuclear family, therefore, is not the result of individual intentions as such. These intentions are a necessary component of social action, but can only really be understood within the context of an established social practice (getting married) that has such an influence that many people intend to get married, and, in doing so, reproduce the structure of the nuclear family.

---

[3] Bhaskar 1989a, pp. 34–5.
[4] Chodos and Hay, p. 29.
[5] Bhaskar 1989a, p. 35.

This highlights the need for critical realism to move away from a simplistic version of the 'duality of structure' (as the medium and outcome of human action), a model that is promoted by Giddens and which is sometimes used in Bhaskar. It is inadequate simply to give structure and agency equal weight without taking account of the effects of social stratification and the complex mediations that take place, 1) through established practices; 2) through what Andrew Collier calls structurata (if structures are deeper mechanisms, structurata are those concrete entities which are structured);[6] 3) by a structure's relation to other structures; 4) by a structure's relations to other agents; 5) by a practice's relation to other structures; and so on.

To develop the aspect of structures relating to other structures, it is not correct, as Chodos and Hay argue, that we can radically transform social relations through democratic reform. This view again depends on the one-to-one model of social transformation whereby an agent acts upon a structure. But these structures are related to other structures – they form an articulated ensemble, a totality. And this totality has a structured hierarchy within which the productive relations are most important. It is not possible radically to transform a particular set of social relations without calling into question the totality. Otherwise, the transformation is not a genuinely radical transformation, but is no more than a radical amelioration of a state of affairs that does not alter the fundamental dynamics of the social formation but perhaps makes them more palatable, when conditions allow. So it might be possible to change a structure, but only in the context of that structure's relation to a hierarchy of other structures, ie. the capitalist system.

The result is that Chodos and Hay's 'creative component' to politics is severely limited by social relations. The idea that a new set of political interests or identities can be realised in the right emergent context relies too much on the 'duality of structure' model where the 'belief-dependent emergent capacities' tend to be individualised in the agent rather than complexly mediated though collectives, practices, structurata, and, of course, the determination of the totality. It is certainly right to say that by transforming a certain structure, new interests, expectations and desires can be created. But if this transformatory approach is limited to certain structures, but not the wider ensemble of such structures, then the politics will inevitably also be negatively determined – that is, by the lack of wider transformatory action and by the dominant dynamics of the totality. We can transform structures and create new political dynamics, but we must also recognise that these structures are related to wider structures and that the bigger picture is more powerful than the localised one. That is why Leninism directs itself at the *totality* of social relations and seeks to do this through the leading role of the state. It cannot be done piecemeal through the 'capturing' of different structures, one after the other.

---

[6] Collier 1989, p. 85.

In short, while the transformational model of social activity is an important guide, it only retains its validity if it is seen in a stratified and mediated social context. And this stratified, mediated context is precisely the reason why I believe that Leninist rather than 'creative politics' is still valid.[7]

Is Leninism realist?

I do not want to go into a detailed discussion about the rights and wrongs of Leninist practice or the particular groups that claim to represent it. Even if we do decide to defend something in Leninism we should always have a critical attitude towards it. However, it is not enough to denounce Leninism as undemocratic *in practice* without showing why this should *intrinsically* be the case.

The theory of democratic centralism is widely regarded as the outdated product of Tsarist Russia. Many on the left now call for this to be replaced with some sort of 'democratic pluralism'. The correct view that the world has significantly changed since Lenin's time is conflated with the incorrect (irrealist) view that today's world is somehow more complex, more diverse and less intelligible than it was eighty years ago.

From here it is not that far a distance to more explicitly postmodern or post-structuralist arguments such as Derrida's call for a 'new international' belonging only to anonymity,[8] or Laclau and Mouffe's discursive version of political strategy. The social identities necessary to organise a political project melt into the air. Instead of community and solidarity we get a plurality based on fractured identity and fragmentary discourse. Inspired by Foucault and others, political struggle disappears into the microstructures of power. This brand of creative and spontaneous politics effectively goes along with the plurality of today's world and theoretically reinforces the fragmentation, division and alienation that today's objective conditions impose.

By contrast, Leninist forms of organisation do recognise the complexity of the social. But it is precisely because society is structured in a stratified, overdetermined way that organisational discipline is necessary if any significant political intervention is to occur.

---

[7] It is also worth noting that the arguments for a creative politics, combined with a focus on the individual come, to a degree, from Chodos's one-sided reading of Lenin. In Chodos 1992 he argues that the problem is Lenin's understanding of the relationship between spontaneity and consciousness and that we need to challenge Lenin's mechanical view that social consciousness reflects social being. In reaction to this Chodos argues that we need to pay more attention to the non-mechanical nature of individual interests. The problem is that Chodos focuses exclusively on Lenin's early book *Materialism and Empirio-Criticism*. In the later *Philosophical Notebooks*, thought's 'reflection' of reality is given a more complex basis, developed through abstractions, concepts and laws, acting much more as a mediation (Lenin 1961, p. 182). Thought and politics are given a more dynamic, creative character. In critical realist terminology, we could say that Lenin gives more weight to the transitive domain of thought and practice.
[8] Derrida 1994, p. 90.

Leninist politics *can* therefore be compatible with critical realist arguments. For Leninist organisation constitutes not a rejection, but a recognition that both structures and agents are complexly stratified and socially mediated. The difficulties involved in pursuing a transformatory project, and its need to stretch across a range of different structures, practices and agents, necessitate a strong form of political organisation and the need for clear leadership. The process by which this leadership and direction is achieved requires the fullest democracy and freedom of discussion. But in the end we also need unity of action.[9]

A realist theory of the social world sees a plurality of social structures, generative mechanisms, human practices and stratified agents. However, to embrace plura*lism*, or celebrate difference, is to leave everything as it is. What is required of Marxism is to develop a socialist strategy in relation to its understanding of the objective features of the social world — structures, practices and the like. To talk of the possibility of changing structures in the context of their inter-relation and stratification requires an analysis of what structures are dominant within the social formation and which agents are best strategically located to enact a transformatory project.

To go back to Chodos and Hay, they are correct to say that in the course of a political project, new interests and ideas will be generated and a creative element activated. This is in line with a realist theory of emergent powers, possibilities and liabilities. But it is also necessary to see the limitations of this as imposed by the objective social context within which political practice operates. This, to use Bhaskar's terminology, is due to the relatively enduring character of social structures and practices, their relative intransitivity and transfactuality. We never act afresh. Political practice is always mediated through other established practices, traditions and bodies, through our relations with concrete social structurata, and through the emergent effects of structures. Agents may have emergent capacities, but the emergent properties of structures are more forceful.

Lenin's theory of political organisation seeks to establish what possibilities and limitations are presented by this differentiated social context. The stratification of both structures and agents requires a centralised approach, both in terms of organising the party, and in organising society. The interconnectedness of different structures means that a transformatory project must be aimed at a wide body of structural relations and that this must be organised through the centralising function of the state.

On the question of the state, I would point to two crucial factors that make it a key focus for a Leninist project. First, it enjoys what might be called a functional relationship to the economy or mode(s) of production. Second, it is a strategic terrain and the locus for various political projects, alliances and strategies. Whatever the importance of

---

[9] Lenin 1962, p. 380.

the transformational model of social activity, it is surely the case that the state remains the most important body for enacting social change.[10]

Lenin's theory of organisation does not start from some abstract idea of pure democracy or democratic pluralism. Rather, his starting point is based on an assessment of the objective conditions under the imperialist phase of capitalism, and (following the *April Theses*) the conditions in Russia of combined and uneven development. As a result of these conditions, new social compositions are formed, new classes created, new social tensions developed. These conditions require an active, interventionist party that is able to give leadership to the most dynamic class, to unite other social groups behind it, and to direct its energies to winning and consolidating state power − in other words, a *vanguard* party.

Vanguard politics

The theory of democratic centralism is far more than a few guidelines for internal organisation. The appropriateness for today of many of the specifics in, for example, *What Is To Be Done?* can be questioned. What is really important is the idea of the party in relation to the wider layers of society. This is contained in Leninism's idea of a vanguard party.

The Leninist approach starts from the actually existing social divisions, recognising the different layers or strata of social groups and classes, and seeking to relate to and activate the most advanced ones. Leninism therefore recognises the stratification of classes based on their various relations to different structures and practices. It seeks to unite the different fractions of the working class on the understanding that productive relations are the most fundamental relations within society and that, under capitalism, the working class enjoys the most intimate relationship with the productive process. Leaving aside the debates over who creates value and what constitutes productive or unproductive labour, we can define the working class quite straight-forwardly as that class which is forced to sell its own labour-power.[11]

But by rejecting the crudest forms of economic determinism and teleology, Lenin and others recognise that class is not something uniform or homogenous, but is also affected by other forms of social determination. This creates different class fractions and social groups.[12] The strategic aim of Leninism is not just to take power, but to do so through the necessary construction of a complicated set of alliances.

---

[10] I do not have the space to go into detail on these aspects of the state but I would refer readers to my article 'In Defence of Critical Realism' (Joseph 1998), which deals with these issues at greater length. I would also recommend Colin Hay's excellent book on the state (Hay 1996), although I have major reservations about 'Jessopian' and regulation approaches also dealt with in the above.

[11] For example Marx 1981, p. 1025.

[12] These terms have a ring of Poulantzas to them and indeed a study of his work on class fractions is a rewarding exercise despite his rigid over-formalisation of these categories and his political movement towards Eurocommunism.

This means working through the leadership of the vanguard and the most advanced workers in order to reach through to wider layers; not just to the working class but also to what might be called supporting classes (the peasantry, petite bourgeoisie etc.) who have to be won over from the bourgeoisie. Then we have to deal with the category of special oppression and the social differentiation that this takes, recognising the right that these groups have to some form of organisational autonomy within the revolutionary movement.

If we look at the Leninist approach today it seems immensely difficult for the small forces of the Left to relate directly to the masses without succumbing to populism, outright reformism, or something like a 'gradualism' that stands somewhere between a reformist and revolutionary approach. In periods like this, it would seem that we are limited to the struggle to win over the political vanguard and the most advanced workers, and to attempt to develop a strategy which, through them, might reach out to wider layers.

This should not be seen as élitist or undemocratic. Rather, by recognising actual divisions within society, and by seeking to organise those forces best able to enact social change, Leninism is potentially the *most* democratic form of organisation. Social democracy depends upon a passive relation between party, members and wider electorate, excluding the wider layers from political participation. Creative or spontaneist politics often ends up substituting symbolic acts for genuine mobilisation. Leninism by contrast sees organisation in an active and organic sense. Its role is not just to relate to the different layers, but to organise them.

We can (indeed should) argue over actual historical examples of Leninist parties or practices, but essentially what we should be in favour of is democratic accountability. If the members of a group have a discussion and as a result decide to implement a decision, then it should be done. Of course this should be interpreted sensibly. It would be wrong to think that a political group had to take a decision on every single question. Imagine, for example, a group deciding that critical realist philosophy was counter-revolutionary and that no member should give it public support.

But at the same time, if a group was to decide a line for a political intervention, for a workers' campaign against the single currency, for example, and members broke the line by campaigning alongside Tory Euro-sceptics, then there are serious implications. Surely, in a democratic organisation, people should know exactly where they stand and what they should do? By contrast, in a pluralist group, there is no accountability, and everyone will do exactly what suits them. There is no obligation for important discussions to be followed up or for decisions to be implemented. What occurs, in effect, is that it provides a platform for bigwigs, bureaucrats, theoretical gurus and the like to get up and do exactly what they like.

An essential part of the Leninist approach should be the fight for reforms that better the conditions of the working class and oppressed. We should never forget that socialists 'have no interests separate and apart from the proletariat as a whole'.[13] If this is implemented correctly, then there should be no need for a 'gradualist' approach. A correct and non-sectarian application of tactics and the method of the united front should mean that Leninists can fight for reforms without having to embrace even a gradualist version of reformism.

In the current period, the important gains that the working class has made, like the welfare state and trade union rights, have to be defended against increased attacks. Ultimately, these gains do come up against the limits of the system. That means that we must be prepared to confront that system *as a whole*, and Leninism would seem to be the only means of organisation capable of doing this. It is no surprise that many attempts at Leninist organisation have failed, for the problems we face are immense. Uniting a set of diverse agents and their interests, collectivising these struggles into a unified movement directed at the system as a whole, while at the same time attempting to employ the broadest democracy and accountability: these are the problems we face, and there is no getting away from them. Given the powerful nature of the social structures we need to deal with, the socially and historically ingrained character of human practices, and the stratified differentiation of the agents we have to mobilise, we need a clear strategy[14] for winning power that can mobilise agents in united action. I would argue that some critical form of Leninism is the only realistic way to do this.

References

Archer, Margaret 1995, *Realist Social Theory: The Morphogenetic Approach*, Cambridge: Cambridge University Press.

Bhaskar, Roy 1989a, *The Possibility of Naturalism*, Hemel Hempstead: Harvester Wheatsheaf.

Bhaskar, Roy 1989b, *Reclaiming Reality*, London: Verso.

Bhaskar, Roy 1993, *Dialectic*, London: Verso.

Bhaskar, Roy 1997, *A Realist Theory of Science*, London: Verso.

Chodos, Howard 1992, 'Epistemology, Politics and the Notion of Class Interest in Lenin, Luxemburg and Gramsci', *Journal of History and Politics*, 10: 35–60.

Collier, Andrew 1994, *Critical Realism*, London: Verso.

Derrida, Jacques 1994, *Specters of Marx*, New York: Routledge.

Giddens, Anthony 1979, *Central Problems in Social Theory*, London: Macmillan.

Giddens, Anthony 1984, *The Constitution of Society*, Cambridge: Polity Press.

---

[13] See *The Communist Manifesto*, Marx 1973, p. 79.

Hay, Colin 1996, *Re-Stating Social and Political Change*, Buckingham: Open University Press.

Joseph, Jonathan 1998, 'In Defence of Critical Realism', *Capital & Class*, 65: 73–107.

Laclau, Ernesto and Chantal Mouffe 1985, *Hegemony and Socialist Strategy*, London: Verso.

Lenin, V.I. 1950, *What is to be Done?*, Moscow: Progress Publishers.

Lenin, V.I. 1961, *Philosophical Notebooks* in *Collected Works* Volume 38, Moscow: Foreign Languages Publishing House.

Lenin, V.I. 1962, *Collected Works*, Volume 10, Moscow: Foreign Languages Publishing House.

Lenin, V.I. 1975, *Imperialism, the Highest Stage of Capitalism*, Peking: Foreign Languages Press.

Lenin, V.I. 1976, *One Step Forward, Two Steps Back*, Peking: Foreign Languages Press.

Lenin, V.I. 1976, *Materialism and Empirio-Criticism*, Peking: Foreign Languages Press.

Lukács, Georg 1974, *Lenin*, Cambridge, Massachusetts: MIT Press.

Marx, Karl 1973, *The Revolutions of 1848*, Harmondsworth: Penguin.

Marx, Karl 1981, *Capital* Volume III, Harmondsworth: Penguin.

Poulantzas, Nicos 1973, *Political Power and Social Classes*, London: New Left Books

Poulantzas, Nicos 1975, *Classes and Contemporary Capitalism*, London: New Left Books.

Trotsky, Leon 1973, *The Transitional Programme for Socialist Revolution*, New York: Pathfinder.

Dialectics, 'the Party' and the Problem of the New Society

Peter Hudis

1. The problem of organisation in contemporary Marxism

This is an especially auspicious moment to reconsider the problem of organisation in Marxist theory. This is not needed for the sake of rehashing old debates about which strategy or tactic can best 'make' the revolution. In a century that has seen many revolutions come to power but none lead to the creation of a new society we have different reasons for exploring the problem of organisation. The question is, what kind of organisation, and what relation between organisation, spontaneity, and revolutionary theory, can best combat the tendency of new forms of oppression to emerge after the seizure of power? In other words, what role does revolutionary organisation play in the effort to envision and help work out the new human relations needed to ensure any successful transformation of society?

The importance of this question flows from today's crisis in articulating a viable alternative to capitalism. Global capital is clearly entering a period of instability, and new forms of resistance are likely to arise against it. But it is also clear that there is a void in the effort to spell out a concept of a society free from the domination of capital. This can be seen from many recent statements, even in the mainstream press, on the importance of Marx for grasping the nature of globalised capitalism. Yet while today's realities have led some to realise the cogency of Marx's critique of capitalism, there is much less discussion, even on the Left, of its alternative – revolutionary socialism. As if a return to Marx's critique of capital without any effort to envision its transcendence can somehow break us free of the 'mind-forged manacles' of unfreedom which Blake spoke of in his time, and which so characterise our own!

Political regimes and economic systems do not get overthrown simply because of their oppressive nature. The inspiration and direction obtained from an idea of what might replace them has always been the energising principle for effective political and social action. This was shown by the development of the socialist movement from its beginnings in the 1830s, the movements of Russian populism and Marxism in the late 19th and early 20th centuries, and the third world revolts of the post-World War II era.

The problem we now face in the aftermath of the failure of social democracy and Stalinism to move humanity beyond capitalist exploitation is to articulate a radical alternative rooted not simply in the abolition of private property, the market, or even the state, but in the abolition of capital itself. Without engaging in the formidable labour needed to realise this enterprise, it is hard to see how radical theory and practice can be renewed or even sustained.

This requires subjecting the concepts of organisation in post-Marx Marxism[1] to a thoroughgoing reevaluation, and this must begin with the notion of the vanguard party. Whatever may have been the justifications for the formation of the vanguard party concept in Russian Marxism at the turn of the century, the concept has long outlived its usefulness. Lenin's 1903 formulation that socialist consciousness must be brought to the masses by intellectuals, since the masses can attain only trade union consciousness through their own endeavour, erected a rigid separation between leaders and ranks, workers and intellectuals, process and goal. This has been a noose around the neck of the movement ever since. The problem is not only that the masses often prove themselves to be in advance of the intellectual leadership, as Lenin himself recognised following the 1905 Revolution and in his April Theses of 1917. It is that the tendency of the vanguard party form to divide leaders from ranks, intellectuals from workers, and theory from the practical struggles which are the source of theory; moreover, it impedes the effort to break down the division between mental and manual labour in the course of the post-revolutionary transition.

This was seen in the struggle carried on by Lenin after 1917 to maintain the revolutionary initiative in the face of tremendously difficult objective circumstances. *Contra* the all-too-prevalent myth of Lenin as an unalloyed despot, he posed the need at various points to involve rank-and-file workers in the running of production and the state, conscious as he was of the bureaucratic distortions which threatened the revolutionary process. Yet the vanguard party form, for which he is so famous, ultimately proved an obstacle to such rank-and-file participation. Though it is doubtful that Lenin ever realised the full extent of it, by the end of his life he was painfully aware of the emergence of bureaucratic and repressive tendencies from within the Bolshevik Party. By the time a new stage of world capitalism arose in the 1930s, Stalin had built upon these tendencies to transform the Bolshevik Party into its opposite, turning it into a mechanism of despotic control over the working class in a form that Lenin would never have recognised as his own.

One might expect that the transformation of the Russian Revolution into its opposite would have produced considerable reconsideration of Lenin's concept of organisation among anti-Stalinists. While some, like the council communists, dispensed with the vanguard party concept,

---

[1] I here use Raya Dunayevskaya's phrase 'post-Marx Marxism' rather than 'classical Marxism' or 'Marxists after Marx,' in order, l) to indicate a separation of Marx from 'Marxism', and, 2) to indicate that this separation did not emerge only after his death, but was present even while he lived. For a detailed elaboration of the category of 'post-Marx Marxism', see Dunayevskaya 1982.

much of the anti-Stalinist Left, like the Trotskyists, did not. For the most part they made as much of a fetish of 'the party' as the Stalinists they opposed. In the post-World War II era, the avowal of the vanguard party form by anti-Stalinists as well as Stalinists increasingly came into conflict with the emergence of new revolutionary subjectivities.

Such new movements as rank-and-file workers battling automated production, women opposing sexism, and national minorities confronting racism often found that to advance their agendas they had to remain independent of, or even openly break from, not only the Stalinists but also the parties and grouplets of the anti-Stalinist Left. Far too many were out to lead and far too few were willing to listen. For many it appeared that the concept of the vanguard party had become a way for radical intellectuals to justify their hegemony over the workers, without having to confront the way intellectuals are subject to the most basic class division of all – the separation of mental from manual labour. It led Frantz Fanon to proclaim in *The Wretched of the Earth*:

> 'Leader': the word comes from the English verb, 'to lead,' but a frequent French translation is 'to drive.' The driver, the shepherd of the people no longer exists today. The people are no longer a herd; they do not need to be driven ... The single party is the modern form of the dictatorship of the bourgeoisie, unmasked, unpainted, unscrupulous, and cynical.[2]

In opposition to the vanguard party concept, a rich legacy of spontaneous and decentralised forms of organisation have arisen, ranging from the worker and peasant cooperatives in the Spanish Revolution of the 1930s, to the workers' councils in Hungary 1956, to Poland's Solidarnosc of the early 1980s – a mass workers' organisation which initially opposed centralised party structures. The development of the feminist movement over the past two decades further confirms the vibrancy of decentralised and spontaneous forms of organisation.

Raya Dunayevskaya, founder of Marxist-humanism in the US,[3] noted that such decentralised forms,

---

[2] Fanon 1975, p. 197.
[3] Raya Dunayevskaya was born in Ukraine in 1910 and came to the U.S. in the early 1920s. She was an early participant in the US Trotskyist movement and became Russian-language secretary to Leon Trotsky during his Mexican exile. She broke with Trotsky in 1939 over his position on the Soviet Union, and wrote (beginning in 1941) the first detailed Marxist analysis of Stalin's Russia as a state-capitalist society. Along with C.L.R. James, she was co-leader of the Johnson-Forest Tendency in the 1940s and early 1950s in the US Marxist movement. In the mid-1950s, after separating from James, she founded the philosophy of Marxist-humanism in the US. Her major works are Dunayevskaya 1958, 1973 and 1982. She died in 1987, while working on a new book tentatively entitled Dialectics of Organisation and Philosophy: 'The Party' and Forms of Organisation Born from Spontaneity. For an overall view of her work, see Hudis 1992.

[raise] the crucial question: what kind of organisation is the one needed to achieve freedom in our state-capitalist age, which has seen a counter-revolution emerge out of the greatest of all proletarian revolutions, the Russian Revolution of 1917... The demand for decentralisation involves two pivotal questions of the day and, I might add, questions of tomorrow, because we are not going to have a successful revolution unless we do answer them. They are, first, the totality of the uprooting and the depth of the necessary uprooting of this exploitative, sexist, racist society. Second, the dual rhythm of revolution: not just the overthrow of the old, but the creation of the new; not just the reorganisation of objective, material foundations but the release of subjective personal freedom, creativity and talents. In a word, there must be such appreciation of the movement from below, from practice, that we never again let theory and practice get separated.[4]

For Dunayevskaya, however, decentralised forms, though of crucial importance, do not provide 'the answer' to the problem of organisation. As she put it in a lecture on a planned book on 'Dialectics of Organisation and Philosophy',

[w]hat happens to a small group [of Marxists] who know that nothing can be done without the masses, and are with them, but they are theoreticians and always seem to be around too. So what is the objectivity which explains their presence, as the objectivity explains the spontaneous outburst of the masses?'[5]

The importance of the question flows from the nature of revolutionary transformation itself. Throughout this century, participants in spontaneous forms of organisation have continuously gone in search of organisations other than their own, because, as their struggles intensify, they feel a need to connect with those who possess an understanding of how to transform social relations radically. This occurs even after spontaneous struggles generate a socialist consciousness in its participants. What drives masses of people to search out revolutionary parties and tendencies is their hunger for a comprehensive answer to what happens after the revolution. The problem is that far too often they encounter parties who are more interested in taking them over than seriously answering such questions.

The depth and persistence of this problem makes it important to reexamine the question of revolutionary organisation in light of the Hegelian dialectic of negativity – the principle which posits the pathway

---

[4] Dunayevskaya 1982, p. 108.
[5] This statement is from a presentation given in June 1987 as part of work in progress on the book Dialectics of Organisation and Philosophy. Though left unfinished at Dunayevskaya's death, her notes for it are available in 'The Raya Dunayevskaya Collection – Marxist-Humanism: A Half-Century of its World Development', on deposit at the Walter Reuther Archives of Labour and Urban Affairs, Detroit, Michigan.

to the transcendence of alienation. In Hegel, all movement proceeds through the power of negativity, the negation of obstacles to the subject's self-development. The transcendence of these obstacles is reached not simply through the negation of their immediate and external forms of appearance (which Hegel calls first negation), but through 'the negation of the negation'. In the negation of the negation, the power of negativity gets turned back upon the self, upon the internal as well as external barriers to self-movement. This movement through the negation of the negation, or absolute negativity, is what produces the positive, the transcendence of alienation.

In the chapter on 'The Absolute Idea' in the *Science of Logic*, Hegel calls absolute negativity 'the innermost and most objective moment of life and spirit, by virtue of which a subject is personal and free'.[6] As he puts it earlier in the same book,

> in all this, care must be taken to distinguish between the first negation as negation in general, and the second negation, the negation of the negation: the latter is concrete, absolute negativity, just as the former on the contrary is only abstract negativity.[7]

In his *Economic and Philosophical Manuscripts of 1844*, Marx critically appropriated this concept of transcendence of alienation through second negativity to express the process of emergence of a new society. The first negation, he says, is the abolition of private property. Yet this negation, while necessary, by no means ensures liberation – on the contrary, he refers to it as 'the abstract negation of the entire world of culture and civilisation'.[8] The 'vulgar communist' negation of private property, he says, must itself be negated in order to reach true liberation. Whether this communism is 'democratic or despotic', Marx says, makes no difference; it is still defective because it is infected with its opposite in reducing everything to the question of property. To abolish capital, the first negation, of private property, must itself be negated. Only then, he says, will there arise 'positive Humanism, beginning from itself'. Marx thus defines genuine communism (which he calls 'a thoroughgoing Naturalism or Humanism') as 'the position of the negation of the negation'.[9]

With this conception of self-movement through absolute negativity, Marx projected a truly new world conception which took him far from the positions held by other socialists and communists of the time. The process of revolutionary transformation is seen by him not as a singular act, as the negation of private property and political overthrow of the bourgeoisie, necessary as that of course is, but as a consistently self-critical social revolution, that is, as a process of permanent revolution.

---

[6] Hegel 1969, p. 830.
[7] Hegel 1969, pp. 115–16.
[8] Marx 1975, p. 295.
[9] Marx 1975, p. 306.

Marx thereby extended the target of critique and social transformation to include production relations, the family, man–woman relations, even the entire 'class culture'. A vision of what happens after the revolution was embedded in his transformation of Hegel's revolution in philosophy into a philosophy of revolution.

The problem presented by the history of Marxism is that, for a variety of reasons, the question of organisation was worked out in a separate compartment from any consideration of the dialectic of negativity. This is not simply because Marx himself never explicitly articulated a theory of organisation. Even when he did focus on organisation, his views were not taken as the ground for deliberations on the subject. Though Marx was viewed as the founder when it came to the theory that must guide socialists, he was not seen as the founder of a distinct concept of organisation.[10] To work out the latter, other, decidedly non-Marxian sources were invoked, such as that of Ferdinand Lassalle, who founded the first lasting independent political party of the German proletariat.

The question of organisation was discussed largely in terms of what tactic or strategy is best needed to 'make' the revolution. In the rather rare instances where the question of dialectics was posed in some way, it was not taken up in relation to the role of revolutionary organisation. This separation of philosophy from organisation meant that the search on the part of masses of people for a comprehensive answer to what happens after the revolution all too often went unsatisfied. Yet this does not lessen the objectivity of the search for organisations that can help answer the question of what happens afterwards.

Herein may lie the objectivity of subjectivity, or what gives a Marxist organisation its historic right to exist. The ability of workers spontaneously to come to socialist consciousness, proven over and over again in this century, is not the same as saying that so total a concept of socialism as spelled out in Marx's philosophy of revolution can be reached simply through spontaneous action. Marx, after all, was not simply one among many other socialists; his philosophy of revolution in permanence was distinctive, and contained a distinctive concept of the new society. Grasping that concept, let alone restating it for one's own day, is not something that comes spontaneously, but takes hard, serious, organised labour.

In light of the need for this generation to recapture not only Marx's critique of capital, but also what is needed to effect its abolition and transcendence, it has become newly important to work out a concept of organisation that decisively breaks from the theory and practice of the vanguard party, while at the same time avoiding the problem of relying exclusively on spontaneous forms of organisation.

---

[10] This is reflected in Molyneux 1978, which accuses Marx of suffering from an antiquated notion of organisation: 'Only with Lenin was the concept of a broad party that represents, or is, the working class replaced by that of a 'minority' party ... which is the vanguard of the class ...' (Molyneux 1978, p. 36).

2. Unilinear evolutionism in post-Marx Marxism

What is so very strange is to see how he treats the two of us as a
singular: "Marx and Engels says" etc.

Marx to Engels, 1 August, 1856

Wherein lies the theoretical ground for working out a new relation of
spontaneity and organisation? Does it reside within post-Marx
Marxism, or is it necessary to break with it completely? Are there
dimensions of Marx's work which provide ground for working it out?
While the contributions of Clarke as well as Chodos and Hay make this
a fruitful moment to explore such questions, the contours of the
discussion raise many problems. This is especially seen from the way
they discuss 'Leninism'.

Clark's effort to reduce Lenin's organisational and philosophical
contributions to the inheritance of populism is not sustainable on
historical grounds, or even in terms of the logic of his own argument, as
I will seek to show in a moment. He also fails to distinguish Lenin from
Stalinism, a problem that afflicts Chodos and Hay as well. I single this
out because the identification of Lenin with Stalin has long served as a
distorting lens which hinders efforts at an objective reappraisal of
Lenin's legacy. One side condemns Lenin for giving birth to Stalin,
while the other side, in reaction against this reductionism, affirms
Lenin's contributions without entering into any serious critical
reappraisal of his legacy. The latter tendency is especially evident in
such works as John Molyneux's.[11]

Aside from taking issue with his 1903 declaration of the inability of
workers to come spontaneously to socialist consciousness, Molyneux
uncritically presents Lenin's organisational theory and practice as viable
for today. Yet he does so without any effort to evaluate Lenin's concepts
in light of the realities of the post-World War II era. He simply assumes
that since the Russian Revolution of 1917 was the only successful
proletarian revolution in history and was led by Lenin's party, his
organisational theory remains valid for those committed to proletarian
revolution. He does not ask himself whether the results of the revolution
and others which followed compel one to rethink Lenin's organisational
theory, even if Lenin himself was not responsible for the outcome of
those revolutions. Lenin was surely not to blame for the betrayal of the
Second International in 1914, but that did not stop him from
responding to it by breaking with much of his own philosophical and
political past in his *Philosophical Notebooks* of 1914–15. In light of
Lenin's much-recognised capacity for self-criticism in the context of
new developments, the defensive approach toward Lenin assumed by

---

[11] Molyneux 1978.

those like Molyneux hardly gets us further than reductionist dismissals of him.

Despite these problems, Clarke as well as Chodos and Hay raise a number of important philosophical issues which, when critically explored, can take us beyond the confines of old debates about 'the party'. One of these is Clarke's critique of Plekhanov's concept of 'dialectical materialism'. Insofar as a critique of Plekhanov's concept reveals some of the philosophical limitations underlying post-Marx Marxism, it can allow us to explore whether that legacy contains any ground for working out a dialectical approach to organisation today.

As Clarke notes, 'dialectical materialism' was not a phrase of Marx's but was created by Plekhanov to express a view of history far more wedded to Feuerbach's materialism than Marx's humanism. Central to Plekhanov's dialectical materialism was a rigidly determinist view of history based on a unilinear conception of historical progress. Though the commonly held view is that Plekhanov's determinism derived from a reading of Hegel, one would be hard pressed to find evidence of strict unilinear evolutionism in Hegel's major philosophical works. *The Phenomenology of Mind*, with its complex and intertwined stages of consciousness wherein spirit continuously encounters the pull of prior philosophical standpoints, hardly lends itself to Plekhanov's neat and tidy presentation of how 'reason governs history in the sense of conformity to law'.

The same is true of the *Science of Logic*. The limits of an evolutionist reading of Hegel's *Logic* becomes especially apparent in the chapters on the 'Three Attitudes of Thought Toward Objectivity' in the *Smaller Logic*, the abbreviated and revised version of the *Logic* which Hegel published as the first volume of his three-part *Encyclopedia of the Philosophical Sciences*. The first attitude covers faith, scholasticism and the old metaphysics. The second attitude covers empiricism and Kant's critical philosophy. Given Hegel's alleged view of inevitable historical progress, one would think that the third attitude would cover the movement from Kant to his own dialectical worldview. It does not, however. The third attitude toward objectivity consists of intuitionism and philosophies of immediacy, which Hegel explicitly refers to as a 'regression' from the standpoint of Kantianism.

The chapters on the three attitudes toward objectivity clearly indicate that for Hegel regression is just as integral a part of the historical dialectic as progression. As Harris has argued, Hegel was confident that no second revolution would be needed after 1789 and that no civilised nation which had felt the full impact of that upheaval could possibly fall back into the political despotism which he thought of as barbaric. The experience of this century has shown how badly mistaken he was, but his mistake was essentially empirical. There is nothing in his logical theory to warrant the belief that the motion of consciousness must always be progressive. Every position of consciousness contains the earlier positions in a sublated form, and every position is a stable circle that can maintain itself against criticism. Thus stability is 'natural' and regression is just as possible as progress.[12]

Despite being one of the few theorists of the Second International to write a major essay on Hegel, Plekhanov never commented on Hegel's strictly philosophical works, limiting himself to the *Philosophy of History* and *Philosophy of Right*. His unilinear evolutionism cannot be blamed, therefore, on Hegel himself. It had much more to do with an effort to find a 'philosophical' underpinning for a determinist view of history, which was shared by virtually all Marxists of his generation. As is well known, for the theorists of the Second International capitalism proceeds on a straight path of development. Through a highly selective reading of Marx they held that what drives capitalist development is the contradiction between the 'anarchy of the market' and the social need for planning brought forth by the development of the productive forces. The more capitalism expands, the greater the contradiction between market anarchy and the needs of socialised production. In this model, the contradiction is ultimately resolved by capitalism 'giving way' to socialism, wherein the fetters holding back planned production are finally overcome. This determinist view fits well with a crude and selective reading of Hegel, since his historical works, such as the *Philosophy of History* (published only after his death, not so incidentally), presents a straight progression from 'lower' to 'higher' stages.

But did Plekhanov's historical determinism accord with Marx? Not at all. Marx did not pose the dividing line between capitalism and socialism as the anarchy of the market versus planned production. For Marx 'planning' is an integral part of the capitalist law of value. Volume I of *Capital* speaks of the despotic plan of capital at the point of production:

> Hence the interconnection between their various labours confronts them, in the realm of ideas, as a plan drawn up by the capitalist, and, in practice, as his authority, as the powerful will of a being outside them, who subjects their activity to his will. If capitalist production is thus twofold in content, owing to the twofold nature of the process of production which has to be directed ... in form, it is purely despotic.[13]

For Marx, the absolute opposites are not 'anarchy of the market' versus 'plan', but rather the despotic plan of capital versus the plan of freely associated labour. The latter emerges from the resistance engendered against capital through the growth of cooperation between workers at the point of production. 'The centralisation of the means of production and the socialisation of labour reach a point at which they become incompatible with the capitalist integument.' That is when the 'knell of

---

[12] Harris 1995, p. 107.
[13] Marx 1976, p. 450.

capitalist private property sounds'.[14] In Volume I of *Capital*, Marx provides no more than an intimation of this future state of affairs. No 'iron laws of necessity' bring forth the new society; it instead arises from the conscious actions of living social agents, the workers.

That the Second International's historical determinism rested on a truncated view of Marx is even more evident from its insistence that the 'historical tendency of capitalist accumulation' was a fate destined for the entire world. In fact, as Marx made clear in his critique of Mikhailovsky in *Otechestvennye Zapiski*, Volume I of *Capital* outlines only the direction of capitalism in Western Europe.[15] Yet Marx's insistence that *Capital* 'provides no reasons either for or against the vitality of the Russian commune'[16] and the statement in the Preface to the 1882 Russian edition of *The Communist Manifesto* that the *mir* 'may serve as the point of departure for a communist development'[17] made no impression on Plekhanov, who insisted on presenting 'Marxism' as a 'philosophy' of unilinear evolutionism. Indeed, the letter to *Otechestvennye Zapiski* was left unpublished by the Emancipation of Labour group, and Plekhanov did his best to conceal knowledge of Marx's letter to Zasulich on the Russian peasant commune.[18] That Plekhanov would become a convert to 'Marxism' at the very moment that Marx was projecting the complete opposite of what he held to be the 'Marxist' position is, of course, not without historical irony. It goes to show how deep and organic was the unilinear evolutionism not just of Plekhanov, but of the entire first generation of post-Marx Marxists.

Simply, Plekhanov did not get his determinist outlook from populism. He got it from the received orthodoxy of the Second International. And the prime disseminator of that orthodoxy was Engels. It was Engels, not the populists, who declared that 'Marxism is Darwinism in its application to social science'.[19] It was Engels, not the populists, to whom Plekhanov expressed his intellectual debt in his 1891 essay 'For the 60th Anniversary of Hegel's Death',[20] the most developed presentation of his view of dialectics. And it was Engels, not the populists, who praised Plekhanov's essay highly.[21] Clarke's statement

---

[14] Marx 1976, p. 929.
[15] Marx 1983.
[16] Marx 1983, p. 125.
[17] Marx and Engels 1983, p. 139.
[18] One of several sources that discusses this is Teodor Shanin 1983, pp. 3–39. On p. 19 he writes, 'The 'Letter to Zasulich' written by explicit request to make Marx's views known, was not published by them either ... Much psychologistic rubbish was written in Russia and in the West about how and why those writings were forgotten by Plekhanov, Zasulich, Axelrod etc., and about the 'need for specialized psychologists to have it explained'. It was probably simpler and cruder. Already in Marx's own generation there were marxists who knew better than Marx what marxism is and were prepared to censor him on the sly, for his own sake'.
[19] Engels 1989, p. 467.
[20] Plekhanov 1974 pp. 402–29.
[21] For a fuller discussion, see Anderson 1995, pp. 15–17. John Rees argues that it was Kautsky, not Plekhanov or Engels, who elaborated a strict unilinear evolutionism. He seems not to notice, however, that the phrase from Kautsky that he takes issue with – 'Marx's theory of history was intended to be nothing

that Engels stands 'somewhere in the middle'[22] between Marx and Plekhanov is truer than he realises. Engels was the crucial mediating factor in allowing 'Marxism' to be presented as a form of historical determinism. If Engels had never lived, Plekhanov and Co. would surely have had to invent him. The *geist* of that historic period, unilinear evolutionism, was simply too strong for any of them to resist.

So what does this have to do with organisation? It may seem that Plekhanov's determinist outlook would stand opposed to the voluntarism which later surfaced in Lenin's organisational theory. But the very opposite is the case. For Plekhanov, determinism did not contradict free will, it only gave it an historically determined justification. As he once put it,

> [i]f I am included to take part in a movement whose triumph seems to me a historical necessity, this only means that I consider my activity likewise to be an indispensable link in the chain of conditions whose aggregate will necessarily ensure the triumph of the movement which is so dear to me.[23]

It is often said that determinist philosophies do not account for free will, but that is really not the case at all. The problem is that they account for it too easily. One simply has to read one's subjective inclinations and goals into the historical process, which is then taken to have historical immutability. Plekhanov's determinism did not close off the voluntarist component; it only gave it justification as an integral part of the process of history.

Of course, the extent to which the voluntarist component was emphasised depended upon one's evaluation of the specific political and social realities on the ground to which each revolutionary tendency had to address itself. By 1904, Lenin differed with Plekhanov over the latter's failure to see that Russia's specific economic and social conditions required that intellectuals be subject to greater central discipline than was the case in the West European parties. The ensuing split between Bolsheviks and Mensheviks on the question of what constitutes membership in a Marxist organisation did not involve any dispute over underlying philosophical principles. It was not until his *Philosophical Notebooks* that Lenin broke from Plekhanov's philosophical position. Prior to that, Lenin's philosophical and organisational outlook was completely in accord with 'orthodox' Marxism.

It was not Lenin, but Kautsky, who first conceived that workers can only obtain trade union consciousness through their own endeavour. In *What Is To Be Done?* Lenin made his theoretical affinity with Kautsky clear by quoting approvingly his statement that

more than the application of Darwinism to social development' – is a paraphrase of Engels's comment, quoted above. See Rees 1998, p. 137.
[22] Clarke p. 16.
[23] Quoted in Baron 1963, p. 292.

> [m]odern socialist consciousness can arise only on the basis
> of profound scientific knowledge...The vehicles of science are
> not the proletariat, but the bourgeois intelligentsia.[24]

In his effort to divide off Lenin's approach from that of the 'orthodox'
Marxists, Clarke asserts that '[a]lthough Kautsky's theory gave the
intellectuals a special position in the struggle for socialism, it did not
give them any special authority'.[25] I will leave to Clarke to explain how it
is possible for the pope of Marxism to provide intellectuals with a
'special position' without granting them 'special authority' – especially
when the position involved granting intellectuals the leadership role of
German Social Democracy! No, the fetish of the party did not begin
with Lenin; it began with German social democracy. This is evidenced
by the fact that the very word 'unorganised worker' was a term of insult
and abuse. Such attitudes also dovetailed with the party's backward and
often racist attitudes towards non-Western peoples.

Yet this is not to grant Kautsky with originality when it came to the
concept of the vanguard party. That honour more properly belongs to
Ferdinand Lassalle. It was Lassalle who formed the first lasting
nationwide, independent political party of the German proletariat and
whose impact on the organisation theory and practice of the Second
International was immense. And it was Lassalle who first defined
intellectuals as the 'vehicles of science'. The lineage runs from Lassalle
through Kautsky to Lenin. By tying Lenin's vanguardism to populism,
Clarke obscures its real roots – the Lassalleanism which permeated the
whole of the Second International, and indeed much that came after.
He thereby obscures how implicated post-Marx Marxism was from its
inception in the Lassallean vanguardism which Marx castigated in his
1875 *Critique of the Gotha Programme*.[26]

3. Absolute negativity as new beginning

To see what is really at stake in the differences between Marx and post-
Marx Marxists on the question of dialectics and materialism, we need to
look more closely at the notion that Feuerbachian materialism, and not
Marx's humanism, represented the real philosophical foundation of
post-Marx Marxism.

Feuerbach's materialism has certainly been tremendously influential,
not only on the Second International but upon many Marxists to this
very day. To draw out the difference between Marx and Feuerbach's
position it is necessary to go to the text in which Marx first broke from

---

[24] Lenin 1943 p.61.
[25] Clarke p. 24.
[26] See Mészáros 1995 for a recent discussion of the Critique of the Gotha
Program as expressing Marx's concept of organisation. For a critique of his
overall position, see Hudis 1997.

him – his 1844 'Critique of the Hegelian Dialectic.' Here, Marx does not accuse Hegel of failing to grasp reality. He writes that the sections of Hegel's *Phenomenology* on

> ...'Unhappy Consciousness', the 'Honorable Consciousness', the fight of the noble and downtrodden consciousness, etc., etc. contain the critical elements – although still in alienated form – of whole spheres like Religion, the State, Civic Life, etc.[27]

Marx is sharply critical of Hegel, however, because the structure of the *Phenomenology* and his philosophical system as a whole poses the subject of the dialectic as disembodied thought instead of as live human beings. Since thought, not 'actual corporeal man' is posed as the subject, humanity appears as the result of the dialectical process, rather than its creative agent. By posing thought and not humanity as the subject, Hegel inverts the relation of subject and object. Humanity, the real subject, becomes the object, the mere result of an activity of its own creation – thought. This is the inversion which Marx is striving to correct in his critique of Hegel.[28] As Marx puts it,

> [t]his process must have a bearer, a subject, but the subject emerges only as a result. This result, the subject knowing itself as absolute self-consciousness, is therefore, God, absolute spirit, the Idea knowing and affirming itself. Actual man and actual nature become mere predicates, symbols of this concealed, unactual man, and this unactual nature. Subject and predicate, therefore, have a relation of absolute inversion to each other ...[29]

The notion that Marx is simply counterposing materialism to Hegel's idealism obscures what is really at issue. Marx says that Hegel's *Logic* serves as 'the abstract expression of the speculative value of the thoughts of man and nature. It has become completely indifferent to all actual determinateness'. Hegel, he is saying, gives intellectual expression to a material reality – the subsuming of human sensuousness under a logic of abstraction. The problem is not that Hegel's philosophy fails to express material reality. The problem is that it expresses it all too well. For by posing the subject of the dialectic as abstract self-consciousness, Hegel captures the logic of capital as self-expanding value. This is why Marx says that 'Hegel stands on the basis of modern political economy'.[30]

---

[27] Marx 1958, p. 309.
[28] Contra Clarke, Marx nowhere discusses the need to replace philosophy by 'science' in his 1844 'Critique'. Clarke is reading the late Engels's promotion of scientism and mechanical positivism into the early Marx.
[29] Marx 1958, p. 320–1.
[30] Marx 1958, p. 310.

Most Marxists stop at this point, presuming that Marx's critique of Hegel for expressing the logic of capital is basically his final word on him. But Marx himself does not stop here. He goes on to single out the positive element which nevertheless resides within Hegel's abstractions. Marx sees this positive element as pointing the way to the abolition of capital. That element is the negation of the negation.

Though he is critical of Hegel for acting as if human sensuousness is the result of the negation of the negation, he does not, like Feuerbach, dismiss it as a mystical abstraction. For Marx sees that second negation, or self-referential negativity, expresses the very process by which capitalism is transcended. He spells this out by saying that the first negation – or communism – is still 'infected with its opposite', in that it still defines itself in relation to the property relation which it opposes. It too must be negated in order to get to the real problem of capitalism, alienated labour. In the preceding essay of the *1844 Manuscripts*, 'Private Property and Communism', Marx says that this movement through second negativity is also needed to transform alienated relations between men and women, which he calls the most fundamental relation in society. Marx appropriates Hegel's concept of absolute negativity to develop a philosophy of revolution rooted in the transformation not just of property forms or even class structures, but of human relations. As he puts it, only by undergoing second negativity, through the negation not just of capitalism but also of 'vulgar communism', does there arise 'positive Humanism, beginning from itself'.[31]

Here lies Marx's point of divide from Feuerbach. Since Hegel held that human sensuousness is the result of the second negation, Feuerbach rejected his idealism in favor of materialism. Marx, in contrast, does not counterpose materialism to idealism. He sees that Hegel's idealism contains a materialist element, the negation of the negation. Marx claims that Feuerbach

> conceives the negation of the negation only as the contradiction of philosophy with itself – as the philosophy which affirms Theology (the transcendent, etc.) after having denied it ... But because Hegel has conceived the negation of the negation from the point of view of the positive relation inherent in it ... to that extent he has discovered, though only as an abstract, logical, and speculative expression, the movement of history.[32]

Marx never lets go of the way Hegel 'grasps the meaning of the positive sense of the negation related to itself, even if in an alienated way'.[33]

As he said later in his 'Theses on Feuerbach', idealism is superior to materialism because it expresses the 'active side'. The 1844 'Critique'

---

[31] Marx 1958, p. 306.
[32] Marx 1958, p. 308.
[33] Marx 1958, p. 320.

defines the active side thus: 'The dialectic of negativity is the moving and creating principle'.[34] At the same time, idealism is defective since it poses human sensuousness as a mere result of the dialectical process, rather than as its subject. Marx therefore projects the need for a new '[h]umanism [which] distinguishes itself from both Idealism and Materialism, and is, at the same time, the truth uniting both'.[35]

With this statement Marx achieves a true leap in consciousness, for it marks the birth of a whole new continent of thought which posits the unity of idealism and materialism, theory and practice, philosophy and revolution. Those raised in the 'classical' Marxist tradition as defined by Engels have hardly measured up to the depth and magnificence of this vision. Even where Marx's break from Feuerbachian materialism is noted in some way, Marx's projection of a new humanism based on a unity of idealism and materialism is studiously ignored. This is most recently seen in John Rees's *The Algebra of Revolution*. Though Rees claims to present an accounting of the Hegel–Marx relation, and has a chapter largely devoted to Marx's 1844 critique of Hegel, he neither mentions nor quotes Marx's statement about a 'thoroughgoing Naturalism or Humanism'! Such formulations of Marx get in the way of Rees's concern with 'proving' that the central issue in Marx's critique of Hegel was the counterposition of materialism versus idealism. Rees, like many others, seems discomforted by Marx's sharp critique of materialism in the manuscripts and tries to explain it away as a critique of 'bourgeois' materialism. But if that is so, then why would Marx define his thought as the unity of materialism and idealism? If Rees is correct, Marx is saying his thought represents a unity of bourgeois materialism with abstract (and equally bourgeois) idealism. This is hardly a defensible position, given Marx's sharp critique of both of these traditions.

Rees's position reveals how deeply rooted many remain in the Feuerbachian-inspired materialist critique of idealism which was so influential among the Marxists of the 19th century. He is hardly alone in this. Even Clarke, who attempts to separate Feuerbach's position from Marx and does cite his discussion of a new humanism, dismisses the negation of the negation as 'mystical'. Yet this was Feuerbach's very position. The tendency to skip over, downplay, or dismiss the dialectic of second negativity is clearly not only something that characterised earlier generations of Marxists, but something that remains with us still.[36]

---

[34] Marx 1958, p. 309.
[35] Marx 1958, p. 313.
[36] Even Derrida, for all his presumed originality and distance from the Marxist tradition, has a surprisingly orthodox view of absolute negativity. As he wrote in Glas, 'Marx [in his 1844 critique of Hegel] then sets out the critical moment of Feuerbach and in its most operative stance: the questioning of the *Aufhebung* and of the negation of the negation. The absolute positive ... hence must not pass through the negation of the negation, the Hegelian *Aufhebung* ...' Derrida 1986, p. 201.

There are of course objective reasons why the Marxists of the Second or even Third International paid scant attention to second negativity. Marx's *1844 Manuscripts*, in which he directly delved into the topic, were unknown until the 1930s. Yet more is involved than availability of texts. Concepts like the negation of the negation did not get the attention they deserved because it seemed that capitalism would inevitably be forced, either through the 'laws' of history or the exertion of human will, to give way to socialism. Why worry oneself about abstruse concepts like absolute negativity when the course of history was preparing the way for the new society? The shock induced by the collapse of the Second International in 1914 undermined this certainty and helps explain why Lenin undertook such an extensive reorganisation of his philosophical position in his 'Abstract of Hegel's *Science of Logic*'. Whereas he was earlier a prime exponent of vulgar materialism and the photocopy theory of reality, he now exclaimed that 'Man's cognition not only reflects the objective world, but creates it'.[37]

But even though he broke with his philosophical past and went so far as to explore the chapter on 'The Absolute Idea' in the *Logic* – untouched by any Marxist up to that point – he did not emphasise the concept of second negation.[38] His 16-point definition of dialectics refers to the negation of the negation as 'the apparent return to the old' and places it beneath the transition of quantity into quality.[39] As Dunayevskaya put it in a reevaluation of his *Philosophical Notebooks* in 1986, '[o]utside of Marx himself, the whole question of the negation of the negation was ignored by all "orthodox Marxists"'.[40]

Even for Lenin in 1914–15, the dialectic of second negativity was not concrete.[41] Why? The reason may lie in the fact that he neither lived to see nor anticipated Stalinism. For all of his embrace of such Hegelian concepts as 'transformation into opposite', Lenin did not anticipate that the counter-revolution would come from within the revolution itself. The compulsion to make the dialectic of second negativity explicit and concrete as the very banner of a reconstituted Marxism did not and perhaps could not be concretely felt until there was historic proof of the non-viability of perspectives based on first negativity. In any case, to the extent that Lenin did explore the dialectic of negativity in 1914–15, it never impacted his conception of revolutionary organisation. Though he

---

[37] Lenin 1961, p. 212.
[38] The fullest treatment of the concept of absolute negativity occurs in Hegel's Philosophy of Mind – a work which Lenin never explored.
[39] Lenin 1961, p. 222.
[40] Dunayevskaya, 1991, p. xxix.
[41] This was addressed by the Scottish Marxist-humanist Harry McShane, in a letter to Dunayevskaya: 'Having lived during the First World War period I recall [that] the steady development of the movement prevented one from giving thought to dialectics. Socialism was certain. Lenin lived in this period. It took a world war before the worship of the Second International came to an end ... Let me ask, Raya, did Lenin have hopes that the Russian social democracy would one day be able to operate in the same way as in West Europe? I think the attitude of social democracy to dialectics deserves some attention'. McShane 1990, C29.

modified his 1903 theory of the party on numerous occasions, he never broke from the organisational precepts inherited (albeit indirectly) from Lassalle. The question of organisation remained in a separate compartment from his consideration of dialectics.

In contrast, by the time a new stage of workers' revolts emerged against Stalinism in the 1950s, theoreticians such as Dunayevskaya felt compelled to turn directly to the dialectic of absolute negativity in Hegel and Marx. It led her to develop an original body of ideas, Marxist-humanism, rooted in the concept of 'absolute negativity as new beginning'.[42]

Dunayevskaya argued that the social content of new revolutionary forces in the post-World War II era showed that masses of people were striving to move beyond political perspectives based on first negativity. Workers involved in the wildcat strikes against automated production asked such questions as 'What kind of labour should people perform?', thereby giving new life to Marx's emphasis on the need to articulate an alternative to alienated labour. Women involved in the various new feminist movements asked what kind of new man–woman relations could be created in the course of the struggle for a new society. Blacks and other minorities involved in the civil rights struggles asked how relations of reciprocity and consciousness of selfhood could be engendered in the very course of the struggle against racism. Instead of waiting until the revolution to pose such critical questions, the movements from practice were striving to raise the issue of 'what happens after?' long before the seisure of power. The 'abstract' question of second negativity took on new life. For Dunayevskaya, this challenged theoreticians to meet the movements from practice with a movement from theory deeply rooted in the dialectic of absolute negativity.

Whatever the reasons earlier generations of Marxists shied away from the dialectic of absolute negativity, one thing should be clear: Our generation has little excuse to do so. The collapse of Stalinism as well as the profound impasse of social democracy and the anti-Stalinist Left provides abundant proof of the insufficiency of defining one's political perspectives on the basis of the mere negation of private property, the market, and capitalist relations of distribution. Whether it be the collapse of the Soviet Union, the coexistence of statist repression and 'free market' economy in China, or Cuba's increasing entry into a world market defined by commodification of human flesh through a burgeoning prostitution industry, history has shown, without any shadow of doubt, that revolutions defined by first negativity have in each and every instance become a transition point, not toward a new society, but back to the capitalism of old.

After all that has transpired in the aborted and unfinished revolutions of this century, it is hard to imagine that masses of people

---

[42] See Dunayevskaya 1991 for the development of this concept.

will feel impelled to transform society on the basis of perspectives which focus on abolishing private property and the anarchy of the market. Indeed, what has become utopian today is not the projection of a liberating vision of the future that points to the negation of capital, but rather the assumption that we can afford to delay doing so for the sake of focusing on the immediate objects of oppression. The need to begin from the second negation has become concrete.

Certainly, this cannot mean overlooking the need to negate such immediate objects of oppression as inequities of property and income fostered by market relations. Yet such targets of critique and social transformation must be conceptualised within a much broader perspective. This must centre upon the need to effect a direct negation of the capital relation on the immediate aftermath of the revolutionary seizure of power, and to prefigure such relations in the very form and content of revolutionary organisation itself. In this sense, the question facing our generation is: will we respond to 'spirit's urgency' by working out a perspective of social transformation rooted in working out a new beginning from the dialectic of second negativity, or will we instead cling to the stageist models and perspectives which have characterised post-Marx Marxism?

4. Beyond post-Marx Marxism

Chodos and Hay make a potentially valuable contribution when they write that

> [w]ithout an ever more concrete and complex conception of a viable socialism based on an ever-more concrete and complex critique of the contours of contemporary capitalism, no self-radicalising – far less revolutionary – political momentum can be generated.
>
> This presents a considerable challenge for the party itself.[43]

The question is whether this can be achieved within the perimeters of a discussion of form of organisation without getting to the philosophical concepts needed to guide it. Though they speak of the need for 'the party [which] bridges the gap between between the future and the present, translating long-term goals into concrete action today, and ascribing meaning to more immediate political action in terms of such goals',[44] their rather indeterminant use of the phrase 'the party' as well as their underlying theoretical concepts risks hemming the discussion into some old dualities.

---

[43] Chodos and Hay, p. 39.
[44] Chodos and Hay, p. 31.

This is especially seen in Chodos and Hay's advocacy of 'radical reformism'. After criticising the social-democratic Left for its abandonment of socialist advocacy, they argue that

> there is little chance of Marxists 'making a difference' without first establishing (governmental) credibility by demonstrating themselves capable of realising immediate, not necessarily radical goals.[45]

To avoid the pitfalls of the social-democratic tradition, they propose that 'the party' combine a gradualist agenda with 'a self-radicalising critique both of its own practices and of capitalism itself'.[46] This indicates that Chodos and Hay may not have absorbed the full lessons of the failure of social democracy.

Proposing that a party have a 'self-radicalising critique both of its own practices and of capitalism itself' is all fine and good, but the question is whether such a perspective can sustain itself once 'the party' enters the corridors of power. If the history of this century proves anything, it is that once 'socialists' assume the position of helping to manage the hierarchies of capital, the exigencies of power and politics inevitably eat away at any effort to maintain socialist ideals. The power of the idea always appears less efficacious than the contingencies of the real – once that is, one decides to insert oneself into the structures of domination.

But Chodos and Hay do not just leave the door open to an eventual watering down of socialist ideals. It already occurs in their piece. In discussing the difference between socialism and communism, they define the former as distribution based on egalitarian remuneration and the latter as the regulation of individual needs. Aside from the fact that Marx did not demarcate socialism and communism as distinct historical stages but used them interchangeably, which renders their critique of Marx's 'stageism' rather superfluous, their definitions offer a rather thin vision of a new society.

Like the post-Marx Marxists of old, for them, socialism centers on a change in the mode of distribution. The nature of communism is left rather vague, posed as 'an attitude, a way of life'. Nowhere do they mention the need to transform production relations, abolish alienated labour, uproot oppressive relations between men and women, end relations of racist domination, etc. In other words, all the things which result from the negation of the negation. Philosophically speaking, Chodos and Hay stop dead at the first negation. Despite their effort to integrate organisation with 'the vision of the long-term goal toward which we are striving', the lack of exploration of 'the dialectic proper' renders their discussion abstract and formalistic.

---

[45] Chodos and Hay, p. 40.
[46] Chodos and Hay, p. 39.

What then does it mean to rethink revolutionary organisation along the lines of second negativity? Though it is impossible to do justice to such an expansive question here, there are several aspects we can point to. As noted earlier, the concept of the vanguard party has long outlived its usefulness. This does not mean, however, that Marxists can presume that 'spontaneous' forms of organisation hold all the answers. The borderline between spontaneity and organisation is never absolute in any case, since spontaneous upsurges are often accompanied by some kind of organised intervention on the part of conscious revolutionaries. Moreover, history indicates that participants in spontaneous upsurges repeatedly go in search of organisations other than their own in order to obtain a fuller grasp the path needed to create a truly new society. The need for an organisation of Marxist revolutionaries remains as objective as ever. The task, however, is not to synthesise the vanguard party form with spontaneous movements, but rather work out a new form of non-vanguardist organisation rooted in the dialectic of absolute negativity.

This means, first of all, that the form of organisation must strive to embody the content of the new society by breaking down the basis of all class divisions – the separation of mental from manual labour. Instead of intellectuals possessing the prerogatives of 'leadership', it becomes essential for working people to guide both the political and theoretical direction of the organisation. Just as intellectuals must break from their own class position by learning to listen, so workers must break from theirs by becoming theoreticians. Breaking down of the division between mental and manual by overcoming the one-sidedness of both workers and intellectuals allows an organisation to project an alternative vision of the future in its very form of functioning.

Secondly, it becomes just as essential for any revolutionary organisation to embody and articulate the content of the array of social forces needed to abolish capital. Capital has invaded every nook and cranny of modern existence. Though it is central to the production process, it is by no means limited to that sphere. Without the articulated subjectivity of workers, women, national minorities, youth and others opposing the logic of capital, the system cannot be fundamentally transformed. Revolutionary organisation must demonstrate this truth by projecting as expansive a concept of liberation as the content of the social forces themselves. As against the notion that focusing on 'movements in solidarity with the third world, to students in revolt, to black power, to women's liberation' involve 'remaining within and adapting to a petty-bourgeois milieu',[47] the underlying reason of these social forces is essential to the forward movement of any revolutionary organisation

Crucial as it is, the form of organisation is not the whole. Form divorced from the content of a philosophy of liberation inevitably becomes hollow and barren. The contingencies of organisation must not

---

[47] Molyneux 1978, pp. 139–40.

predominate over the principles of Marx's philosophy of revolution in permanence. Just as the principles of revolution in permanence must inform the very form of organisation, so must its content be articulated anew for our era. Though the unity of philosophy and organisation remains an untrodden path in the history of post-Marx Marxism, it is through this praxis that a new beginning from the dialectic of second negativity can be made.

Lenin once said that creating a new International cannot be achieved on the basis of a crude or vulgarised Marxism. Neither can the working out of a new relation of spontaneity, organisation and philosophy, which opposes the 'party to lead' while avoiding the tendency to saddle spontaneous forms of organisation with all of the responsibility for working out a concept of a new society. Though the dominance of the unilinear evolutionism which characterised 'orthodox Marxism' is not as predominant as it once was, especially in light of the scathing critiques of it made by critical theorists, feminists, and postcolonial thinkers, the need to grasp the full implications of Marx's transformation of Hegel's revolution in philosophy into a philosophy of revolution in permanence is still very much before us. In lieu of that, efforts to fill the void in the projection of an alternative to capitalism will hardly prove viable.

As Dunayevskaya put it in one of her last writings in 1987:

> The dialectic of organisation, as of philosophy, goes to the root of not only the question of the relationship of spontaneity to party, but the relationship of multilinearism to unilinearism. Put simply, it is question of human development, be it capitalism, pre-capitalism or post-capitalism. The fact that Stalin could transform so great a revolution as the Russian Revolution of 1917 into a state bureaucracy tells more than just the isolation of a proletarian revolution in a single country. The whole question of the indispensability of spontaneity not only as something that is in the revolution, but must continue its development after; the question of different cultures, as well as self-development as having a non-state form of collectivity – makes the task much more difficult and impossible to anticipate in advance. The self-development of ideas cannot take second place to the self-bringing-forth of liberty, because both the movement from practice that is itself a form of theory, and the development of theory as philosophy, are more than just saying philosophy is action. There is surely one thing on which we should not try to improve on Marx – and that is trying to have a blueprint for the future.[48]

---

[48] Dunayevskaya 1996, p. 107.

References

Anderson, Kevin 1995 *Lenin, Hegel and Western Marxism: A Critical Study*, Champaign-Urbana: University of Illinois Press.

Baron, Samuel H. 1963 *Plekhanov, the Father of Russian Marxism*, Stanford: Stanford University Press.

Derrida, Jacques 1986 [1974], *Glas*, Lincoln: University of Nebraska Press.

Dunayevskaya, Raya 1958, *Marxism and Freedom, From 1776 Until Today*, New York: Bookman.

Dunayevskaya, Raya 1982, *Rosa Luxemburg, Women's Liberation, and Marx's Philosophy of Revolution*, Champaign-Urbana: University of Illinois Press.

Dunayevskaya, Raya 1989, *The Philosophic Moment of Marxist-Humanism*, Chicago: News and Letters.

Dunayevskaya, Raya 1991, *Philosophy and Revolution, from Hegel to Sartre and From Marx to Mao*, New York: Columbia University Press.

Dunayevskaya, Raya, 1996. 'A Post-World War II View of Marx's Humanism, 1843–83; Marxist Humanism in the 1950s and 1980s,' in *Bosnia-Herzegovina: Achilles Heel of Western 'Civilization'* edited by Peter Wermuth, Chicago: News and Letters.

Engels, Frederick 1989, 'Karl Marx's Funeral,' in Marx and Engels, *Collected Works* Volume 24, New York: International Publishers.

Fanon, Frantz 1975, *The Wretched of the Earth*, New York: Grove Press.

Harris, H.S. 1995, *Hegel: Phenomenology and System*, Indianapolis: Hacket.

Hegel, G.W.F. 1969, *Science of Logic*, New York: Humanities Press.

Hudis, Peter, 1992, 'Introduction' in *The Marxist-Humanist Theory of State-Capitalism: Selected Writings by Raya Dunayevskaya*, Chicago: News and Letters.

Hudis, Peter 1997, 'Conceptualizing an Emancipatory Alternative: Istvan Mészáros' Beyond Capital,' *Socialism and Democracy*, 11, 1: 37–55

Lenin, V.I. 1943, *What Is To Be Done* in *Selected Works* Volume 2 Moscow: International Publishers.

Lenin, V.I. 1961, 'Conspectus of Hegel's Science of Logic,' in *Collected Works*, Volume 38. New York: London: Lawrence & Wishart.

McShane, Harry 1992, 'The Harry McShane Collection, 1959-88', National Museum of Labour History, Manchester, England.

Marx, Karl 1958, 'Critique of the Hegelian Dialectic', in *Marxism and Freedom, From 1776 Until Today* by Raya Dunayevskaya, New York: Bookman.

Marx, Karl, 1975, *Economic and Philosophical Manuscripts of 1844*, in *Collected Works* Volume 3, New York: International Publishers.

Marx, Karl 1976, *Capital*, Volume I, New York: Vintage.

Marx, Karl 1983, 'A Letter to the Editorial Board of *Otechestvennye Zapiski*', in *Late Marx and the Russian Road* edited by Teodor Shanin, New York: Monthly Review.

Marx, Karl and Engels, Frederick 1983, 'Preface to the Second Russian Edition of the Manifesto of the Communist Party', in *Late Marx and the Russian Road* edited by Teodor Shanin, New York: Monthly Review.

Mészaros, Istvan 1995, *Beyond Capital: Towards a Theory of Transition*, New York: Monthly Review Press.

Molyneux, John 1978, *Marxism and the Party*, London: Pluto Press.

Rees, John, 1998 *The Algebra of Revolution: The Dialectic and the Classical Marxist Tradition*, London: Routledge.

Plekhanov, Georgi 1974, 'For the 60th Anniversary of Hegel's Death' *Selected Philosophical Works*, Vol. I Moscow: Progress.

Teodor, Shanin 1983, 'Late Marx: Gods and Craftsmen' in *Late Marx and the Russian Road,* edited by Teodor Shanin, Monthly Review: New York.

Actuel Marx

Revue internationale consacrée au marxisme
publiée aux Presses Universitaires de France
avec le concours de l'Université Paris-X Nanterre et du CNRS

Sommaire du n° 24 - 1998/2

Actuel Marx : http ://www.u-paris10.fr - E-mail : ActuelMarx@u-paris10.fr

PRIX DU NUMERO 180 francs
ABONNEMENT (2 numéros par an)
France 300 francs - Etranger 350 francs

Paiement par virement postal à PUF CCP 392 33 A - PARIS, ou par chèque bancaire
libellé à l'ordre de PUF :14, avenue du Bois-de-l'épine - BP 90 - 91003 EVRY - FRANCE

Labour, Eco-Regulation, and Value: A Response to Benton's Ecological Critique of Marx

Paul Burkett

Introduction

In an earlier article, I responded to Ted Benton's charge that Marx and Engels, upon realising the political conservatism associated with Malthusian natural limits arguments, retreated from materialism to a social-constructionist conception of human production and reproduction.[1] I showed that Benton artificially dichotomises the material and social elements of historical materialism, thereby misreading Marx and Engels's recognition of the historical specificity of material conditions as an outright denial of all natural limits. In place of Marx and Engels's materialist and class-relational approach to population issues and the reserve army of the unemployed, Benton employs a partially Malthusianised Marxism heavily reliant on ahistorical notions of natural limits.

It remains to consider Benton's critique of Marx's *Capital*, the ecological shortcomings of which, according to Benton, go a long way towards explaining the tense and often conflictual relationship between Marxists and environmentalists. My earlier article considered Marx's *Capital* only as necessary to deal with the relationship between Marx and Malthus. Benton's ecological critique of *Capital*'s labour-process analysis, and his detection of an anti-materialist bias in Marx's labour theory of value, were temporarily left out of account. The present article demonstrates that these criticisms again apply a false material/social dualism to Marx's analysis.

I first take up Benton's suggestion that Marx's labour-process analysis understates the dependence of human production on irreplaceable natural conditions, especially in 'eco-regulatory' practices such as farming where the intentional action of human labour is necessarily interrupted by organic processes. It is shown that Benton's argumentative strategy combines an artificial denaturalisation of Marx's analysis with a desocialised reading of Marx's conception of human labour – leading to various contradictions in Benton's argument. I then demonstrate that Benton dematerialises Marx's value analysis by drawing a false dichotomy between value and use-value. Finally, Benton's distortion of *Capital*'s value analysis is shown to reinforce the

---

[1] Burkett 1998a, and Benton 1989.

technological determinism and de-classed ecological politics built into his reconstruction of historical materialism.

The labour process and natural conditions

Benton's ecological critique of *Capital* centres on 'the "labour process" as a transhistorical condition of human survival,' as demarcated in Chapter 7 of Volume I: 'The elementary factors of the labour-process are 1, the personal activity of man, ie., the work itself, 2, the subject of that work, and 3, its instruments.'[2] Benton argues that this classification

> under-represents the significance of non-manipulable natural conditions of labour-processes and over-represents the role of human intentional transformative powers vis-à-vis nature ... Marx does, indeed, recognize such activities as felling timber, catching fish, extracting ore, and agriculture as labour-processes ... But in recognizing the necessity of [natural] conditions, Marx simultaneously fails to recognize their significance by including them *within* the category of 'instruments of production'. These conditions cannot plausibly be considered 'conductors' of the activity of the labourer.[3]

In short, Benton's complaint is that

> the conceptual assimilation of contextual *conditions* of the labour-process to the category of 'instruments of production' has the effect of occluding the essential dependence of all labour-processes upon at least some non-manipulable contextual conditions ... [T]he subjection to human *intentionality* which is implicit in the concept of an 'instrument' is precisely what *cannot* be plausibly attributed to these contextual conditions of production.[4]

This critique is based on a partial dematerialisation of Marx's labour-process conception. Specifically, it blurs Marx's internal differentiation of the 'instruments' category to explicitly incorporate natural conditions that are *not* direct conductors of human labour:

> In a wider sense we may include among the instruments of labour, in addition to those things that are used for directly transferring labour to its subject, and which therefore, in one way or another, serve as conductors of activity, all such objects as are necessary for carrying on the labour-process. These do not enter directly into the process, but without them it is either impossible for it to take place at all, or possible only

---

[2] Benton 1989, p. 64, and Marx 1967a, p. 178.
[3] Benton 1989, pp. 64, 66, 72.
[4] Benton 1989, p. 72.

to a partial extent. Once more we find the earth to be a
universal instrument of this sort, for it furnishes a *locus standi*
to the labourer and a field of employment for his activity.[5]

Curiously, Benton *partially* quotes this passage – mentioning only that
'Marx proposes to include ... the earth itself (which "furnishes a *locus
standi* to the labourer and a field of employment for his activity") ...
among the instruments of labour ("in a wider sense")'.[6] Benton thus
conceals Marx's recognition of 'all such objects as are necessary for
carrying on the labour-process' as a distinct ('universal') category of
productive instruments. This category includes not only 'the earth' as 'a
locus standi and field of employment', but all natural conditions which,
while not directly conducting human labour, are necessary for the
labour process. This follows from Marx's terminology (not mentioned
by Benton) in which the earth encompasses all forces and elements of
terrestrial nature.[7] The universal instruments category accords with
Capital's earlier analysis of *commodity* use-values, where Marx
emphasises not only that 'if we take away the useful labour expended
upon them, a material substratum is always left, which is furnished by
Nature without the help of man', but also that labour 'is constantly
helped by natural forces'.[8]

In short, far from *assimilating* natural conditions to a predetermined productive instruments category, Marx *consciously
variegates* the instruments category so as to distinguish those natural
conditions which do not directly conduct human labour from those
means of production which do serve as labour conductors. Similar
problems emerge when Benton extends his rather liberal translation of
Marx's Chapter 7 from the instruments to the subjects of labour:

> Marx concedes that some very elementary transactions with
> nature do not require artificial implements, and here human
> limbs themselves can be regarded as playing the part of
> 'instruments of production'. The 'subject' of labour – the
> thing or material worked on – may be 'spontaneously
> provided by nature', or, more commonly, it will have been
> 'filtered through past labour', in which case Marx speaks
> (somewhat misleadingly) of 'raw material'.[9]

Benton's description of produced instruments as 'artificial' leaves the
incorrect impression that, for Marx, produced instruments have no
natural basis or substance. Similarly, Benton contrasts the
'spontaneously provided' and the ('more common') 'filtered' subjects of
labour – reinforcing the impression that, for Marx, labour somehow
negates the natural characteristics of its nature-given subjects or

---

[5] Marx 1967a, p. 180
[6] Benton 1989, pp. 65–6.
[7] Marx 1967a, p. 183, 1967c, p. 774.
[8] Marx 1967a, p. 43.
[9] Benton 1989, p. 65.

reduces the importance of these characteristics for human production. Indeed, Benton's statement seems to suggest that Marx limited the importance of nature-provided means of production to those cases in which labourers use no instruments other than their own limbs! Here again, a far more general picture emerges from Marx's text:

> The soil (and this, economically speaking, includes water) in the virgin state in which it supplies man with necessaries or the means of subsistence ready to hand, exists independently of him, and is the universal subject of human labour. All those things which labour merely separates from immediate connection with their environment, are subjects of labour spontaneously provided by nature.[10]

Notice that Marx in no way limits the role of 'spontaneously provided subjects of labour' to 'very elementary transactions with nature' in which labour uses no produced instruments; nor does Marx give any impression that the natural characteristics of these 'universal subjects' become less important as a result of their being subjects of human labour.

Evidently Marx needs to be reconstructed because, instead of using terms such as 'non-manipulable contextual conditions,' he refers to natural conditions as universal 'instruments and subject[s] of labour ... means of production'.[11] This despite Marx's emphatic insistence on the irreplaceability of natural conditions by human labour:

> It appears paradoxical to assert, that uncaught fish, for instance, are a means of production in the fishing industry. But hitherto no one has discovered the art of catching fish in waters that contain none.[12]

> In so far then, as its instruments and subjects are themselves products, labour consumes products in order to create products ... But, just as in the beginning, the only participators in the labour-process were man and the earth, which latter exists independently of man, so even now we still employ in the process many means of production, provided directly by Nature, that do not represent any combination of natural substances with human labour.[13]

In sum, Benton's critique seems to confuse terminological preference with conceptual assimilation. Certainly Benton fails to demonstrate 'defects in Marx's *concept* of the labour-process' from the standpoint of 'non-manipulable contextual conditions'.[14]

---

[10] Marx 1967a, p. 178.
[11] Benton 1989, p. 72, and Marx 1967a, p. 181.
[12] Marx 1967a, p. 181.
[13] Marx 1967a, p. 183.
[14] Benton 1989, pp. 72, 76. My emphasis.

Benton's awkward attempt to partially dematerialise Marx's labour-process analysis runs side-by-side with a desocialised interpretation of this same analysis. This is not surprising, insofar as asocial conceptions of material life can only be maintained by abstracting from the material content of social relations. Crude materialism and idealism always represent two sides of the same undialectical coin.[15]

Hence, the only characteristics of specifically human labour explicitly recognised by Benton are: (1) the use of instruments of production produced with the help of labour, and, (2) subjection of the labour process to human intentionality. It is true that these features are highly *characteristic* of human labour; but they do not exhaust Marx's transhistorical conception. For Marx, human labour is defined first and foremost by its 'social character', because 'from the moment that men in any way work for one another, their labour assumes a social form'.[16] The fact that Marx first 'consider[s] the labour-process independently of the particular form it assumes under given social conditions', that is, in terms of the elements 'common to ... every social phase of [human] existence', does not mean that he is not talking about a social labour process here.[17] Marx starts with a conception of human labour as an essential part of the 'life-process of society', albeit in transhistorical terms 'independent of every [particular] social phase' of human existence – so that 'it was ... not necessary to represent our labourer in connexion with other labourers; man and his labour on one side, nature and its materials on the other, sufficed'.[18]

The reason Marx highlights the social character of human labour is not to engage in a social-constructionist downgrading of the role of nature. Rather, it is to emphasise that it is in and through specific social relations of production that the particular characteristics of human labour (intentional determination of outcomes; use of produced instruments of production) are developed, and with them the wealth-creating powers latent in nature and cooperative human labour.[19] Benton's desocialisation of Marx's conception is clear from the former's interpretation of the intentional character of human labour:

> Now, it is immediately clear that the intentional structure of the labour-process is, for Marx, a transformative one. It is plausible to suppose that Marx's model is handicraft production of some kind ... With some modifications, the representation might do for productive labour-processes in general, though with the important reservation that in industrial labour-processes the intentionality which assigns each element to its place in the structure is not that of the individual agents in the process.[20]

---

[15] Marx 1976b, p. 615; Marx and Engels 1980, p. 159.
[16] Marx 1967a, pp. 71–2.
[17] Marx 1967a, pp. 177, 184.
[18] Marx 1967a, pp. 80, 184.
[19] Compare Engels 1964, pp. 175–7.
[20] Benton 1989, p. 66.

This statement is incorrect because Marx's transhistorical conception by definition focuses on those factors which are 'independent of every social phase ... or rather, [are] common to every such phase' of human history.[21] Since Marx's conception does not represent the labourer in connection with other labourers in any historically specific way, it is not based on any specific 'model' of human-social production – handicraft or otherwise. Hence, Marx's labour-process classification does not hinge upon any particular conception of the intentionality of human labour as individual or collective, or as coercive versus non-coercive. This is evident from Chapter 16 of *Capital*, Volume I, where Marx conducts a 'further development' of his analysis of human labour 'as a process between man and Nature' – a process he had earlier analysed 'in the abstract, apart from its historical forms'. Here, Marx makes it quite clear that his transhistorical conception of human labour does encompass those forms where 'the product ceases to be the direct product of the individual, and becomes a social product, produced in common by a collective labourer'.[22] Indeed, if this were not the case, Marx would not have been able to refer to various kinds of industrial labour not reducible to individual handicraft work as *examples* of specifically human labour in Chapter 7 of *Capital*, Volume I.[23]

By contrast, Benton's desocialised interpretation of the intentionality of human labour leads to serious inconsistencies. The 'handicraft model' has Marx stupidly adopting a conception of human labour inapplicable to industrial capitalism. Further, Benton does not demonstrate how the individual intentionality of handicraft production can be specified independently of specific social relations; that is, he fails to show how it could qualify as a transhistorical characteristic of human labour. Similarly, Benton's 'industrial' interpretation mistakenly treats a historically specific form of intentionality (that 'which assigns each element to its place in the structure' *apart from* the intentions 'of the individual agents in the process') as a general characteristic of industrial labour.[24] This ignores the possibility of a more directly associated form of industrial intentionality where the 'combination and co-operation of many in pursuance of a common result' is simultaneously individual and collective.[25]

Benton's desocialised conception of human labour explains other curious aspects of his ecological critique. For instance, he argues that Marx's emphasis on the intentionality of human labour in itself 'prevented [Marx] from adequately theorising ... the necessary dependence of all forms of economic life upon naturally given preconditions'.[26] This argument truncates the transhistorical

---

[21] Marx 1967a, p. 184.
[22] Marx 1967a, p. 508.
[23] Marx 1967a, pp. 181–3.
[24] Benton 1989, p. 66.
[25] Marx 1967c, p. 387.
[26] Benton 1989, pp. 64–5.

intentionality of human labour to include only that kind of intentionality which ignores labour's dependence on natural conditions – an arbitrary procedure from Marx's perspective, in which use-values (the needs and purposes served by labour and production) are socially *and* materially determined. At one stroke, Benton denies the human race the possibility of ever intentionally building the recognition of its own ecological dependence into the social processes governing wealth production!

A parallel difficulty afflicts Benton's argument that 'Marx's intentional ... classification' downgrades the importance of *unintentional* environmental impacts, and that 'insofar as this class of properties did not figure in Marx's characterisation ... he shared the blindness of agents themselves to the sources of *naturally* mediated unintended and unforeseen consequences of specific practices upon nature'.[27] Benton neglects the fact that to treat unintentional environmental effects as a transhistorical characteristic of human labour is to arbitrarily deny the possibility of an ecologically rational production in which actual and intended consequences coincide.[28] In this sense, too, Benton's 'intentionality' argument seems to implicitly naturalise the kinds of ecological disruptions generated by capitalism and other class societies where production is still anarchically organised for private gain rather than being subjected to 'a real social communality ... posited by society'.[29]

The labour process and eco-regulatory production

Benton also suggests that 'Marx's abstract concept of the labour-process ... assimilates all labour-processes to a "productive" model' by not adequately encompassing 'eco-regulatory' processes such as agriculture, where

> human labour is not deployed to bring about an intended transformation in a raw material. It is, rather, primarily deployed to sustain or regulate the environmental conditions under which seed or stock animals grow and develop. There *is* a transformative moment in these labour-processes, but the transformations are brought about by naturally given organic mechanisms, not by the application of human labour.[30]

---

[27] Benton 1989, p. 73.
[28] This possibility need not require complete control or even knowledge of all environmental impacts of all feasible patterns of production, since there is the additional possibility – unfulfillable under capitalism but arguably contained in Marx and Engels's projections of communism – that society could consciously and collectively decide to forego any such changes in the production process as have unknown or uncertain consequences for natural conditions. See Burkett 1997, pp. 172–3, and 1999a, Chapter 14, for further discussion.
[29] Marx 1973, p. 276.
[30] Benton 1989, p. 67.

Benton's point is that farming and other eco-regulatory labour processes have 'an intentional structure which is quite different from ... productive, transformative labour-processes' where the processing of the subjects of labour bears a more direct correspondence, both temporally and materially, with the direct operation of human labour on these subjects. Eco-regulatory labour 'is primarily ... a labour of sustaining, regulating and reproducing, rather than transforming' – a labour that

> is applied primarily to optimizing the *conditions* for transformations, which are themselves organic processes, relatively impervious to intentional modification. The 'subject of labour' ... is therefore *not* the raw material which will become the 'principal substance' of the 'product' but, rather, the conditions within which it grows and develops.[31]

An obvious feature of eco-regulatory labour is that the 'spatial and temporal distributions of labouring activity are to a high degree shaped by the contextual conditions of the labour-process and by the rhythms of organic developmental processes'. As discussed earlier, Benton argues that these conditions and processes are 'not readily assimilable to Marx's tripartite classification (labour, instruments of labour, raw materials)'.[32]

Responding to Benton's claim that *Capital* inadequately encompasses eco-regulatory processes, Grundmann suggests that 'for Marx human interventions into ... natural processes also count as transformative actions, since prepared ground is quite different from untouched nature'.[33] On one level, I agree with Grundmann on this point. It is true that for Marx, the utilisation of natural conditions and processes for the production of use-values must involve some contact of human labour with these conditions and processes at one moment or another – even in cases where such labour is limited to eco-regulation or, for that matter, primary appropriation (on which more below). This necessary role of human labour in the production of use-values explains why Marx is able to categorise the elements of the labour process in terms of their respective positions vis-à-vis the intended outcome(s) of this process.[34] The fact that many conditions and processes of production are provided by nature does not change the fact that their appropriation and use is subject to human intentionality.

At the same time, I disagree with Grundmann's outright denial of any 'significant difference between transformative and "eco-regulatory"

---

[31] Benton 1989, pp. 67–8.
[32] Benton 1989, p. 68.
[33] Grundmann 1991, p. 108.
[34] 'Hence we see that whether a use-value is to be regarded as raw material, as instrument of labour, or as product, this is determined entirely by its function in the labour-process, or by the position it there occupies; as this varies, so does its character' (Marx 1967a, p. 182).

labour processes'.[35] Grundmann's dismissal of Benton's argument does not establish that Marx formally recognises the special role of natural conditions and processes in eco-regulatory production. Specifically, Grundmann fails to address one obvious question raised by Benton's critique. That is, if Marx's labour-process analysis inadequately encompasses eco-regulation, how is it that Marx was able to use eco-regulated practices (agriculture, livestock raising, and the preparation of conditions for chemical and biological processes in industry) as *examples* of human labour in Chapter 7 of *Capital*, Volume I?[36]

Part of the answer to this apparent puzzle is provided by the categorical distinctions Marx employs to differentiate eco-regulatory processes from other forms of production. Marx observes, for example, how 'a particular product may be used in one and the same process, both as an instrument of labour and as raw material', as in the case of 'the fattening of cattle, where the animal is the raw material, and at the same time an instrument for the production of manure'.[37] Similarly, when referring to forestry and livestock production, Marx indicates that the 'supply – a certain amount of standing timber or livestock – exists ... simultaneously as instruments of labour and material of labour, in accordance with the natural conditions of its reproduction under proper management'.[38] Meanwhile, in order to grasp the distinctive features of industrial eco-regulatory processes, Marx differentiates those 'raw materials' forming 'the principal substance of a product' from those which 'enter into its formation only as an accessory':

> An accessory may be consumed by the instruments of labour, as coal under a boiler, oil by a wheel, hay by draft-horses, or it may be mixed with the raw material in order to produce some modification thereof, as chlorine into unbleached linen, coal with iron, dye-stuff with wool, or again, it may help to carry on the work itself, as in the case of the materials used for heating and lighting workshops. The distinction between principal substance and accessory vanishes in the true chemical industries, because there none of the raw material re-appears, in its original composition, in the substance of the product.[39]

Given Marx's categorisation of the earth as the universal instrument and universal subject of labour, the above categorical distinctions can be applied to all natural conditions and processes 'necessary for carrying on the labour-process' in eco-regulatory contexts.[40]

Another distinction ignored by both Benton and Grundmann is that between labour and production. Indeed, Benton's 'eco-regulation'

[35] Grundmann 1991, p. 108.
[36] Marx 1967a, pp. 181–2.
[37] Marx 1967a, p. 182.
[38] Marx 1967b, p. 244.
[39] Marx 1967a, p. 181.
[40] Marx 1967a, p. 180.

critique presumes that Marx identified the production process with the labour process. Actually, Marx specifies the 'labour-process [as] human action *with a view to the production* of use-values', and as a *'necessary condition* for effecting exchange of matter between man and Nature' – a *'universal condition* for the metabolic interaction between nature and man'.[41] That Marx does not reduce the production process to the labour process is clear from the examples of eco-regulatory production in Chapter 7 of *Capital*, Volume I, where Marx speaks of the 'gradual transformation [of] animals and plants ... under man's superintendence', as well as the 'modification' of (accessory and principal) raw materials by organic processes in industry.[42]

The labour/production distinction is clarified in Volume II of *Capital*, where Marx states that 'the time of production naturally comprises the period of the labour-process, but is not comprised in it'. Excesses of production time over labour time are not only due to 'interruptions of the labour-process necessitated by natural limitations of the labour-power itself ... by night for instance'.[43] Rather,

> the process of production may itself be responsible for interruptions of the labour-process, and hence of the labour-time – intervals during which the subject of labour is exposed to the action of physical processes without the further intervention of human labour. The process of production, and thus the functioning of the means of production, continue in this case, although the labour-process, and thus the functioning of the means of production as instruments of labour, have been interrupted. This applies, for instance, to the grain, after it has been sown, the wine fermenting in the cellar, the labour-material of many factories, such as tanneries, where the material is exposed to the action of chemical processes. The time of production is here longer than the labour-time.[44]

Notice that Marx expressly states that during the excess of production time over labour time, means of production continue to function – ie. continue to produce use-values – even though their functioning as instruments of labour has been interrupted.[45] In other words, Marx's analysis is quite capable of handling eco-regulatory processes based on

---

[41] Marx 1967a, pp. 183–4, and 1988, p. 63. My emphases.
[42] Marx 1967a, p. 181.
[43] Marx 1967b, pp. 121, 238.
[44] Marx 1967b, p. 122.
[45] Marx had already developed the distinction between production time and labour time in the *Grundrisse*: 'In agriculture (and to a greater or lesser degree in many another branch of production) there are interruptions given by the conditions of the production process itself ... The time required here for the product to reach maturity, the interruptions of work, here constitute conditions of production. Not-labour time constitutes a condition for labour time, in order to turn the latter really into production time'. This 'non-identity of production time with labour time can be due generally only to natural conditions, which stand directly in the path of the realisation of labour' (Marx 1973, pp. 602, 668–70).

his distinction between labour and production. Indeed, Marx often uses this distinction to emphasise the more naturally constrained role of human intentionality in eco-regulatory processes. For example:

> The difference between production time and working time becomes especially apparent in agriculture. In our moderate climates the land bears grain once a year. Shortening or lengthening the period of production (for winter grain it averages nine months) itself depends on the alternation of good and bad seasons, and for this reason cannot be accurately determined and controlled beforehand as in industry proper. Only such by-products as milk, cheese, etc. can steadily be produced and sold in comparatively short periods.[46]

It is true that in *Capital*, Marx only fully develops the above categorical distinctions applicable to eco-regulatory processes *after* Chapter 7, Section 1 of Volume I, ie., mainly in the context of analyses of specifically capitalist production. The reason for this is straightforward: the actual development of situations where means of production function as both instruments and raw material, of production processes involving different combinations of accessory and principal raw materials, and of the corresponding deviations between production time and labour time, can only be analysed in relation to the specific social relations of production in and through which such developments occur. The alternative is to conceive of eco-regulatory labour and production along neo-Malthusian lines, ie., as subject to 'given' natural limits conceived independently of historically specific social relations of production.

In this last connection, Marx's labour-process classification in Chapter 7 of *Capital*, Volume I could not incorporate eco-regulation as an intrinsic element for the simple reason that eco-regulatory labour is not a transhistorical element of human-social labour. If we follow Benton's suggestion and treat eco-regulation as transhistorical, we arbitrarily bypass the possibility (and the historical fact) of human production on the basis of practices such as simple hunting and gathering – practices which do not require any 'human labour ... deployed to sustain or regulate the environmental conditions under which seed or stock animals grow and develop'.[47] Such primary-appropriative practices do, however – if socially organised – conform to Marx's conception of human labour, which is precisely why Marx includes them as examples of human labour in Chapter 7, Section 1 of *Capital*, Volume I.[48]

---

46 Marx 1967b, p. 240.
47 Benton 1989, p. 67.
48 Marx 1967a, pp. 178–83. Notice that, insofar as Benton's transhistorical conception of human labour does not recognise the possibility of human production on the basis of primary appropriation, it is in fact a more 'productivist' conception than Marx's! It is also worth mentioning that eco-

In short, since eco-regulation is not transhistorical in the sense demanded by Chapter 7, Volume I of *Capital*, it does not constitute a legitimate basis for an ecological critique of Marx's transhistorical specification of human labour. However, as noted above, this does not mean that *Capital* contains no analyses of eco-regulatory processes. To see the logic of these analyses one must remember the ordering of economic categories employed by Marx.[49]

To begin with, insofar as capitalistic eco-regulation involves historically specific distinctions and relations between labour time and production time, it could only be formally treated in Volume II where Marx analyses the circulation and turnover of capital. The subject of Volume I is the basic class-exploitative nature of capitalist production, and capitalism's reshaping of the material process of production is dealt with in this volume only insofar as is absolutely necessary to establish the historical specificity of capitalist exploitation and accumulation.[50] However, the fact that Volume I formally abstracts from divergences between production time and labour time does not mean that this volume ignores eco-regulatory processes. Volume I's treatment of capitalism as a specific class form of production includes analysis of capital's appropriation of natural conditions as a necessary condition of accumulation.[51] In this context, Marx refers to 'the purely mechanical working of the soil itself ... on the amount of the product' as one of the 'circumstances that ... determine the amount of accumulation'.[52] Indeed, Marx includes 'a fruitful soil', along with 'natural wealth in the instruments of labour, such as waterfalls, navigable rivers, wood, metal, coal, etc' as elements of the 'natural basis' of surplus value itself – the idea being that 'without a certain degree of productiveness' of labour as supported by natural conditions, 'no surplus-labour, and therefore no capitalists'.[53]

In analysing how with industrial capital accumulation, 'a radical change in the mode of production in one sphere of industry involves a similar change in other spheres', Volume I of *Capital* deals with the capitalist division of labour between agriculture and industry.[54] This

---

regulatory labour as such does not – absent the element of conscious pre-positing in and through society – distinguish human labour from that of other life forms, eg., the eco-regulatory operations of food-burying squirrels or dam-building beavers. See Engels 1964, pp. 177, 181–2.

[49] Rosdolsky 1977, pp. 41–50, and Burkett 1991.

[50] As Marx puts it: 'An exact analysis of the process [of exploitation and accumulation] demands that we should, for a time, disregard all phenomena that hide the play of its inner mechanism'. This meant abstracting from any complications arising from the 'forms the circulation of capital' takes on as 'the same phases are continually gone through in succession' (1967a, pp. 564–5). In other words, 'the various forms which capital takes on in its different stages ... were discussed in Book I only in so far as this was necessary for an understanding of the process of production of capital' as a specific class-exploitative form of production (Marx 1967b, p. 23).

[51] For a detailed overview, see Burkett 1999b and 1999a, Chapters 3 and 6.

[52] Marx 1967a, p. 599, 604.

[53] Marx 1967a, pp. 511–12. For a fuller discussion of this 'natural basis of surplus value' in Marx's analysis, see Burkett 1999a, Chapter 3.

[54] Marx 1967a, p. 383.

includes the promotion of technological changes in agriculture by advances in eco-regulatory industrial methods and *vice versa*,[55] and the attendant 'separation between town and country' which, by 'upsetting the naturally grown conditions for ... the circulation of matter', winds up 'sapping the original sources of all wealth – the soil and the labourer'.[56]

Eco-regulation is placed under a more powerful microscope in Volume II, where 'excess[es] of the production time over the labour-time' arising from capital 'functioning in the productive process without taking part in the labour-process' are a central concern in Marx's investigation of the circulation of capital.[57] Here Marx conducts detailed analyses of

> interruptions independent of the length of the labour-process, brought about by the very nature of the product and its fabrication, during which the subject of labour is for a longer or shorter time subjected to natural processes, must undergo physical, chemical and physiological changes, during which the labour-process is entirely or partially suspended. For instance grape after being pressed must ferment awhile and then rest for some time in order to reach a certain degree of perfection. In many branches of industry the product must pass through a drying process, for instance in pottery, or be exposed to certain conditions in order to change its chemical properties, as for instance in bleaching. Winter grain needs about nine months to mature. Between the time of sowing and harvesting the labour-process is almost entirely suspended. In timber-raising, after the sowing and the incidental preliminary work are completed, the seed requires about 100 years to be transformed into a finished product and during all that time it stands in comparatively very little need of the action of labour ... In all these cases therefore the production time of the advanced capital consists of two periods: one period during which the capital is engaged in the labour-process and a second period during which its form of existence – that of an unfinished product – is abandoned to the sway of natural processes.[58]

Chapter 13 of Volume II analyses many cases where 'differences between production time and working time' arise – a phenomenon which 'admits of many variations' in terms of its effects on the

---

[55] 'Thus spinning by machinery made weaving by machinery a necessity, and both together made the mechanical and chemical revolution that took place in bleaching, printing, and dyeing, imperative. So too, on the other hand, the revolution in cotton-spinning called forth the invention of the gin, for separating the seeds from the cotton fibre; it was only by means of this invention, that the production of cotton became possible on the enormous scale at present required' (Marx 1967a, pp. 383–4).
[56] Marx 1967a, pp. 352, 505–7. For details, see Burkett 1998b and 1999a, Chapter 9, and Foster 1997.
[57] Marx 1967b, p. 122.
[58] Marx 1967b, pp. 238–9.

circulation of capital materially and socially. Numerous such analyses occur in other chapters of this volume, as when Marx discusses how 'many raw materials, semi-finished goods, etc., require rather long periods of time for their production ... especially ... raw materials furnished by agriculture', or when Marx observes how in eco-regulatory spheres 'varying amounts of capital [have] to be invested in different working periods, as for instance in agriculture'.[59] These analyses show great sensitivity to the special role of 'contextual conditions' and 'organic developmental processes' in eco-regulatory production and capital circulation.[60] The distinctive conditions of eco-regulatory capital circulation are, in fact, central to Marx's grasp of how 'the economic process of reproduction, whatever may be its specific social character, always becomes intertwined ... with a natural process of reproduction'.[61]

Even in Volume II, however, eco-regulation is treated in abstraction from the distinct roles of landed property, rents, and price fluctuations associated with market competition – all of which are only dealt with in Volume III. It is in the latter volume that Marx analyses 'the violent price fluctuations of one of the main elements in the process of reproduction ... raw materials taken from organic nature ... vegetable and animal substances whose growth and production are subject to certain organic laws and bound up with definite natural time periods'.[62] Marx roots both the origins and the materially disruptive effects of such price fluctuations in the contradiction between competitive capital accumulation and rational, sustainable agricultural practices.[63] Volume III also extends Marx's analysis of the capitalist separation of town and country, paying close attention to the role of naturally variegated conditions in influencing the different forms of eco-regulatory production and corresponding rents.[64]

When analysing the productivity of agricultural investment, for example, Marx insists that 'the peculiar nature of agriculture must be taken into account', since 'it is not only a matter of the social, but also of the natural, productivity of labour which depends on the natural conditions of labour'; indeed, Marx emphasises that 'the increase in social productivity in agriculture' may 'barely compensate, or not even compensate, for the decrease in natural power'.[65] Near the beginning of the section on differential rent, we find Marx emphasising 'climactic

---

[59] Marx 1967b, pp. 246, 143, 259.
[60] Benton 1989, p. 68.
[61] Marx 1967b, p. 359. Benton also quotes this last sentence, but only as evidence of how Marx 'comments approvingly on Quesnay's statement' of the dependence of capitalist production on 'labour-processes which appropriate energy, raw materials, and means of subsistence from nature' (Benton 1989, p. 85). It is strange that Benton employs *Capital*, Volume II as his primary source on Quesnay and Adam Smith without so much as mentioning Marx's detailed analyses of eco-regulatory production in this volume.
[62] Marx 1967c, pp. 119–21.
[63] For details, see Mayumi 1991, and Burkett 1998b and 1999a, Chapter 9.
[64] For further elaboration, see Foster 1997, pp. 283–7, and Burkett 1999a, Chapters 7 and 9.
[65] Marx 1967c, p. 766; compare pp. 691, 708–10, 733.

factors', differences in 'the chemical composition of the top soil', and 'location of the land' as factors – 'quite independent of capital' – that influence 'the unequal results of equal quantities of capital applied to different plots of land of equal size'. This is all quite consistent with Marx's definition of a rent-yielding natural condition as a 'monopolisable ... condition for an increase in the productiveness of the invested capital that cannot be established by the production process of the capital itself'.[66] No sign of social constructionism here! Indeed, given that some of Marx's richest treatments of eco-regulation occur in his analysis of rents, Benton's failure to even mention Marx's rent theory is quite curious.

Value and nature

Finally, Benton argues that, from an ecological standpoint, the 'economic theory' in *Capital* is handicapped by the 'labour theory of value, which Marx adopted, albeit with important modifications, from his predecessors in Classical Political Economy'. The problem, says Benton, is that 'the labour theory of value either excludes natural scarcity from consideration, or allows it to be recognised only in the form of its displaced manifestation within the internal social-relational structure of the economy'.[67] Here Benton neglects Marx's most important modification of classical value theory, namely his analysis of value as a specific social form of material wealth or use-value.[68] This value-form analysis is the bridge connecting Marx's historical materialism to *Capital*'s analyses of exploitation and accumulation; and it makes the latter an application of the former.

The materialist premise of *Capital*'s value analysis is simply the material production required for all forms of social reproduction. Indeed, the reason why *Capital* 'must ... begin with the analysis of a commodity' is that under capitalism, material wealth 'presents itself as an immense accumulation of commodities'.[69] Material production

---

[66] Marx 1967c, pp. 650–1, 645.
[67] Benton 1989, pp. 76–7.
[68] 'It is one of the chief failings of classical political economy that it has never succeeded, by means of its analysis of commodities ... in discovering that form under which value becomes exchange-value. Even Adam Smith and Ricardo, the best representatives of the school, treat the form of value as a thing of no importance, as having no connexion with the inherent nature of commodities. The reason for this is not solely because their attention is entirely absorbed in the analysis of the magnitude of value. It lies deeper. The value-form of the product of labour is not only the most abstract, but is also the most universal form, taken by the product in bourgeois production, and stamps that production as a particular species of social production, and thereby gives it its special historical character. If then we treat this mode of production as one eternally fixed by Nature for every state of society, we necessarily overlook that which is the differentia specifica of the value-form, and consequently of the commodity-form, and of its further developments, money-form, capital-form, &c.' (Marx 1967a, pp. 80–1). Benton, like the classicals, 'treats the form of value as a thing of no importance', and 'is entirely absorbed in the analysis of the magnitude of value'.
[69] Marx 1967a, p. 35.

involves a social division (allocation) of useful labour enmeshed with natural conditions. Under capitalism, where social production is organised in mutually autonomous 'private' units, this 'social character of each producer's labour does not show itself except in the act of exchange', so that 'the labour of the individual asserts itself as a part of the labour of society, only by means of the relations which the act of exchange establishes directly between the products, and indirectly, through them, between the producers'.[70]

Despite Marx's insistence that nature and labour both contribute to the production of material wealth, *Capital* treats commodity exchange-values as 'a definite social manner of expressing the *amount of labour* bestowed upon an object'.[71] Far from an inconsistency or a step away from materialism on Marx's part, however, this paradox represents a contradiction of capitalism itself; indeed, it is a most important form of the contradiction between exchange-value and use-value.[72] This contradiction is firmly rooted in the basic class relations of capitalism, under which the producers are socially separated from natural and other necessary conditions of production. It is this separation that enables capitalism's valuation of natural conditions according to the wage-labour time required for their appropriation, rather than according to nature's real contribution to wealth. The under-valuation of nature is a necessary feature of a system which, having alienated necessary conditions of production vis-à-vis the producers, develops these conditions in line with the dictates of competitive accumulation of exchange-value rather than individual and collective human needs. It is, in short, an integral part of capitalism's reduction of people, nature, and society to mere conditions of monetary accumulation. Benton's critique blames Marx for this reduction when the real culprit is capitalism itself.[73]

Bypassing the value-form approach which distinguishes Marx from the classical economists, Benton misses the fact that for Marx, value is a contradictory 'unity of use-value and exchange-value' – one in which 'use-value,' involving 'the individual's relation to Nature,' takes the social form of 'exchange-value ... command over the use-values of others'. As such, value must be 'represented in use-value; and use-value is a pre-requisite for the creation of value'.[74] By ignoring the interconnections among value, exchange-value, and use-value, Benton falsely dematerialises *Capital*'s value analysis. This helps explain his curious critique of Volume II's reproduction schemas:

> Marx's theorization ... involves him in a direct recognition of the pertinence of broad categories of *use-values* in the products and materials employed by these individual capitals.

---

[70] Marx 1967a, p. 73.
[71] Marx 1967a, p. 82. My emphasis.
[72] For further discussion, see Burkett 1996b and 1999b.
[73] See Burkett 1996a and 1999a, Chapters 5 and 7.
[74] Marx 1973, p. 267, 1987, p. 458, and 1967c, p. 817.

> Marx's distinction between Departments I and II (production of means of production and articles of consumption, respectively) does precisely this ... However, although Marx's account does embody a recognition that these reproduction requirements include both 'the value as well as the substance of the individual component parts' of productive capital, his representation of these conditions is conducted *primarily in value terms.*[75]

On this basis, Benton suggests that Marx's value analysis precludes us from 'perceiv[ing] in crises of disproportion the mediated and displaced manifestations of crises of an ecological nature whose source is located in those labour-processes such as extraction and eco-regulation which are at the "interface" between the total social capital and its natural preconditions'.[76] But this suggestion hinges on Benton's dematerialised conception of value. The notion of Marx's reproduction analysis being 'conducted primarily in value terms' itself presumes that the reproduction and circulation of values can be separated from their material embodiments as means of subsistence and means of production. Yet, in Part III of *Capital*, Volume II, Marx continually emphasises the necessary materiality of means of consumption and means of production even considered as values.

Benton's social/material dichotomy prevents him from realising that the whole motivation of Marx's Volume II schemas is the investigation of reproduction simultaneously in terms of value and use-value, ie. in terms 'not only [of] a replacement of value, but also a replacement in material' – an investigation 'as much bound up with the relative proportions of the value-components of the total social product as with their use-value, their material shape'.[77] An analysis 'primarily in value terms' – which Benton takes as abstracting from use-value – would have been useless since Marx's very object of investigation was the 'total process compris[ing] both the productive consumption (the direct process of production) *together with* the conversions of form (*materially considered*, exchanges) which bring it about, and the individual consumption *together with* the conversions of form or exchanges by which it is brought about'.[78] Marx conceptualises his investigation in this way not only because 'with few exceptions ... means of production and articles of consumption are wholly different ... products of entirely different bodily or use-forms', but also because of the variegated material forms of constant capital, many of which directly involve primary appropriation or eco-regulation, through which value circulates and which are treated in this context.[79] Indeed, it is to highlight the role of such material forms of value – and to simplify the analysis – that the Volume II schemas 'assume that products are exchanged at their values

---

[75] Benton 1989, pp. 84–5. Last emphasis mine.
[76] Benton 1989, p. 85.
[77] Marx 1967b, p. 394.
[78] Marx 1967b, p. 352. My emphases.
[79] Marx 1967b, p. 430; see pp. 355–8, 449–50, 468, 479–80, 495, 521–2.

and also that there is no revolution in the values of the component parts of productive capital'.[80] We thus see that value and capital are indeed 'represented in use-value' in Marx's reproduction analysis *precisely because* this analysis is conducted 'in value terms'.[81]

Interestingly, Benton does not explain how Marx could have analysed reproduction in anything other than 'value terms' – ie., in terms other than the money, commodity, and capital forms in and through which this reproduction occurs under capitalism – while still talking about a specifically capitalist form of reproduction. This quandary is the flip-side of the strange notion that Marx somehow analysed reproduction 'in value terms' abstracting from use-value. Once again, Benton's social/material dichotomy appears as an artificial dematerialisation of Marx's social-relational analysis alongside Benton's own desocialised conception of human production.

By contrast, Marx's value-based approach, insofar as it encapsulates the contradiction between capitalism's social under-valuation of and material reliance on nature, is quite capable of handling environmental crises in historically specific materialist *and* social-relational terms. For example, if a useful natural condition of production becomes increasingly scarce (and this includes decreases in its utility due to its degradation), the average productivity of the labour appropriating or utilising this natural condition is, by definition, reduced in terms of material use-values producible per hour of work, *ceteris paribus*. The *values* of the commodities produced with the increasingly scarce natural condition are, accordingly, increased due to the greater amount of social labour time now required to produce the same use-values. (This includes any additional necessary labour expended in the appropriation and utilisation of *substitute* natural conditions.) These effects are clearly set out in Marx's discussions of the productivity of labour, the natural basis of surplus value, and capital's free appropriation of natural conditions.[82] They play a key role in Marx's value-theoretic materialist analyses of accumulation crises rooted in 'crises [of] extraction and eco-regulation'.[83] In Volume III of *Capital* and Part 2 of *Theories of Surplus Value*, for example, Marx treats 'fluctuations in the price of raw materials, and their direct effects on the rate of profit' as well as 'interruption[s] in the production process through scarcity and dearness of raw material'.[84] Here, Marx analyses the combined effects of reductions in the available quantity, and increases in the unit value, of raw materials in the wake of crop failures. These effects involve

[80] Marx 1967b, p. 393.
[81] As Rosdolsky indicates, 'the basic presupposition of the schemes of reproduction in Volume II [is] that the relations of exchange between the two main departments of social production must accord with one another, both from the point of view of value, and from that of use-value, if equilibrium conditions for the reproduction of total social capital are to be maintained'. He adds: 'We have to stress this necessary condition of the schemes, since it is, unfortunately, too often forgotten in marxist literature' (1977, p. 457).
[82] See Burkett 1999a, Chapters 3 and 6, and 1999b.
[83] Benton 1989, p. 85.
[84] Marx 1967c, pp. 105, 128.

'disturbances in the reproduction process' in both material and value terms, the reason being that materials shortages not only raise the value of constant capital (thereby reducing the rate of profit) but also physically disrupt production by 'making it impossible to continue the process on the scale required by its technical basis'. As a result, 'a part of fixed capital stands idle and a part of the workers is thrown out on the streets'.[85] In short, it is simply untrue that Marx's value theory 'excludes natural scarcity from consideration, or allows it to be recognised only in the form of its displaced manifestation within the internal social-relational structure of the economy' where the latter structure is conceived in non-material terms.[86]

That Benton's critique rests on a false social/material dichotomy is clear from his treatment of 'the distinction between capitalist production considered as a process of producing use-values and as a process of producing exchange-values'. Here, 'the value-maximizing intentional structure' of capital accumulation is described as having an 'indifference to the concrete character of the process' of production and its material conditions:

> In its [value-creating] aspect, capitalist production is a process of exploitation of 'abstract' labour which aims at a quantitative increase in exchange-value. The second intentional structure is considered to be abstract in the sense that the material properties of the product, the character of the labour which shapes it, and the nature of the want it satisfies are all quite irrelevant to the central purpose of a purely quantitative increase in the value of the product ... [The] value-maximizing intentional structure must be superimposed upon, and predominate over, the intentional structure of production in its aspect as a utility-producing labour-process.[87]

Benton treats value and use-value production as essentially two separate processes, with the former 'superimposed upon', and even 'indifferent to the concrete character of', the latter. For Marx, however, 'the difference between labour, considered on the one hand as producing utilities, and on the other hand, as creating value, *a difference which we discovered only by our analysis of the commodity*, resolves itself into a distinction between *two aspects of the process of production*'. Marx conceptualises the labour process not as two separate processes, but as the contradictory 'unity of the labour-process and the process of creating value', ie., as a further determination of the contradictory unity of exchange-value and use-value basic to the commodity form.[88] As Marx indicates, 'the valorisation process is in reality nothing but the

[85] Marx 1968, pp. 515–16, and 1967c, p. 109. For further discussion, see Burkett 1998b and 1999a, Chapter 9.
[86] Benton 1989, p. 77.
[87] Benton 1989, pp. 70, 83.
[88] Marx 1967a, p. 197. My emphases.

labour process in a particular social form ... not, as it were, two distinct real processes, but *the same* process, viewed at one time in terms of its content, at the other time according to its form'.[89] The connection with Marx's analysis of commodities is clear from his observation that 'if use-value is the product of the labour process, exchange-value must be regarded as the product of the valorisation process, and thus the commodity, the unity of exchange-value and use-value, must be regarded as the product of both processes, which are merely two forms of the same process'.[90]

Benton's interpretation of the labour process has serious implications for the conception of capitalist development, class conflicts and ecological phenomena. When referring to 'the distinctively capitalist tendency to replace living labour with machinery, and to transform the technical basis of the labour-process,' for example, Benton suggests that Marx's 'crucial interest was in the consequences of these tendencies for capital accumulation considered in value terms, and for the development of the antagonism between capital and labour'.[91] We have already debunked Benton's 'in value terms' notion; the new difficulty is Benton's treatment of the capital–labour antagonism and capital accumulation as mere 'consequences' of mechanisation and technological change – as if capitalism's basic social forms and class antagonisms were not themselves fundamental forces driving the mechanisation of production, as well as shaping the whole pattern and content of capitalism's metabolism with nature. Benton's social/material dichotomy here takes the form of a technological-determinist conception of production and class relations. This technological determinism is the flip-side of Benton's characterisation of capital's 'value-maximizing intentional structure' as simply 'indifferent to the concrete character' of labour and production.

Marx's approach is quite different. True, Marx argues that, under capitalism, the values of commodities and of all means of production, including useful natural conditions and processes, are determined by the amount of abstract labour time which they embody. However, Marx also recognises that despite value's social abstraction from wealth's natural basis and substance, capital still has a use-value requirement: the appropriation, and social realisation through commodity exchange, of 'the use-value of labour-power, or in other words, labour'. This 'special service that the capitalist expects from labour-power' requires that 'labour must be expended in a useful manner'.[92] Therefore, capital

[89] Marx 1988, p. 140.
[90] Marx 1988, p. 81. Elsewhere, Marx describes the 'process of production' as 'the *immediate* unity of labour process and valorization process, just as its immediate result, the commodity, is the *immediate* unity of use-value and exchange-value' (1977, p. 991). Altvater notes that Marx's analysis of the 'dual character of labour ... creates the possibility of grasping economic processes at once as *transformations of values* (value-formation and valorization) and as *transformations of materials and energy* (labour process, "metabolic interaction" between man and nature)' (1993, p. 188).
[91] Benton 1989, pp. 70–1.
[92] Marx 1967a, p. 193.

must have access to material conditions (including natural conditions) under which surplus labour can be extracted and objectified in vendible use-values, based first and foremost on the social separation of the producers from these necessary conditions of production. Besides, exploitable labour-power is itself a 'natural force of human beings' requiring definite natural conditions for its survival and reproduction.[93]

Within this framework, it is the dependence of value accumulation on extraction of surplus labour from workers capable of subjective activity (the basic capital–labour antagonism) which underpins capital's tendency toward scientifically engineered deskilling, division, mechanisation and intensification of labour – practices paralleled in the ever expanding extraction, fragmentation, and poisoning of the natural conditions required as material vehicles of the same process of accumulation.[94] This exploitative process is enabled by the social separation of the producers vis-à-vis natural conditions of production, which allows capital, with the help of social labour and science, to develop (and despoil) the productive forces latent in nature to a much greater degree than previous economic forms.[95]

In short, Marx's conception of value accumulation cannot be adequately understood in terms of a non-dialectical 'indifference' or 'insensitivity' to material conditions. In Marx's view, capitalist value production has a specific material *and* class-relational character deriving from capital's exploitative appropriation of the use-values of both labour-power and nature, as rooted in the specifically capitalist separation (and continuous re-alienation) of the producers vis-à-vis natural conditions of production. Benton's material/social bifurcation of the labour process prevents him from seeing that for Marx, what stamps the people–nature relation as capitalistic is not an actual material severing or supersession of this relation, but the alienated form in which the producers and nature are brought together in a production process governed by the imperative of monetary accumulation.[96]

Political implications

We have seen that Benton's social/material dichotomy manifests itself in his treatment of material production and value production as two distinct processes that are not mutually constituted. Although Benton suggests that the goal of value accumulation is 'superimposed upon, and predominate[s] over, the ... utility-producing labour-process', he nonetheless maintains that the material forms of production are 'irrelevant' to capitalism's 'value-maximizing intentional structure' – the latter which maintains an 'indifference to the concrete character of the

---

[93] Marx 1967c, p. 813. See Burkett 1999a, Chapter 4, for Marx's analysis of labour-power as a natural and social force.
[94] See Burkett 1999a, Chapter 7.
[95] Burkett 1997, pp. 173–4.
[96] See Marx 1967b, pp. 34–5.

process'.[97] Having dichotomised use-value and value production, Benton prioritises the former in 'naturist' and technological-determinist fashion. Essentially, he distorts Marx's base-superstructure metaphor by imposing a one-way causality from a desocialised material base to the political and ideological superstructure – unlike Marx for whom the base represents a complex mutual constitution of class and material forms.[98] This conceptual break is evident from Benton's suggestion that:

> Different technical bases for society can be understood ... as delimiting specific alternative patterns of possibility for further human development. Theorising such alternative possibility spaces can help in thinking about 'development' ... in terms of a range of qualitatively different ways of realising human social possibilities ... By giving explicit theoretical recognition to relatively or absolutely non-manipulable conditions and elements in labour-processes, one throws into relief a distinction between technologies which enable a *transcendence* of naturally imposed limits and technologies which enhance *adaptability* in the face of natural conditions impervious to intentional action.[99]

Here, Benton assigns the 'delimiting' role in 'human development' to 'technical bases' and 'non-manipulable conditions', with social relations relegated to the category of 'human social possibilities' whose range is a passive function of the natural and technical base. This strictly circumscribes the role of class relations in determining the degree and the forms in which the wealth-creating powers of nature and labour are released or destroyed. As a result, Benton is forced to adopt a false dichotomy between transcendence of and adaptation to natural limits (as if either one could occur by means other than knowledge and utilisation of natural conditions and processes) as well as an ahistorical notion of 'intentional action'. While recognising that each mode of production has 'a specific form of nature/society interaction ... its own distinctive ecological "niche"', Benton downgrades the possibility that the material content of each niche manifests the class character of each mode, eg., in terms of the class-differentiation of people–nature relations.[100] He thus tends to lump the working class together with capital as ecologically incorrect agents of capitalist civilisation – as in the assertion that the 'dominant labour-processes of industrial capitalism' are 'liable to sustain spontaneous ideologies in their economic agents which exclude or occlude their dependence upon contextual conditions and limits'.[101]

In this way, Benton's material/social dichotomy presses him toward a politics reliant on moralising arguments grounded in spontaneous

---

[97] Benton 1989, pp. 70, 83.
[98] Compare Vlachou 1994, p. 118, and Burkett 1998a, pp. 121–3.
[99] Benton 1989, p. 79.
[100] Benton 1989, p. 81.
[101] Benton 1989, p. 83.

technological and even ideological developments, rather than in the conflicting positions vis-à-vis wealth production occupied by capital and labour in capitalist society. We are told, for example, that the recognition 'that specific social and economic forms of life encounter real natural limits

> ... may provide the beginnings of a powerful argument for
> *transforming* the prevailing patterns of nature/society
> interaction ... A strategic focus on adaptability-enhancing
> technologies may be no less emancipatory, and is certainly
> likely to be far more sustainable than the transformative focus
> which predominates in our civilization.[102]

There may be nothing wrong with 'adaptability-enhancing technologies' per se (although it is important to recognise that even 'ecologically correct' technologies may serve as instruments of capitalist exploitation); but it is doubtful whether a movement capable of revolutionising production, so that it is no longer dependent on exploitation of labour and nature, can be built upon the motto of overcoming 'the transformative focus which predominates in our civilisation'. Aside from the fact that 'transforming the prevailing patterns of nature/society interaction' is an incredibly transformative task, these patterns are class-differentiated, which means that any such transformation is a matter of class struggle rather than powerful arguments in support of particular technologies conceived in non-class terms. Given that notions of 'adaptability' and 'sustainability' are socially *and* materially defined, it cannot be assumed that the terms of debate and conflict over the prevailing patterns of production will be agreed upon *a priori* on the basis of some shared conception of natural limits.[103]

The basic problem here is that Benton's material/social dichotomy prevents him from explicitly recognising the alienated form of the unity of the producers and nature that exists under capitalism – thus closing off all political channels toward a disalienated form of the same unity under a post-capitalist, associated mode of production. Once one dichotomises concrete and value-creating labour, it is impossible to ground any conception of an ecologically sustainable mode of production in the producers' self-objectification in and against capital's alienated form of labour.[104] Given that it is social labour that initiates human production, any disalienated and ecologically sustainable mode must 'restore the original union' of the producers and the conditions of production 'in a new historical form'. This 'new and fundamental revolution in the mode of production' can only be achieved by the producers and their communities struggling for a cooperative-

---

[102] Benton 1989, pp. 79–80.
[103] See Enzensberger 1974, and Foster 1996.
[104] Kamolnick 1988.

democratic appropriation and development of the conditions and results of their own objectively social labour.[105]

The artificial dichotomisation of value and use-value prevents one from making these politically crucial social-material connections. This helps explain Benton's recent endorsement of James O'Connor's 'two contradictions' approach, which basically treats the capital–labour and capital–nature contradictions as two *separate* contradictions rather than two forms of the capital relation as a material and social whole.[106] Like O'Connor, Benton ultimately fails to overcome what David Harvey has termed the 'false opposition' or 'duality of *anthropocentrism* and *ecocentrism*' that artificially divides red and green movements.[107] One can only agree with Benton's conclusion that 'the point is to change it'; but Benton's material/social (use-value/exchange-value) dichotomy seriously hampers the grounding of such change in the *'practical, human-sensuous activity'* of the whole society of producers – an activity which, despite capitalism's alienating social forms, still determines 'social life [as] essentially *practical*'.[108]

In the end, Benton's work does shed important light on the paradox of 'so much bad blood between Marxists and ecologists' despite Marx and Engels's materialism, though not in the way he intended.[109] With its social/material dichotomy, its 'naturism' and technological determinism, and its denunciations of capitalist civilisation without regard to class distinctions, Benton's reconstruction of Marx closely mirrors the intellectual outlook of official, Stalinist Marxism. Inverting Stalinism's affirmation of humanity's historical 'progress' *against* nature (as buoyed by the unilinear development of desocialised productive forces), Benton's Malthusian dualism basically takes the side of nature *against* society. Both interpretations one-sidedly distort Marx's dialectical social-material approach to human production. By illustrating the ecological and social shortcomings of both dualistic Marxisms, Benton unconsciously points toward an important source of the red/green tension, namely, the historical reification and desocialisation of Marxism in ideological service of institutionalised class power. Any investigation of this history from an ecological point of view requires that we first 'examine to what extent one is dealing with original elements of Marxist thought or with later deformations of theory'.[110] My evaluation of Benton's 'critique and reconstruction' will have served its purpose if it has provided a useful starting point for such an examination.

---

[105] Marx 1976a, p. 39. For an elaboration, see Burkett 1999a, Chapter 13.
[106] O'Connor 1998, and Benton 1997, p. 43; compare Burkett 1999c and 1999a, Chapter 12.
[107] Harvey 1993, p. 37.
[108] Benton 1989, p. 86, and Marx 1976b, pp. 616–17.
[109] Benton 1989, p. 55.
[110] Enzensberger 1974, pp. 37–8.

References

Altvater, Elmar 1993, *The Future of the Market*, London: Verso.

Benton, Ted 1989, 'Marxism and Natural Limits: An Ecological Critique and Reconstruction', *New Left Review*, 178: 51–86.

Benton, Ted 1997, 'Beyond Left and Right? Ecological Politics, Capitalism and Modernity', in *Greening the Millennium?*, edited by Michael Jacobs, Oxford: Oxford University Press, 34–46.

Burkett, Paul 1991, 'Some Comments on "Capital in General and the Structure of Marx's *Capital*"', *Capital & Class*, 44: 49–72.

Burkett, Paul 1996a, 'On Some Common Misconceptions About Nature and Marx's Critique of Political Economy', *Capitalism, Nature, Socialism*, 7, 3: 57–80.

Burkett, Paul 1996b, 'Value, Capital and Nature: Some Ecological Implications of Marx's Critique of Political Economy', *Science & Society*, 60, 3: 332–59.

Burkett, Paul 1997, 'Nature in Marx Reconsidered', *Organization & Environment*, 10, 2: 164–83.

Burkett, Paul 1998a, 'A Critique of Neo-Malthusian Marxism: Society, Nature, and Population', *Historical Materialism*, 2: 118–42.

Burkett, Paul 1998b, 'Marx's Analysis of Capitalist Environmental Crisis', *Nature, Society, and Thought*, forthcoming.

Burkett, Paul 1999a, *Marx and Nature: A Red and Green Perspective*, New York: St. Martin's Press (in press).

Burkett, Paul 1999b, 'Nature's "Free Gifts" and the Ecological Significance of Value', *Capital & Class*, forthcoming.

Burkett, Paul 1999c, 'Fusing Red and Green', *Monthly Review*, forthcoming.

Engels, Frederick 1964, *Dialectics of Nature*, Moscow: Progress Publishers.

Enzensberger, Hans Magnus 1974, 'A Critique of Political Ecology', *New Left Review*, 84; reprinted in *The Greening of Marxism*, edited by Ted Benton, New York: Guilford, 1996, pp. 17–49.

Foster, John Bellamy 1996, 'Sustainable Development of What?', *Capitalism, Nature, Socialism*, 7, 3: 129–32.

Foster, John Bellamy 1997, 'The Crisis of the Earth: Marx's Theory of Ecological Sustainability as a Nature-Imposed Necessity for Human Production', *Organization & Environment*, 10, 3: 278–95.

Grundmann, Reiner 1991, 'The Ecological Challenge to Marxism', *New Left Review*, 187: 103–20.

Harvey, David 1993, 'The Nature of Environment: The Dialectics of Social and Environmental Change', in *Socialist Register 1993: Real Problems, False Solutions*, edited by Ralph Miliband and Leo Panitch, London: Merlin, pp. 1–51.

Kamolnick, Paul 1988, *Classes: A Marxist Critique*, Dix Hills, NY: General Hall.

Marx, Karl 1967a, *Capital* Volume 1, New York: International Publishers.

Marx, Karl 1967b, *Capital* Volume 2, New York: International Publishers.

Marx, Karl 1967c, *Capital* Volume 3, New York: International Publishers.

Marx, Karl 1968, *Theories of Surplus Value*, Part II, Moscow: Progress Publishers.

Marx, Karl 1973, *Grundrisse*, New York: Vintage.

Marx, Karl 1976a, *Value, Price and Profit*, New York: International Publishers.

Marx, Karl 1976b, 'Theses on Feuerbach', in *The German Ideology*, by Karl Marx and Frederick Engels, Moscow: Progress Publishers, pp. 615–20.

Marx, Karl 1977, 'Results of the Immediate Process of Production', in *Capital*, Volume I, New York: Vintage, pp. 948–1084.

Marx, Karl 1987, 'From the Preparatory Materials', in *Collected Works, Karl Marx and Frederick Engels*, Volume 29, New York: International Publishers, pp. 430–532.

Marx, Karl 1988, 'Economic Manuscript of 1861–63, Third Chapter', in *Collected Works, Karl Marx and Frederick Engels*, Volume 30, New York: International Publishers, pp. 9–346.

Marx, Karl and Frederick Engels 1980, *The Holy Family, or Critique of Critical Criticism*, Moscow: Progress Publishers.

Mayumi, Kozo 1991, 'Temporary Emancipation from Land: From the Industrial Revolution to the Present Time', *Ecological Economics*, 4, 1: 35–56.

O'Connor, James 1998, *Natural Causes: Essays in Ecological Marxism*, New York: Guilford.

Rosdolsky, Roman 1977, *The Making of Marx's 'Capital'*, London: Pluto Press.

Vlachou, Adriana 1994, 'Reflections on the Ecological Critiques and Reconstructions of Marxism', *Rethinking Marxism*, 7, 3: 112–28.

The Politics of Novelty

Werner Bonefeld

The 'politics of novelty' seems a somewhat strange if not straightforwardly bizarre topic. What is meant by 'novelty' and under what sort of conditions would one be able to think of 'novelty' in terms of a politics? What does politics have to do with 'novelty', and conversely, 'novelty' with 'politics'?

Over the last 25 years, since the mid-1970s, new and even newer research agendas and organising terms such as risk society, postmodernism, disorganised capitalism, post-industrialism, and post-Fordism and globalisation, have been introduced. The social sciences have shown a quite breath-taking innovative capacity. The proponents of these new concepts and research agendas claim that these are required to supply an adequate understanding of contemporary changes. Yet, at the same time as the 'new left' appears to be desperately abandoning its Marxist heritage, the capitalist world has re-discovered its liberal roots. I say 're-discovered' not because these liberal roots had ever been abandoned but because, especially during the 1950s and 1960s, liberalism was dressed up as Keynesianism. Keynesianism did not amount to a theory and practice of a 'third way' between laissez-faire capitalism and planned socialism. The importance of Keynesianism was its ideological projection of a reformed and tamed capitalism that offered salvation in the name of democracy and citizenship. The re-discovery of liberalism during the 1970s was thus not a 're-discovery' as such but involved, in fact, a return to basic principles without the ideological projections presented by Keynesianism. In conclusion, then, while the new left is seeking to leave behind its Marxist roots, the capitalist world unashamedly and unsurprisingly has returned to its roots, celebrating the achievements of Adam Smith and arguing that his theory of the invisible hand supplies a solution to capitalist crisis. In other words, while the political Right turns backwards to find salvation in the future, the new left has abandoned Marx and replaced the principled critique of Smith with terms and theoretical perspectives that seem to indicate that capitalism is no longer capitalism.

The world of the new left appears as a post-industrial world, as a postmodern world, as a post-class world; in other words, as a world beyond the confines of political economy. Some might respond that this is true for post-industrialism etc., but that recent theories of globalisation and post-Fordism pose issues that belong firmly in the tradition of political economy, including Marx's critique of political economy. This response is well-founded and yet it is misleading. I will argue that recent theories of globalisation and post-Fordism are firmly embedded within neoliberalism's agenda and project of, no less, a world tailored around neoliberal principles. Of course, the new left does not like the unfettered operation of market forces proposed by neoliberalism. But whether one 'likes' something is ultimately no more than an aesthetic question.

The argument, then, is that even new left proposals of a political economy kind are tainted by the abandonment of 'politics' and thus, fundamentally, by the abandonment of the notion of 'totality', a notion crucial not only to Marx but, also, to Adam Smith. While the political right has always felt happy to ridicule Marxism for its totalising thought, its own strategies and ideologies were themselves totalising: the market is all and everything, and all and everything is derived from the market itself. In fact, liberalism has always had great trust in the power of the market, a trust so great that it abandoned the study of the social constitution of the market by claiming it is governed by an invisible hand. The trust in the invisible as an effective, efficient, and fair power of an almighty sort has been unbroken since the inception of capitalist social relations. Marx, and the tradition based on his writings, provided a critique of invisible principles. This critique, I will argue, has been abandoned by theories of globalisation. In this way, new left political-economic inquiries have become part and parcel of neoliberalism's worship of invisible principles. While the new left might not 'like' the invisible's hard-hitting 'hand', it is forced to accept it because the acceptance of the 'market' entails that the cunning of reason amounts to no more than the invisible's own project.

I shall first give a brief outline of the development of the 'Left' since the 1960s. There then follows an introduction to contemporary theoretical conceptions of 'novelty'. The conclusion reassesses the meaning of the 'politics of novelty'.

A short guide to the Left, post-1960

During the late 1960s Marxism appeared rejuvenated. By the mid-1970s cracks appeared as erstwhile followers of Marxist study showed themselves as followers of fashion. In the 1960s, Marxism was in vogue, was fashionable, and by the mid-1970s it no longer was. New 'isms' such as post-industrialism, the first blossoms of postmodernism, and studies examining the crisis of the welfare state appeared. These no longer aspired to the rigour of Marxist analysis. The crisis of capitalist reproduction, showing itself, for example, as a crisis of the state and its social-democratic outlook, seemed to demand a more 'realistic' approach which took the form of value-free academic study (as in the case of Offe and other so-called second-generation critical theorists). Others focused on 'new forms' of struggle stressing the 'marginal' as the essence of going beyond capitalism without even touching on the relations of exploitation. This approach, known as post-industrialism or post-materialism, emphasised ecology and lifestyles as the centre of political concern.

The farewell to the working class was proclaimed and Marxism, where it persisted, showed itself as structuralism – a form of thought which reduces all social practice to an agency whose lively existence is said to be able to reproduce the capitalist structures of exploitation. Thus, Aglietta's important study, which gave rise to the growth industry associated with the Regulation School and its notion of a transition from Fordism to post-Fordism, was solely interested in the mechanisms required to secure capitalist reproduction.[1] The study was originally published in French in 1974. Most commentators agree that the breakdown of the Bretton Woods system between 1971 and 1973 had profound consequences for political stability and that the oil-crisis of 1974 accelerated and emphasised the already existing deep crisis of capitalist overaccumulation on a global scale. The date of Aglietta's study is thus significant.

Thus, while post-industrialists and post-materialists proclaimed their farewell to the working class, Marxist-inspired work on political economy, such as Aglietta's, stressed the requirements that had to be observed to regulate the accumulation of human bodies in the name of capitalist self-expansion.

Those to whom the renewal of Marxist critique in the 1960s was more than just a fashionable exercise experienced the 1970s as a particularly burdensome decade. The 'hot autumns' of 1977 in Italy and Germany showed the danger involved in the continuous project of an enlightened and enlightening Marxism. For some, loss of employment in the civil service, if not prison, beckoned; others felt obliged to sign declarations expressing their loyalty to the basic principles of state and society. The witch-hunt against leftist intellectuals and scholars had a profound effect on the intellectual climate and precipitated a 'change in values', leading to greater dominance of liberal ideas and interpretations.

The coming into power of neo-conservative parties, and the monetarist turn-around of socialist parties in office, sharpened the belief that rigorous Marxist critique was best replaced by a strategy of avoiding the likely consequences of neoliberal policies. Furthermore, the maturing, especially in Germany, of the green movement into an electorally successful Green Party renewed the conflict over extra-institutional versus institutional struggles. While the Greens were successfully institutionalised, the erstwhile 'radicals' became newborn parliamentarians endowed with a sense of responsibility towards parliamentary democracy. Habermas, who only a decade earlier was vilified for his denunciation of the student Left as a 'left-fascism', could now advocate a politics of constitutional patriotism without risk of

---

[1] Aglietta 1974.

opposition. Eurocommunist parties, too, became submerged or, rather, reasserted their integration into the political system; either through coalition governments (as in France) or through a politics of historical compromise (as in Italy, though it was never formalised after the assassination of Aldo Moro). The zeitgeist of the 1980s was fundamentally different from that of the 1960s. Indeed, by the late 1970s, Althusser proclaimed that Marxism was in crisis. For him, this crisis was, of course, a crisis of structuralist Marxism. While one should not be dismayed about this crisis, it nevertheless indicated a profound change in the left intellectual climate. Poulantzas committed suicide and Althusser himself 'opted' for mental death: he, quite literally, went mad.

Against this background, the new politics of postmodernism, post-industrialism and post-materialism, as well as liberal versions of feminism, gained greater and greater credibility as academic research areas. Marxism's totalising critique, its emphasis on the commodity as a fetish, and its critique of economic categories was turned against itself. The use of the concept of totality was criticised as totalitarian, the critique of fetishism was criticised for endorsing productivity for the sake of productivity; the critique of economic categories was criticised as Marxism's economism. Most disturbing of all, Marx's critique of Ricardo's labour theory of value was said to endorse a productivist perspective in which only male, industrial labour is deemed to be of social value! Of course Marx endorsed this view. It was endorsed because capitalist social relations constitute human social practice in precisely this constrained productivist way. However, his endorsement did not entail acceptance. Rather, the reduction of 'labour' to no more than a factor of capitalist production was criticised *in toto*. Even a cursory glance at his writings would make this clear. However, his critique of political economy was turned against Marx, followed by the argument that Marx's was not a critique of political economy but a different system of economics, an economics that projects the constitution of a workers' republic, a republic of labour. Such vilification confused capitalism's reduction of labour to human machines with Marx's critique of capitalism's perversion of labour. Thus, the 'new left' of post-something engaged in a denunciation of Marxism which, in the past, had been carried forward by Marxism's enemies: the bourgeoisie and its chattering intellectual 'classes'. The 'new left' proclaimed itself to be in favour of 'minority' emancipation, including animals and plants. Identity politics and the focus on 'lifestyle', so much emphasised in the 1990s, have their roots in the 1970s. Their legacy is the endorsement of individualist notions of self-determination and of the autonomy of the self, a demand that fitted well with the projections of the neoliberal Right. Of course, individuals should be encouraged to self-determine themselves. However, in a society that expands 'wealth' by imposing poverty upon those without property, self-determination of the individual can go forward only on the basis of individual competitiveness.

On the whole, the new Marxist Left of the post-1960s proclaimed in favour of socialism without committing itself to any blueprint of what such a society might look like. Its major preoccupation was to criticise the endeavour to bring new life into Marx's critique of political economy. Blueprints were few and far between. However, the endorsement of socialism was not tantamount to the endorsement of 'really existing socialism' in the then Eastern bloc. The new Marxist Left post-1960 was, if anything, a more rigorous critic of really existing socialism than conservative critics. Their source of inspiration was Rosa Luxemburg, not Lenin.

Yet, the fall of the Berlin Wall in 1989 has been taken by many to indicate that there is no alternative to capitalism. The implication is thus that the post-1960s socialist Left saw, in fact, really existing socialism in the East as its utopia. One should not be surprised if the end of history, the end of socialism, is proclaimed by proponents of capitalism. These proclamations are, as it were, their profession and business. However, the proclamation of the death of socialism, and the endorsement of the spectre of capitalism has been, on the whole, most vigorously argued by those who are usually seen to belong to the Left. Claus Offe, to mention just one author, feels that his position of the 1970s has been vindicated: there is no alternative to liberal democracy and to market-centred systems of production.[2] Joachim Hirsch calls for the end of 'negative critique' because it is outdated, for the moment at least, and difficult times demand positive political proposals such as the renewal of liberal-democratic values in the face of globalised capitalism.[3]

The collapse of really existing socialism, in short, was seen as being synonymous with the end of socialism, as if the socialist post-1960s Left was a really existing socialist Left and as if this Left was implicated by association. The collapse of really existing socialism was thus not seen as an opportunity for freeing Marx but, rather, as a means of burying him, and not only him but the whole anti-Leninist tradition associated with negative critique. In sum, the fall of the Berlin Wall made it possible to formalise what had, in fact, taken place a long time ago, namely the new 'Left's' abandonment of negative critique. The fall of the Wall, then, allowed the new 'Left' to free itself from Marx.

Risk and related topics

According to Ulrich Beck, we no longer live in a class society but in a risk society.[4] The old class antagonism between capital and labour, based on accumulation and exploitation, is seen to have created something of a positive-sum game in that the wealth of nations increased, allowing everybody to get a bigger slice of the cake. But the

---

[2] Offe 1996.
[3] Hirsch 1995.
[4] Beck 1992.

consequence was the submergence of the original class divisions which drove economic expansion. Thus the growing 'cake' society was replaced by a negative-sum game characterised by something called 'collective self-injury'. Everybody is thus 'injured'; risk treats everybody equally and there seems no escape. Thus Beck's notion of a unity between perpetrator and victim. Although some members of society have an advantage over others, this advantage is one of degree only; it is a matter of reducing disadvantages rather than escaping injury. Some are able to reduce disadvantages by shifting them to others, but still the congruence between perpetrator and victim holds. Thus there is, in Beck's argument, no social-political vantage point that might provide a privileged point from which to initiate a sort of 'causal therapy'. This, it is argued, was possible in class-based societies. But in our society, in our risk society, nothing can be done: all are injured and nobody, no group is able to effect a policy that supplies a solution to 'risk'. Risk, then, is institutionalised, irresistible and here to stay. Beck concludes that there is no reliable theoretical knowledge as to which actions and non-actions might place heavy burdens of risk on whom, and in what temporal horizon risk might impose itself upon the innocent and the ugly. The degree of risk can not be investigated. The only knowledge is that it is there. All social connections are thus 'homogenised' as they all become 'Angst'-connections!

The notion that our society is a classless society is not new; indeed, it is as old as capitalism. That our society is at risk, a risk society, is not new, either; Spengler made it the starting point of his distasteful diatribe. Yet other leftist intellectuals such as Offe and Hirsch, while endorsing Beck's view on risk, do not go all the way. For Offe, socialism as a structural formula for a truly emancipated social order is operationally empty, and has been for some time. The fall of the Berlin Wall has vindicated democracy's values and the Left, in the face of risk and neoliberal solutions to the crisis of the welfare state, is encouraged to demand guarantees of social and economic minimums rather than demanding maximums: the Left is asked to pursue avoidance strategies so as to secure minimum wages and basic welfare entitlements. However, avoidance criteria are difficult to determine: again, as with Beck's risk society thesis, theory does not provide reliable knowledge as to what action is wanted and on whose behalf action should be demanded. Avoidance criteria can only be defined case by case and applied according to the available options by means of the appropriate procedures and institutions.

Thus, Offe argues against his old 'theoretical fathers'. Against the tradition associated with Adorno and Horkheimer, he argues that the Left should not seek to attain certain concrete final ends; he rejects Adorno and critical theory as irrational because this form of theorising is seen to block every road towards a theory of rational morality; he renounces reason's claim to revolution because it is destructive for the creation of a rational morality. Reason should be used for attainable aims and not for the undermining of liberal democracy. Theoretically, Offe and Beck are set to destroy any notion of theory as a totalising force concerned with the mode of existence of essential relations, that is relations between humans and therewith between humans and nature. Of course, Offe appears less determined than Beck, insofar as he advocates the notion of a moral rationality. However, Offe argues his case without any theoretical investigation into the social and historical constitution of 'moral rationality'. It is construed in an *a priori* fashion, as a categorical norm. Thus, Offe reintroduces 'totalisation' through the back door by elevating 'moral rationality' to a normative obligation that is universally applicable. It is as if the nice forms of equality, liberty, freedom, citizenship-rights, etc., exist externally to their social content, that is, as norms of exploitation and domination.

Hirsch's contribution to the 'new' Left's abandonment of negative critique is based on the notion that capitalist society exists in and through a plurality of antagonisms such as racism, sexism, wage-labour conflict, ecological struggles, etc. These struggles individualise society and make it less able to resist the forces of globalisation. He too argues that there is at present no alternative to capitalism and the Left has to accept this in order to avoid the consequences of a neoliberalism's politics of globalisation. These consequences are portrayed with reference to Beck's notion of a risk society, which Hirsch addresses in terms of a politics of global social apartheid. In Hirsch's work, the only really existing subject is 'capital'. Social relations are too fragmented and relate antagonistically to each other, undermining any viable alternative within the framework set by 'capital'. Thus, in Hirsch's argument, too, we find that the reintroduction of a notion of totality. For Hirsch it is 'capital' as a *begreifendes Subjekt* (knowing subject), that is a universal, all-defining, and autonomous subject. Again, capital is perceived as a universal category constituted by powers internal to itself. Opposite to capital is no-thing, only a plurality of distinct social interests, social groups, and social conflicts.

In sum, since the mid-1970s, Marxist theorising has undergone, as far as the mainstream Left is concerned, important and significant changes. Whether it be risk society, rational morality, capital as subject – all reject the notion that in order to determine social existence one has to negate the independence of the particular so as to see it as distinct-in-unity. At the same time as negative critique stands rejected, all these approaches reintroduce the notion of 'totality' by arguing either in terms of 'universal risk', 'universal moral rationality', or a 'universal capitalist subject'. None provides an analysis of their 'universal' categories in terms of their social and historical constitution. All assume the existence of their universals in *a priori* fashion. As *a priori* assumptions, their 'existence' and 'power' derive from principles that are beyond critical judgement. It is as if these principles emerge from invisible spaces.

All these approaches, whatever their specific form, rest upon three mutually dependent developments:

1) All claim to have discovered new significant developments that cannot be analysed adequately within the Marxist theoretical tradition. Marxist theory appears, at worst, overtaken by events and thus outdated, or, at best, in need of substantial revision to accommodate that which is deemed to be new. On closer inspection, though, the charges against the Marxist theoretical tradition are not new but do have, in fact, a long established tradition of 'rejection' associated, in the past, with liberal thinking. Furthermore, the claim that developments have overtaken the horizon of Marxism's theoretical grasp is also quite old. What is new about a 'risk' society? Workers have always faced the risk of injury, unemployment, wage cuts and so on. And the capitalists: of course, bankruptcy has always been their likely risk. Indeed, the exploitation of the worker, in a way, impresses itself, as a systemic necessity, upon the individual capitalist through competition. Failure to impose 'risk' on the worker might mean 'risk' for the capitalist.

2) All new left approaches since the mid-1970s depend on the rejection of Marxism's negative critique as a way of determining different phenomena as distinct moments in unity. This rejection goes hand in hand with the adoption of a value-neutral standpoint. Thus, negative critique is dismissed for its 'negativity' and thus for its apparent irrationality. Furthermore, the rejection of negative critique is tantamount to the rejection of Marxism's totalising view. Instead, the new left approaches focus on particular 'instances' and induce from these general judgement on the world. Their organising methodology consists in an inductive epistemology, causal connections and a value-free research perspective, as if such a perspective is not already, and emphatically so, a value-decision. In other words, their organising methodology, and back-door notions of totality, are theoretically at ease with the form of positivist social theory popularised by Parsons.

3) All new left approaches since the mid-1970s claim to have developed an alternative to Marxism's negative critique, an alternative that is firmly embedded within the epistemological parameters and constraints of (vulgar) economic theory. Economic theory, at least since the marginalist revolution at the turn of this century, no longer sought to establish 'economics' as a science as Smith and his contemporaries still did. Instead, economics started to base itself on set assumptions about certain economic variables. These are interpreted as individual elements within a mathematical equation. In distinction to Marx's notion that everything is constituted as mutually dependent and mutually penetrating moments of a dialectical totality, economics treats each case separately and brings these individual cases back into an equation, thereby creating model-like relations. Thus, everything is reduced to quantity and everything is related to each other in an external, causal, sum game.

Modern new 'leftist' theories, it seems to me, do just that. Their rejection of Marxism's claim of a dialectical totality finds its other side in the treatment of social relations as: relations of racism; relations of gender; relations of wage labour; relation of nature; relations of ... etc etc. The new left's endorsement of identity politics, of 'lifestyle', of postmodernist indifference to resistance as being of no more than empty significance, of risk society where everybody is a victim – all depend on the notion of individual circumstances and cases, cases that are brought into relation with each other as if each existed independently from the other, as if social relations as a whole are no more than the sum of many individual cases. In other words, the theoretical claims of new left social theory are those of marginalist economic theory and its social and political companion, positivist thought. Is this too strong a statement? Possibly. Yet, marginalism depends on universals, namely the market, capital etc. It depends on assumptions. New left theory seems to depend on assumptions, too, as well as on universals: it endorses capital as a universal subject, or rational morality as a universal value-free norm, or catastrophe as a universally applicable power that produces risk. All these, capital, rational morality, and universal catastrophe are merely assumed: the constitution of their 'existence' is not questioned. Both, marginalism and new left thinking depend on separating 'genesis' from 'existence'; this separation, according to Horkheimer constitutes the blind spot of dogmatic thought.[5] Dogmatism, of course, feels most at home in approaches that refuse to understand the social world we live in as a world constituted in and through social practice, however perverted this practice might be. There is thus a considerable irony: the new left, which has battled so hard to appear respectable by ridding itself of any association with negative critique, ends up where it projected 'Marxism' to be, namely in the camp of dogmatism.

Conclusion

The paper started with the notion of a 'politics of novelty'. Is this notion appropriate? In a way I would like to think that it is and I have argued long and hard in its favour. However, perhaps it is inappropriate after all? Would it not make sense to argue that there is something more fundamental involved, something that the notion of a politics of novelty serves to hide?

I have argued that the 'politics of novelty' amounts to the Left's abdication of negative critique in favour of new and newer concepts which are based on the theoretical tradition of positivism. In this way the Left has lost its theoretical 'home' and has tailored its conception according to its 'enemy's' theoretical agenda. True, there are differences between neoliberalism and Offe's project of a moral rationality, though

---

[5] Horkheimer 1947.

these differences are distinct only as variations on a common theme. The 'politics of novelty' thus could be argued to amount to no more than a crisis of theory, a crisis which is informed by and informs – as its theoretical expression – the social and political crisis that beset capitalist social relations since the late 1960s. However, a crisis of theory has to be more than just an objective reflection of 'social and economic crisis'. There are choices that can be made and have been made. Thus, the politics of novelty also amounts to something else, to something hidden behind itself. This something, I suppose, would be best emphasised by two interrelated thematic issues.

The first is fashion. There is no doubt that social theory, especially of a new left sort, is fashion-driven. The invention of new research agendas, the proposal of new research themes and so on is highly lucrative in terms of outside research funding, reputation, book sales, etc. Innovation produces a name and not only a name. It also supplies the social sciences with 'significance'. It legitimises the social sciences as a worthwhile social activity and so gives it academic 'respectfulness'. In this way, then, the new constructive manifestation of new left thinking has assumed the role of a social servant: *ancilla constitutionis*.

The second issue is that of commodification: the fashion-driven nature of much of social theory takes away theory's claim to comprehend, understand, conceptualise and criticise social existence. The Enlightenment's notion, 'doubt everything', its summoning of social critique as a destructive critique, has been replaced by servitude to – an analogy of Adorno's critique of the culture industry – the academic industry.[6] 'Left' social theory, in this view, is a theoretical expression of the zeitgeist, a zeitgeist which theoretical fashions seek to reinforce and exploit. Zeitgeist does not provide good theory but it does supply theory with a market for all categories of readers whose views and 'Angst' it does not wish to challenge – this would not only reduce sales prospects but might, also, entail 'risk'. Thus, I would argue that much of today's left theory has embraced the profitable road to market success. Surely, market development is connected with the development of political currencies. Yet, I have already argued that, to me, much of late 1960s Marxism showed itself as 'fashion' when confronted with the political climate of the 1970s. The connection between theory-production, theme-production, zeitgeist and sales prospects is vital. The casualty in all of this is 'theory' and therewith the understanding of social practice: in this sense we do indeed witness a profound crisis of theory.

References

---

[6]See Agnoli 1992, pp. 43-51.

Aglietta, Michel 1974, *Accumulation et regulation du capitalism en longue periode. L'exemple des Etats-Unis (1870-1970)*, Paris: Insee.

Agnoli, Johannes 1992, 'The Determination of the Scholar in Miserable Times is Destruction', *Common Sense*, 12: 43–51.

Beck, Ulrich 1992, *Risk Society: Towards a New Modernity*, London: Sage.

Hirsch, Joachim 1995, *Der nationale Wettbewerbsstaat*, Berlin: id-edition.

Horkheimer, Max 1947, *The Eclipse of Reason*, New York: Oxford University Press.

Offe, Claus 1996, *Modernity and the State*, Cambridge: Polity.

Transformation

Marxist Boundary Work in Theory, Economics, Politics and Culture

Marxism Queer Theory, Gender

Vol. 2

Transformation
Mas'ud Zavarzadeh, Editor
Teresa L. Ebert, Co-Editor
Donald Morton, Co-Editor

Box 7302 University Station
Syracuse, New York, 13210-7302

Single copy $15.00

Saving Private Ryan: Realism and the Enigma of Head-Wounds

John Roberts

In Ernst Friedrich's *Krieg dem Kriege*[1] there is a large section of photographs of survivors of World War I with the most hideous disfigurements of the face: jaws are missing, gaping slashes stare out where mouths should be. Friedrich leaves this gallery of 'untouchables' to the end of the book as if to achieve the maximum debasement of military glory and heroism. The head and face are obviously the most vulnerable part of the body in warfare – brutal wounds to the face and decapitations are common. In World War I, a number of hospitals were set up to deal solely with head-wounds, developing the basis of what we now know as plastic surgery. Yet, in the representation of combat on screen, even in the most candid and unsentimental of war films, such as *Hamburger Hill* and *Platoon*, injuries to the face are rare or non-existent. This absence has something to do with the difficulty of producing convincing prosthetic wound-cavities on the head; blown-off limbs can obviously be created with ease through covering up the actor's extant limb with padded clothing; bloody disembowellings can be simulated with the judicious use of imitation innards and the illusionistic application of broken flesh, and so on. But the problems of modelling head-wounds clearly only half-explain the consistency of the absence.

In conventional film narrative, the representation of the actor's head as the source of discernible emotion is considered sacrosanct, even in death, for what narrative cinema always fears to lose is our full and attentive identification with the fate of the actor. In order for the loss of life or able-bodiedness to secure its emotional force, the face has to retain its expressive integrity: the face cannot be obliterated and silenced completely; in scenes of import the character has to remain cognisant of his or her fate through speech, or at least sound. If our identification with the passing life of the character is to expose us to the emotional truth of the scene, we cannot be forced to look away, or ironise our revulsion as if we were watching a horror movie. Indeed, it is the horror film where the aesthetics of the gruesome head-wound reside, for in the horror film human disfigurement is never believable. Interestingly, this problem of the head-wound becomes the actual subject of a scene in one of the best war movies of the 1950s, Stanley Kubrick's *Paths of Glory* (1957), which deals with the outcome of would-be cowardice at

---

[1] Friedrich 1924.

the French front during World War I. Two French soldiers are talking in their bunker about the impending push forward of the French army, and about ways in which they would least like to die. One of the soldiers is indefatigable: he does not want to die through being shot in the head – anything but that. This short scene could stand as an allegory on war and cinema. For, everything the soldier fears about the obliteration of identity through the head-wound seems to have been internalised by the makers of modern war movies.

It is no surprise, therefore, to note that in Steven Spielberg's recent film *Saving Private Ryan* (1997), a film that has been lauded for its unparalleled realism, gruesome head-wounds are absent. Indeed, one is even more surprised by this given the ferocity and unrelenting visceralness of the combat scenes, and more significantly, the fact that despite the films ostensible theme – the search for an American soldier by the US army after the D-Day landings – the film has little interest in the relationships between the film's characters or any ideological position on the fight against fascism in Europe. This is a film about the experience of modern warfare, about the barbarous penetration of steel through flesh, about panic, about losing the ability to fix a position, about the failure of 'seeing' as an invitation to death. This means that the film discards many of the conventions of the World War II buddy-movie or mission movie, in which the trials and dangers of a group of soldiers are narrated as part of a larger story about the defeat of fascism – as in *Object Burma* (1944), starring Errol Flynn. Furthermore, in *Saving Private Ryan*, there is little time and effort devoted to the narration of the psychological effects of combat on the soldiers: when we witness trauma it is the immediate consequences of death on the battle field. There is little dialogue about the loss of comrades, about the horrors of combat; and, when its impact is touched on, the result is baleful and cursory, even cliché-ridden, as in the sequence towards the end when Private Ryan and a group of soldiers are reminiscing about home and listening to Edith Piaf on a gramophone. This stilted threnody of doomed desire is highly revealing of where Spielberg's interests lie. That is, what concerns him is not how well his protagonists narrate their own experience to the audience – which, in this scene, is crassly done – but the authenticity of how we experience the experience of combat itself.

It has been commented that watching the film is exhausting – and so it is. The cacophonous level of sound, the bloody close-ups, the shared sense of apprehension, of waiting-for-the-worst, conduce a level of physical stress that only modern cinema can achieve. As such, we should look to the technologies of wide-screen cinema in order to understand the impact and significance of the film. Indeed, where Spielberg shows a disinterest in narrating the effects of war, he makes up for it in his mimesis of the point of view of the soldier under fire. In this respect, *Saving Private Ryan* is as close as any film-maker has come recently to exploiting the relationship between cinema and violence. By this I mean the mimetic capacity of modern cinema to subject the audience *to* the violence of a scene – its brutality and disorientation – by moving the camera into and through the action, and not just as the witness to a violent act or scene. If these techniques have contributed to the 'realist' effects of recent war films, they have rarely been used so extensively and relentlessly as in *Saving Private Ryan*. Thus Spielberg's primary concern is to bring the spectator in direct alignment with the industrialisation of warfare, into the space of its absolute destructiveness and shocking derealisation of perception. In the 1920s and 1930s, Ernst Jünger, in such works as *Storm of Steel* (1920) and *Der Gerfahrliche Augenblick* (1931), expressed and celebrated these effects as the inevitable consequence of technological development. But if modern cinema has embraced this industrialisation as a central part of its narrative machinery, it has rarely – because of censorship, lack of technical capability and the demands of story-telling – focused on what such industrialisation actually does to bodies and perception. Hence, seventy years on, there is a way of reading Spielberg's soldier-as-camera in the centre of the battle, as the director's adaptation of a modernist, Jüngerian derangement of the senses within a technologically transformed and ideologically less constrained Hollywood cinema. For, without doubt, Spielberg sets out to subjugate the audience, to push the spectator back into his and her seat, without respite, without the comforts of anecdotal asides and character-building.

The film's major set piece and claim to unprecedented realism is the opening sequence, which narrates the D-Day landing on Omaha Beach on 6 June 1944 by American 2nd Rangers. Under severe machine gun and mortar fire, the Rangers were required to secure the beach for the rest of the landing. Four thousand six hundred and forty-nine men were killed or wounded. In fact, so severe was the German fire, that hundreds of soldiers were killed as soon as the doors of the troop carriers were lowered. Spielberg shows this to brutal effect. Indeed what is so powerful about this sequence is the way in which the German machine guns and mortars overwhelm the action. This allows Spielberg to focus not just on their violent effects, but on the sheer confusion of the soldiers, and their inability to move, pinned down by heavy enemy fire. The Omaha sequence lasts for thirty minutes or more, in effect covering in 'real-time' the broken advance of the Americans up the beach. This putative realism is instated immediately. As the troop-carriers approach the beach we see in close-up two soldiers throwing up, and Tom Hanks, who plays Captain Miller, the officer who later leads the search for Ryan, shaking profusely – a nervousness which is replayed on a number of occasions through the film. On the beach, the camera then adopts the uncertain position of the advancing soldiers, ducking, weaving, collapsing, crawling. Spielberg has gone on record as saying that one of the main visual reference points for the opening sequence was Robert Capa's fuzzy, shaky photographs of the D-Day landings, the only extant images of the attack. Similarly, there is much in Spielberg's camera angles that borrows from the hand-held camerawork of World War II combat documentaries, such as John Huston's 1944 fox-hole short. Both Capa and Huston invoke the viewpoint of the soldier under fire. But, in the case of Spielberg, the camera is *in* and *amongst* the soldiers, in a way that signifies both a startling verisimilitude that documentary filming is unable to achieve and the impossibility of that verisimilitude. As such, it is the choreographed illusionism of the sequence – Spielberg' s marshalling of ballistic skills, prosthetics and logistical arrangements of men and equipment – that produces what we take to be the unprecedented realism of the attack sequence. For instance, as part of the sequence's hypersensitivity to the effects of gun-fire on bodies (bodies dismembered, shattered) Spielberg focuses on the trajectory of bullets – their penetrative power. As the attack begins we see two soldiers who have submerged themselves in the water shot as they are trying to free themselves of their heavy packs. The bullets zip through their bodies creating red tracers in their wake. When one thinks of the way shooting into water in films is usually handled – as ineffective – this attention to the hidden velocity of heavy fire gives a gruesome scientificity to the death of the soldiers. Similarly, injuries are given a forensic focus, as with the extraordinary moment – straight out of *Night of the Living Dead* – when one the soldiers returns, as if dream-walking in hell, to pick up his arm which has been shot off. These moments of trauma and chaos show Spielberg montaging the carnage through a sequence of disturbing, disconnected images. There is no internal dramatisation of the advance amongst the protagonists, no meaningful actions or words that would provide a clue to the objective of the attack. It is only when they pass beyond the barbed wire and are sheltering in front of the pill-box that orders become intelligible. Just before this point we also witness a key motif of the chaos of combat in the film, and perhaps of all war-movies – the brief loss of discipline or failure of perception as an invitation to death. Crouching beneath the sea wall, one of the Rangers takes his helmet off, and, as we anticipate, in that moment he is shot in the head. However, this is not to contradict my opening claim; on the contrary, this kind of death is invariably a 'clean one', in which the single shot to the head brings poignancy, even doomed beauty on occasions, to the soldier's fate. The latter is emblematic in *All Quiet on the Western Front* (the 1930 original directed by Louis Milestone and the 1979 remake) when, at the end, Paul Bäumer, the 'everyman' soldier, is shot when he takes a moment's respite – and indulges in a momentary loss of discipline – in the trenches to watch a butterfly, or, in the remake, to draw a bird. This poignancy lies in the failed attempt on the part of the soldier to recover his humanity by de-militarising his behaviour. This kind of 'clean death' is also said to have accounted for the last Allied fatality in World War I. After the battle of Mons, Canadian Private George Price took off his helmet as he bent down to pick up some flowers given to him by Belgian children, and was shot in the head by a German sniper. There is also the poignancy of the shot-to-the-head against all odds, in which the head of the enemy becomes the trophy of the sniper. Spielberg employs this as the Rangers fight their way up the beach to capture the German positions. The cool and highly religious sharp-shooter of the platoon scores an improbable and beautifully symmetrical shot into the forehead of a German Grenadier inside his pill box. The 'cleanness' of the death allows Spielberg to dwell on it for effect: for what he wants to register on the dead soldier's face is utter surprise. The Americans have broken through! From that moment on the attack moves in the favour of the Rangers.

After the Rangers have captured the German position, Captain Miller is ordered by US high-command to form a platoon to search for Private Ryan (Matt Damon), one of four brothers who were fighting in the US Army. Unbeknown to Ryan, his three brothers have all been killed, prompting the high-command to the unprecedented step of saving Ryan for the sake of his traumatised mother. The middle section of the film is taken up with this implausible challenge, involving Miller's platoon in a number of violent confrontations, before they eventually find Ryan holed up in a French village with his platoon – he is unsurprisingly unwilling to leave his comrades – waiting for the advancing Wehrmacht. The final sequence is another conflagatory set-piece, as the Americans successfully delay the German advance. In these two sections of the film, the viewpoint of the sniper, and of rifle sight-lines generally, become increasingly important as the action is given over to hand-to-hand fighting. However, what maintains the momentum of the violence and derangement of the senses of combat through to the final battle is a series of death-tableaux.

The death-tableau is something the modern war film borrows from the photographic archive and history painting, in which the moment of death is a reminder to the living of the ungiving temporality of all things.[2] In film-making, though, the tableau is either produced in an active form – the consequence of a given action, as in the final scene of *All Quiet On the Western Front*, or in Sam Fuller's highly stylised combat movies – or in passive form – the outcome of events recently past, which soldiers stumble on. The latter kind of scene – as atrocity or accident – is invariably a way of bringing soldiers to consciousness of a situation or given task, as is familiar from a number of Vietnam films. In *Saving Private Ryan* Spielberg uses both forms.

---

[2] I am also reminded of the gap between what Spielberg does with the tableau and the filmic transposition of the tableau in the contemporary use of photography. One such photographic death-tableau that comes to mind is Jeff Wall's *Dead Troops Talk: A Vision after an Ambush of a Red Army Patrol, near Moqor, Afghanistan, Winter 1986*, (1991–2) which depicts the corpses of a Red Army unit transformed into zombies after a Mujahideen attack. Wall's history-painting scale photograph incorporates a number of head-wounds, simulated in fact by Hollywood make-up artists, reinforcing my point about manifest head-wounds being dependent on the aesthetic grotesqueries of the horror film. Here the Red Army zombies are joking, smiling, playing-up.

Still searching for Ryan, Miller's platoon stops to rest at a village occupied by the Germans. In a dilapidated building, one of the soldiers sits down to rest on a pile of rubble and knocks a beam against the back wall bringing the wall down. Behind the wall is a group of German soldiers also resting. There is a frozen stand-off with guns at the ready, until the Rangers open fire. All the Germans are killed, producing a disconcertingly 'domestic' tableau of death – one of the soldiers is shot sitting on table, and slumps forward still seated. This visual complicity between death and sleep in photographic representation of corpses is, of course, commonplace. But why does Spielberg bother to create this effect in what appears to be a completely arbitrary act of violence? Why didn't he have the soldiers move on after resting, or fight the remaining Germans at a distance? He does not, because, as becomes clearer as the film unfolds, the soldiers' – and our – exposure to violence is being subjected to different experiences of dying and death. *Saving Private Ryan* functions indirectly as a compendium of modes of dying in combat and experiencing dying in combat; in this, it brings to the viewer abreactively the shocks of conflict; and the tableau, at one level, advances this. So, in the middle section of the film, we also see Miller and his platoon discover the decomposing bodies of a number of GIs just before the platoon is about to attack an important German radar station. Similarly, after the attack, the camera lingers on a dead German machine-gunner, still seated behind his gun.

This brings us to the final sequence, and the core of the claims for the film's realism. Before discussing this sequence, we need to remind ourselves of the claims of the classic realist text from 1970s film theory. As with all Spielberg's recent populist history films, he mixes historical events and scholarly research with what he takes to be legitimate artistic licence. In fact, Spielberg is less interested in the veracity of historical detail and the plausibility of actions and relationships than in the panorama of human conflict. Critics of this populist historiography have rightly attacked his work – *Schindler's List*, *Amistad* – for its abandonment to melodrama, feel-good images and historical 'gawping'. In *Amistad*, for instance, Spielberg's ostensibly anti-racist account of slave resistance in the eighteenth century, the white abolitionists are portrayed as epicene and untrustworthy, in order that the film appeals over the head of 'scholarly opinion', to a contemporary multicultural US audience, who want positive and uplifting images of racial self-emancipation, no matter how historically implausible. So too, in *Schindler's List*, Spielberg films the experience of the Holocaust from the perspective of Schindler and his Nazi associates, in order to secure a wholly conservative view of Jews as a redeemed people; to film from inside the Shoah would court too many spectres of division and complicity. These elisions and aporias, of course, are the basis of what customarily is referred to as the ideological closure of the classic realist text, a critique which was largely formulated in the pages of *Screen* in the early 1970s when neo-Brechtian film critics such as Colin MacCabe and Stephen Heath looked to Althusser and Pierre Macherey, and later Lacan (via Althusser), to rethink the ideological conditions of spectatorship. From this perspective, the classic realist text is structurally incapable of incorporating contradiction as means of subjecting the notion of the camera as a neutral agent and the construction of the spectator as objective witness of historical events to critique.[3]

Since the late 1970s, this view of the essentially closed nature of the classic realist text has received a great deal of criticism from inside and outside film theory, as Althusser's theory of ideological interpellation has come under gainful attack and neo-Brechtianism has lost its sheen. Principally, these criticisms have been twofold: the ideological hierarchies internal to the conventional narrative form of the classic realist text are not fixed, and therefore open to ideological revision; and the relationship between the spectator and film's dominant ideology is never secure, as a result of the preformation of the subject as divided; the subject is not hailed by the dominant ideology of the film, it 'works' through it, resisting and identifying in an unfolding process of avowal and disavowal.

In 1980s, the direct outcome of this shift was a move to reception theory in theories of spectatorship – largely developing out of psychoanalysis – and a celebration of non-realist forms of film production, such as fantasy, melodrama and comedy as a counter to the would-be 'vanguard' status of realist aesthetics. As a result, the main interests of film theory shifted to theories of consumption – to the political unconscious of the film text, its utopian glimpses – and, consequently, a less ideologically parsimonious view of Hollywood film. Accordingly, whereas in the 1970s the form of classic realist film was criticised for its conservatism, its conservatism was now seen as securing a progressive function through its ideological hierarchies. If the failure of the classic realist text to articulate its own constructedness was once a familiar refrain, the slogan now became: 'There can be no progressive film in which only the dominant have a facility.'[4]

But as this Left or progressive populism gained advocates in the face of what was seen as the terminal crisis of 1970s Left avant-gardism, the culture that might have sustained such a project went into decline, splintering in the face of the downturn in class struggle, the rise of postmodernism and the massive changes in the American film industry: the return of the big studios and the culture of account-led, technology-obsessed spectacles. Thus, when Raymond Williams entered the debate on realism in the late 1970s, defending his own version of a progressive classical realism, the moment of realignment had gone. Indeed Williams's idea of a subjunctive realism, a counter-narration of the everyday that was neither futurist nor utopian, yet moved the narration of events beyond the positivistic defence of what was deemed

---

[3] MacCabe 1974.
[4] For example, Lovell 1980.

historically feasible or plausible, had nothing but good will to underwrite it.[5]

In terms of the long-term decline and crisis of this progressive classic realist tradition, Spielberg is in equal measures a compelling and frustrating film-maker. For, in terms of the dominant tendencies within late 1980s and 1990s Hollywood cinema, he represents something of an anomaly: unlike the majority of his peers in the late 1980s he has turned to a 'public cinema' in which the historical consciousness of modernity and the experience of the American peoples are a given sweeping narrative form as the basis for the widest possible critical consumption of modern history. In terms of one of the principle ideals of the classic realist text, this conforms to an idea of public cinema as the 'conscience' of social democracy. That is, the 'dominant ideology' of the film is seen to conflict with, or call into question, the 'dominant ideology' of bourgeois society, thereby securing the film's progressiveness. In *Schindler's List* and *Amistad*, this rests on the broadest of ideological base: cinema has a responsibility to the past, given that historical consciousness is what modernity – and modern American cinema – derogates. However, this simple accord with the ethics of remembrance carries little political weight. For there is nothing inherently dissident or speculative about the themes of Spielberg's movies that would render them fundamentally out of step either with contemporary liberalism or American state policy. In this sense, their 'progressiveness' is a kind of metaprogressiveness. By this I mean that the very fact that Spielberg is prepared to defend a 'cinema of history' in the 1990s is sufficient to give his work a critical aura. In these terms, the conventional account of the classical realist text does not apply in any strict sense. For Spielberg's history films are a result of the incorporation of the critique of the classical realist text within its forms.

As mentioned, the early critics of the closure of the classical realist text accepted that classic realist cinema was never an ideologically stable form. However, these critics could not have anticipated the extent to which the theory of realism as articulation would, in a radically amended – depoliticised – form, come to open up the aesthetics of realism and commercial film-making generally in the 1980s. The film-within-a-film, the scattergun reference to other films, the open parody, the use of discontinuity and internal montage, have all played their part in heightening the fictiveness of the cinematic experience and dissolving the 'truth-effect' of the classic realist text. This 'postmodernisation' of film viewing is highly evident in Spielberg's recent films, in particular in relation to how he approaches the representation of history. In short, Spielberg has internalised the widespread and conventional postmodern view that historiography is a form of storytelling in which the truth-claims of the story are dependent on the powers of the storyteller. Historical film-making, therefore, is concerned with the business of

---

[5] Williams 1979.

telling good stories, and not trusting in notions of historical objectivity, or even plausibility. But if Spielberg wants to be thought of as, in his words, 'a magician' , he is not a disinterested teller of yarns: on the contrary, he remains committed to some notion of film as a space of historical explanation. Thus, as a film-maker narrating verifiable historical events and experiences (genocide and the slave trade), he must respect the historical truth of those events and experiences in order for the films to produce their progressive effects. Consequently, the internalisation of the postmodern idea of history as a set of competing micro-narratives (histories of relative value) comes into conflict in his films with the deeper claims of historical memory: that, without the acknowledgement of suffering, historical remembrance is the language of barbarism. Above all else, *Schindler's List* is a film about the incontestability of the suffering of a people; and, as such, despite Spielberg's acceptance of the elision between the fictiveness of film-making and the 'fictiveness' of historical construction, this is a film which refuses to give an inch to those who say that these events are past and therefore worth forgetting, or, following Lyotard in his barbarous-positivist mode, that these events will no longer exist once all the remaining survivors and witnesses of the camps are dead. The outcome is a film-maker who is conservative and sentimental on matters of human conflict, indifferent to historical precedent, non-confrontational on questions of politics, yet committed to a version of classic realism as a public cinema. This may be confusing and not much of a recommendation. But there is always something awkward about his embrace of classic realism that undercuts it, dispels its seamlessness in the process of staging its seductive effects. That is, Spielberg directs history self-consciously as an historical spectacle, but without denying the possibility that such spectacles might play a part in the critical recovery of historical memory. And it is in this way that Spielberg could be said to be 'postmodernising' the ideological effect of the classic realist text, for, by embracing spectacle and melodrama, the historical referent is coded on two fronts simultaneously: on the one hand, as a fictive experience; but, on the other, as a fiction that has the power to draw us into historical truth. Or as Michael Rogin puts it, discussing *Amistad*, the film 'claims power over history in the name of fidelity to it'.[6] The result is that Spielberg makes no pretence at historical complexity at the level of the script, but prefers a populist 'blocking in' of events, scenes and emotions. If this leaves the characters of his films particularly unengaging, it also makes his films formally heterodox. In fact, it is these deflections from the classic realist text that actually saves his film-making; and no more so than in *Saving Private Ryan*.

As pointed out earlier, in *Saving Private Ryan* Spielberg is neither interested in narrating the story of the group of soldiers who set out to save Private Ryan nor the story of Private Ryan himself. This leaves the

---

[6] Rogin 1998, p157.

structure of the narrative ragged, and strangely indifferent to the advertised content of the film. Indeed, the film's narrative dissolves in indifference to the requirements of convincing character development. From this it is unclear why Spielberg has set out to make a war movie without engaging with the lives of those who are involved in the fighting. Thus, as the film unfolds, we expect a conflict we never really get: the conflict between a group of reluctant soldiers and their officer sent on an impossible and reckless mission. For a Howard Hawks, for example, this would generate all kinds of ethical dilemmas and emotional intricacies as the soldiers try to survive in an alien environment. Spielberg will have none of it; in fact the fundamental tension between the laudable aims of the mission and its excessive human cost – the majority of the platoon are killed – is treated with utter superficiality. Hence, when we meet Ryan we are given little sense amongst the men who survived thus far whether the mission is appropriate or not. There is resentment, but at no point is resentment ever allowed to find dramatic shape. Customarily, this would point to the failure of the film; however, once we accept this absence or indifference, we begin to see the shape of a very different – and more interesting – kind of film, and, as such, judge the film in terms of its failure to meet a quite different set of requirements. Essentially, *Saving Private Ryan* is a film that deals with the experience of modern warfare without fully living up to these demands. Consequently, once we accept the incidental character of the narrative of recovery, the violent set-pieces begin to open up their content, as I have attempted to analyse above.

Now, of course, since the 1950s there have many war films which have taken on the experience of combat from the point of view of the soldier. This is now largely conventional for the genre. There have been few films though that used the full weight of cinematic technology to show the soldier in a state of constant subjugation and fear in the process of combat itself. Why should this occur with such candour now, when clearly the technology and will have long been available to produce a comparable kind of film? I believe this has much to do with two related issues: the increasing sensitivity to the limits and demands of masculinity in popular culture; and, correspondingly, an increasing awareness both inside and outside the military of the actual psychological costs of warfare and those who survive it. *Saving Private Ryan*, then, is not so much a film about war, or even about World War II; it is film about trauma. A good indication of this is the opening sequence, when Tom Hanks is shaking. Examples of soldiers shaking and male hysteria are not uncommon in the war-film genre. Yet there is something about Hanks's shaking hand that signifies a masculine vulnerability that rarely finds its expression in the genre, it connotes the wrong 'tone'. In this sense, the shaking enunciates, at the very start of the action, how we are to see the combatants: as men unsure and unprepared for what they are about to experience. It is no surprise, therefore, that the film has been a popular success in the US, where the historical memory of and physical cost of American imperialism is a living source of both massive enmity and patriotic fervour in the current 'crisis of masculinity' debate. As in Britain, the film has prompted discussion of the widespread occurrence of psychiatric casualties in World War II and the Vietnam war. Indeed, the staggering social and psychological cost of the Vietnam war is inseparable from the US reception of the post-1960s American war movie. It is estimated that over 130,000 veterans have committed suicide. Moreover, in the mid-1990s when the US prison population had reached the one million mark, around 200,000 veterans were inmates.[7] On this score it is revealing to note that the considerable influence Hanks himself had on the character of Miller. In a recent interview he confessed that the film started out as a mess. 'Captain Miller was a stock, one-dimensional war hero who'd won the Medal of Honour and chomped on a cigar and said, "Come on, you sons of bitches". There were so many degrees of falsehood'. Hanks talked to Spielberg and 'they changed every word of it'.[8] In this respect, what makes *Saving Private Ryan* a compelling film is that it is not an anti-war film as it might be understood within the confines of classic realism, but a film about being inside the spaces, positions, and trajectories of warfare from the perspective of the front-line soldier. We might say, then, that this constitutes its psychological realism.

I have left a discussion of the final violent set-piece for my concluding comments. In the abandoned French village, the remnants of Captain Miller's platoon and the remnants of Private Ryan's platoon engage with the Wehrmacht in hand-to-hand fighting. The sequence lasts for about thirty minutes, allowing Spielberg to shift from the death-tableau to the geometries and subterfuges of close combat and the bloody actuality of death. Whereas the violence in the opening sequence is based on the American soldiers being in the line of fire, here it is largely reversed. Indeed, the rifle and machine gun sight-lines of the GIs become the point of view of the camera, as Spielberg takes up the firing position of various members of the platoon. For instance, the platoon sharp-shooter, who is secluded in a damaged church tower, is shown firing a rapid succession of shots into the advancing Germans: each clinical shot finding its deathly mark. This triadic identification of the soldier's viewpoint/camera position/spectator's viewpoint is conventionally used to denote the power of the assailant over the enemy; here it functions closer to an act of desperation and panic as the soldier tries to find his bearing in a field of vision – the fast approaching Germans – that is about to overwhelm him. The effect is to produce another look of death, the soldier who falls at distance, 'silent' and

---

[7] Matlin 1997.
[8] Andersen 1998, p. 120. Hanks is maybe thinking of Robert Mitchum's cigar-chomping performance in the Omaha beach sequences in *The Longest Day* (1962).

without any perceivable injury, like a duck on a shooting-range. Much of this sequence is reminiscent of the scene in Sartre's *Iron in the Soul* (1950), the last volume of *Roads to Freedom*, when Mathieu and his comrades hiding in the clock tower hold off, and are eventually overwhelmed by a German armoured division. As with Spielberg's sharpshooter Mathieu fires rapidly, determinedly into the oncoming Wehrmacht.

> He made his way to the parapet and stood there firing. This was revenge on a big scale. Each one of his shots avenged some ancient scruple. One for Lola whom I dared to rob; one for Marcelle whom I ought to have left in the lurch; one for Odette whom I didn't want to kiss ... Beauty dived downwards like some obscene bird. But Mathieu went on firing. He fired. He was cleansed. He was all-powerful. He was free. [9]

Distance numbs the consequences of Mathieu's desperation and sadism. However, in *Saving Private Ryan* this mixture of physical propinquity and psychological distance for soldier and spectator alike is shattered in one of the film's most violent and gruelling scenes. Two members of the platoon are trapped in a room by the Germans. One is shot horrifically in the throat, and, as he grasps for breath in his death throes, the remaining German and the other GI fight to the death on the floor. Spielberg takes his time; the fight is drawn out, until the German drives his bayonet slowly into the chest of the GI. This hideous intimacy has direct echoes of Paul Bäumer's killing of the French soldier in the shell-hole in *All Quiet on the Western Front*. But whereas the latter is a moment of literary reflection on Erich Maria Remarque's part as Bäumer watches the soldier die slowly – ' I have killed Gerald Duvall the printer' – for Spielberg the giving up of life for one person is the possibility of continuing life, no matter how briefly, for another. This, however, does not mean that Spielberg is at all interested in the experience of the Wehrmacht soldiers; surprisingly all they offer to both combat sequences is their bodies. And this is what makes the final combat sequence and the wider ambitions of the film perplexing. There is an American patriotism that underscores the narrative, which is a reflection of what I mean by the film not living up to its demands of being about the experience *of* war. Because, if Spielberg was really serious about destabilising the expectations of the classic realist text – that is, within the ideological bounds of Hollywood cinema – he would have filmed some of the combat sequences from the position of the German soldiers. But this would have divided the sympathies of his US audience, even if it would have reinforced the powerful dementia of the combat scenes. In this respect, Spielberg has almost made a great war film, but his populist instinct always outstrips his better judgement.

---

[9] Sartre 1950, p. 225.

Which is to say that he cannot completely accept the denaturalising force of the violence he depicts. Hence the abreactive power of the combat scenes is almost wholly destroyed by the jump-cut to the Stars and Stripes at the end and the ridiculous morphing of the face of Private Ryan into himself as an old man at the grave of Captain Miller in Normandy. Nevertheless, Spielberg has made a film about combat in a world where the realities of such things are not said to happen, or not said to happen with the ferocity that Spielberg shows. And, in this, I detect one of the better impulses at work in Spielberg's realism: in a US film industry where violence is spectacularly brutal and ethically impoverished at the same time, and in a culture where the concept of the 'electronic battlefield' is practically state policy, Spielberg's combination of a Jüngerian dementia of battle with the point of view of the front-line soldier is genuinely harrowing, and not just simply shocking. Accordingly, I detect an historical consciousness in this dementia that does not so much excuse his sentimental lapses, but allows us to understand their structural origins.

Spielberg is a film-maker who chooses his subjects as a means of bearing historical witness. As such, *Saving Private Ryan*'s re-enactment of trauma cannot be divorced from what I take to be Spielberg's commitment to a popular collective memory of war. In key respects, many of the artistic achievements of the post-war American film industry have been based on the reconstruction and mobilisation of this collective memory: Fuller, Huston, Scorsese, Stone. Indeed, as a theatre of inter- and intra-class and racial conflict within the theatre of war itself, the war-movie has been one of the few significant public sites where the big themes of politics and state, identity and commitment could be dramatised in vivid, critical ways. Hence the social importance of the genre, particularly the Vietnam war film. However, it is has been received opinion in Hollywood in the 1990s that the conventional combat movie is dead, or at least dying. There are a number of persuasive reasons given for this, from the renewed confidence of American foreign policy after the collapse of Soviet communism as 'post-ideological', leaving the 'bad memory' of Vietnam behind, to the fact that the best of 1970s film directors have themselves now worked through the trauma of their generation's experience of the war, and as such, the Vietnam war film has become an historical artefact.

But perhaps a more convincing reason is the impact of the new conditions of computerised or electronic warfare on the narration of warfare itself. In this respect Hollywood seems to have taken Paul Virilio's *War and Cinema* to their hearts. Virilio's well-known thesis is that the new technologies have not only pushed the soldier 'off' the battle field, but transformed military offensive and tactics into a virtual spectacle of pin-point reconnaissance and bombing. For Virilians, the Gulf War remains the exemplary 'electronic' military confrontation, in that the victory of the US was won through superior technological penetration of Iraq's defences and not through the weight of superior forces in combat on the ground. In the 1990s this 'smart weaponry' has had a widespread impact on the representation of military conflict and violence and in popular film, reproducing at the level of the film's narration the subordination of the modern soldier to the invisible power of modern weaponry, the power of modern weaponry to seek and destroy at vast distances separate from the observation of those who operated the technology. This outcome, of course, is not peculiar to computerised weapon systems, but a tendency which has been in place since the large-scale industrialisation of war during World War I: the gradual separation of large-scale combat from planning decisions taken on the basis of a chain of command's close observation of a target. And this is why Jünger's early writing has found a new academic audience, for in his fictional writings about World War I and in his collaborative photo-text archives of 'technological catastrophes' he was one of the few writers on the industrialisation of war to note the structural link within capitalism between the development of technologies of representation and the increasing efficiency of weapon systems. This elision between technology and the body of the (US) soldier has become a functional feature of the new generation of futurist and science fiction films, in which the destructive power of computerised weapons systems outruns the actual need for standing armies and conventional combat skills. Although these conflagratory spectacles are set in highly technologically advanced futures, the implication is that the military body as a mere appendage of technology determines the strategies of the modern battlefield here and now. At the point, therefore, where this elision of the military body and technology has overtaken the content of much popular film and academic discourse on popular culture, Spielberg produces a film which both takes on the industrialisation of war and yet moves ethically away from its contemporary symbolisations. Indeed, Spielberg's return to the World War II combat movie produces an interesting ideological rupture both within the recent narration of the computerisation of warfare on screen and within the conventions of the classic realist war film.

For, if *Saving Private Ryan* is a film which sets out to represent the effects of the industrialisation of warfare on bodies in the wake of the vast technological extension of conventional warfare, it also bears traditional witness to the experience of the combat soldier who defies death and the battlefield through luck and bravery. Hence it can be argued that the unwillingness or inability of Spielberg to follow through the implications of his Jüngerian depiction of combat, is not so much a sentimental failing, but a structural consequence of a deeper commitment to the humanism of the traditional anti-war movie. That is, what defines the 'progressiveness' of the classic realism of the anti-war film is, in fact, ultimately the *separation or distance* between the soldier's body and an alien technology.[10] The soldier-hero/anti-hero *survives* the

---

[10] For a discussion of this separation, see Hüppauf 1993.

derealisation and trauma of combat. And this is why there tends to be an absence of the gruesome head-wound in the genre. Because it is the expressive singularity of the undamaged face which not only secures the emotional identification with suffering on the part of the spectator, but represents the survival of humanity in the face of its destruction. Consequently, Spielberg's representation of combat could be said to have incorporated the technological abstraction of modern warfare into the traditional war-movie genre, at a time when such abstraction has defined itself outside of the genre, but also at a point when the conventions of the traditional World War II war film have themselves run out of ideological steam. Hence *Saving Private Ryan*'s narrative raggedness and the final return to Ryan's emotive (undamaged) face. Yet this heterodox quality is where a critical commitment to a popular collective memory of war is to be found. For the recourse to images of close combat sends an unambiguous message to those who confuse the partial and treacherous computerisation of the battlefield with the smooth and spectacular computerisation of warfare in the contemporary futurist film. In *Saving Private Ryan* there is a direct confrontation with these idealist mediations. In this it certainly teaches a younger audience, who have not grown up with a tradition of anti-war combat films — for all these films' own idealisations — that violence on screen can also carry the obligations of historical consciousness.

References

Andersen, Kurt 1998, 'The Tom Hanks Phenomenon', *New Yorker*, December: 7–14.

Bucholtz, Ferdinand and Jünger, Ernst 1931, *Der gefährliche Augenblick: Eine Sammlung von Bildern und Berichten*, Berlin: Junker and Dunhaupt

Friedrich, Ernst 1980 [1924], *Krieg dem Kriege* , Frankfurt am Main: Zweitausendeins.

Hüppauf, Bernd 1993, 'Experiences of Modern Warfare and the Crisis of Representation', *New German Critique*, 59: 41–76.

Jünger, Ernst 1994 [1931], 'On Danger' , in *The Weimar Republic Sourcebook*, edited by Anton Kaes, Martin Jay, and Eduard Dimendberg, Berkeley: University of California.

Lovell, Terry 1980, *Pictures of Reality: Aesthetics Politics and Pleasure*, London: British Film Institute.

MacCabe, Colin 1974, 'Realism and the Cinema: Notes on Some Brechtian Theses', *Screen* 15, 2: 7–27.

Matlin, David 1997, *Vernooykill Creek: The Crisis of Prisons in America*, San Diego: San Diego State University Press.

Rogin, Michael 1998, 'Spielberg's List', *New Left Review*, 230: 153–60.

Sartre, Jean-Paul 1963, *Iron in the Soul*, London: Penguin.

Wall, Jeff 1993, *Tote Soldaten Sprechen/Dead Troops Talk*, Luzern: Kunstmuseum.

Virilio, Paul 1989, *War and Cinema*, London: Verso.

Williams, Raymond 1979, *Politics and Letters: Interviews with* New Left Review, London: New Left Books.

The Incomplete Marx
Felton Shortall
Aldershot: Avebury, 1994

Reviewed by Michael A. Lebowitz

The Missing Thread

Who could deny that an essential part of Marx is missing from *Capital*? Woven into his work from the time of his earliest writings is the red thread of the self-development of the working class through its struggles. Marx's argument in 1850 that workers would have to go through as many as 50 years of 'civil wars and national struggles not only to bring about a change in society but also to change yourselves'[1] – just as his statement a few years earlier that the process of revolutionary activity was the only way the working class could 'succeed in ridding itself of the muck of ages and become fitted to found society anew'[2] – reflected his conception of 'revolutionary practice': 'the coincidence of the changing of circumstances and of human activity or self-change'.[3]

As Marx was well aware, this focus upon the development of human beings through their activities was the rational core of Hegel's concept of the self-development of the Idea/Spirit, which develops and increasingly realises its nature through the creative destruction of all its successive forms of existence. Hegel's 'outstanding achievement', Marx wrote in 1844, is that he 'conceives the self-creation of man as a process', that he grasps human beings 'as the outcome of man's *own labour*' – although, to be sure, 'the only labour Hegel knows and recognises is *abstractly mental* labour'.[4] In the fluid idealism of Hegel, Marx uncovered the centrality of human activity and practice for human development that was missing from the materialism of his predecessors.[5]

Nor was this critical emphasis upon practice abandoned after some variety of epistemological break marking the chronological separation of teleological humanist from sober scientist. In the labour process, Marx noted in *Capital*, the worker 'acts upon external nature and changes it, and in this way he simultaneously changes his own nature'.[6] This concept of joint products (the changing of circumstances and self-change) was also present in the *Grundrisse* where Marx proposed that in the process of production 'the producers change, too, in that they bring out new qualities in themselves, develop themselves in production,

---

[1] Marx 1979, p. 403.
[2] Marx and Engels 1976, pp. 52-3.
[3] Marx 1976, p. 4.
[4] Marx 1975, pp. 332-3.
[5] Marx 1976, p. 3.
[6] Marx 1977, p. 283.

transform themselves, develop new powers and ideas, new modes of intercourse, new needs and new language'.[7] In all this, too, there remains a clear conception of development; describing the process of co-operation in production, Marx commented: 'When the worker co-operates in a planned way with others, he strips off the fetters of his individuality, and develops the capabilities of his species.'[8]

Self-development, however, for Marx always involved more than just the process of material production. Critically, it also meant development of socialist human beings through collective struggle. Following the defeat of the Paris Commune, he again stressed that to reach their goal of a new society workers must 'pass through long struggles, through a series of historic processes, transforming circumstances and men'. As he had argued in 1853 and 1865, in the absence of struggles against capital, though, the nature of the human beings produced would be predictable: workers would become 'apathetic, thoughtless, more or less well-fed instruments of production' and be 'degraded to one level mass of broken wretches past salvation'.[9] Effectively, they would be merely the products of capital and, as such, conditions of existence of capital reproduced by capital itself: 'In the ordinary run of things, the worker can be left to the 'natural laws of production', ie. it is possible to rely on his dependence on capital, which springs from the conditions of production themselves, and is guaranteed in perpetuity by them'.[10]

In struggling against capital, however, workers produce themselves differently – here, too, just as in the production process, they transform themselves. By co-operating with others in a planned way in the struggle against capital, the workers 'develop [...] the capabilities of [the] species'. Ridding themselves in this way of 'the muck of ages', in short, they produce themselves no longer as results of capital but as presuppositions of a new society.

Yet, whether this focus on the worker as subject and result is called revolutionary practice, 'self-valorization',[11] or, as Felton Shortall proposes in *The Incomplete Marx*, 'the dialectic of human praxis' (p. 119), it is certain that there are only glimpses of this theme in *Capital*. Rather, Shortall argues that the worker appears there as 'mere *object*, ... a *passive* object ... A *mere object of exploitation*' (p. 256). What Marx presents in *Capital* is the 'dialectic of capital', 'the self-development of capital' – ie., the 'objective and positive logic of capital', which proceeds from the perspective of capital; indeed, he notes, 'this *critical perspective of the bourgeoisie* ... reduces the working class to mere object of exploitation' (pp. 120-2). Thus, the dialectic of human praxis, 'the ontological basis for the entire Marxian project' (p. 261), is buried by an emphasis on the objectivist logic of the dialectic of capital (pp. 262-3); in the same way, 'the counter-dialectic of class struggle ... is so

---

[7] Marx 1973, p. 494.
[8] Marx 1977, p. 447.
[9] Lebowitz 1992, pp. 143–4.
[10] Marx 1977, p. 899.
[11] Negri 1991.

evidently suppressed in the exposition of the objective laws of the dialectic of capital that is pursued in the three volumes of *Capital*' (p. 195).

This argument about what is missing in *Capital* is, of course, not unique. Rather, it adds to a growing body of work which challenges the exclusive preoccupation with *Capital* of so many academic Marxists. E.P. Thompson's conclusion that '*Capital* is a study in the logic of capital not of capitalism' and that class struggle stands outside its 'closed system of economic logic';[12] Antonio Negri's assertion that *Capital* 'annihilate[s] subjectivity in objectivity [and] ... subject[s] the subversive capacity of the proletariat to the reorganizing and repressive intelligence of capitalist power';[13] and this writer's argument that presentation of the worker as object for capital but not as subject for herself in *Capital* both yields a one-sided understanding of capitalism and also obscures Marx's own political economy of the working class[14] – all (along with Shortall) stress the distinction between capital and capitalism, insisting that *Capital* leaves out an essential aspect of the latter: class struggle from the side of workers.[15]

But, why and how did this happen? While there are interesting overlaps, the explanations offered differ. For Thompson, the problem is that, in setting out to criticise political economy, Marx became trapped within its premises and proceeded to reproduce its system of closure which excludes human experience.[16] Negri, on the other hand, finds in the *Grundrisse* signs of Marx's larger project which reveal *Capital* as only a fragment of the analysis and, in particular, identifies Marx's intended book on wage-labour as the site of the missing focus on the subjectivity of the worker and class struggle. Also stressing that missing book on wage-labour, and attempting to demonstrate how it would have completed the inner totality of capitalism and redressed the one-sidedness in *Capital*, I have proposed that *Capital* (and, particularly, its first volume) took precedence for Marx because of the critical need to demystify the nature of capital for workers.[17] While elements of all these propositions reappear in Shortall's explanation, *The Incomplete Marx* also introduces new suggestions which deserve close examination because they both support and raise questions about previous arguments.

The necessity of closure

Tracing the changing themes of Marx's project from his earliest writings through the three volumes of *Capital*, Shortall declares that

---

[12] Thompson 1978, 65.
[13] Negri 1991, pp. 18–19.
[14] Lebowitz 1992.
[15] Cf. Colin Barker's discussion of this problem and some of its implications in Barker 1997.
[16] Thompson 1978, pp. 59-60.
[17] Lebowitz 1992, and 1997.

Marx moved from a Young Hegelian thematic of human liberation and ending human alienation, to one of 'capitalism and its overthrow', and from there to one of the 'dialectic of capital and the counter-dialectic of class struggle'. In this account, the first of these shifts is relatively unproblematic: Shortall proposes that, having developed his materialist conception of history, Marx 'preserved and superseded' the Young Hegelian thematic by grasping that revolution by workers against capitalism was a necessary condition for human liberation (p. 31). The second shift, however, is somewhat more problematic. Although Shortall indicates that in the *Grundrisse* 'the Young Hegelian thematic of human alienation and human liberation is not only superseded but preserved within Marx's critique of political economy' (p. 74), it is noteworthy that the political economy which Marx had earlier dismissed as one-sided, considering workers only as working animals, apparently reappears to play an important role in the change of Marx's project into something one-sided, too.

This sets the context for much of *The Incomplete Marx*. The principal problems Shortall sets out to understand are, (i) why Marx substituted for a focus on capitalism and its overthrow 'the dialectic of capital and the counter-dialectic of class struggle'; (ii) why, having proceeded to this point, Marx then stopped his analysis with the 'dialectic of capital' – ie., why there is an apparent closure, why he did not go on to analyse the 'counter-dialectic of class struggle'; and (iii) how precisely this closure was enacted in the *Grundrisse* and the three volumes of *Capital*.

With respect to the first of these issues, Shortall proposes that the critique of political economy became an intellectual necessity as part of Marx's new thematic of capitalism and its overthrow (p. 80) – that, it became, indeed, its *'necessary first moment'*. If Marx was to 'understand how it [capitalism] could be overthrown, he first had to understand how it persisted' (p. 115). Thus, he had to uncover the inner laws of movement of capitalism, the logic of capital, the dialectic of capital (p. 116):

> He had to first of all understand what capitalism *is* and how it perpetuates itself ... The analysis of the dialectic of capital – the objective and positive logic of capital – had therefore to be the *first moment* within his thematic. (pp. 120-1)

Accordingly, Shortall suggests that Marx embarks upon his critique of political economy as the condition of understanding 'the essence of capitalist society'. Why? Because political economy presents the positive laws of capitalism – even though it is from the perspective of the capitalist: 'Marx has to take up, albeit critically, the *perspective of the bourgeoisie*' (p. 122).

The same theoretical imperative that impelled Marx to take up the critique of political economy, Shortall further argues, also would require him to make a provisional closure:

He has to establish the objective laws of capitalist production independently and in abstraction from its subjective determinations. It is in this way that he comes to provisionally assert the dialectic of capital over the counter-dialectic of class struggle as a logical necessity. (p. 263)

In short, adopting the problematic of political economy meant that 'the counter-dialectic of class struggle and the class subjectivity of the proletariat had to be closed off' (p. 130). Shortall's main theme (as will be seen below, there are other explanations he offers), thus, is that the 'counter-dialectic of class struggle' – which delimits the functioning of the dialectic of capital by the manner in which 'the workers in their everyday struggles impose limits on the operation of capital' (p. 129) – disappears from *Capital* as a logical necessity.

Closure as contingent?

Yet, in addition to the argument stressing the logical imperative for Marx as scientist, another image lurks here as well – Marx as socialist actor. Marx, Shortall offers, embarked upon the close study of political economy in order to make his work more scientific than that of competitors in the early socialist and workers' movement. To combat 'the voluntarism of his socialist rivals', Shortall proposes, Marx was 'forced to stress the need for a "scientific" and objective basis for socialist theory and practice' (p. 133). Indeed, Shortall argues that the 'struggle against Proudhonian socialism' became 'the driving imperative of Marx's theoretical efforts'; and 'this proved to be an important catalyst in the development of Marx's theoretical project towards a critique of political economy' (p. 38).

Nor was this true only at the time of writing *The Poverty of Philosophy*, Marx's specific assault on Proudhon; Marx continued to combat the influence of Proudhon and similar theorists among workers at the time of the First International. What drove Marx was 'the political imperative that arose with his confrontation with Proudhon and the artisanal socialism of the mid-nineteenth century workers' movement' (p. 80). It became necessary to provide a solid foundation for his argument: 'Against the voluntarism and utopianism of Proudhon, Marx had to above all stress the historical and economic necessity of the development of capitalism and its contradictions' (p. 44).

Of course, there is no necessary conflict between the picture of Marx as scientist and that of Marx as socialist actor. Yet, distinguishing between the two can be important. Whereas the former stresses what is immanent in the body of Marx's work, the latter situates Marx very clearly in time and space. The distinction takes on importance when we consider Shortall's explanation as to why a closure emerged in Marx's work – why the 'counter-dialectic of class struggle', which delimits the functioning of the dialectic of capital by the manner in which 'the workers in their everyday struggles impose limits on the operation of capital' (p. 129), disappears from *Capital*.

Once Shortall situates Marx as a socialist actor, rather than focusing on logical and theoretical necessities, the explanation of closure becomes Marx's own *inability* to go further – ie., the extent to which 'Marx's theoretical efforts were delimited by the limitations of his own epoch' (p. 2). One such limitation was that 'in the absence of a revolutionary situation Marx had to fight on the terrain of the bourgeoisie' – a terrain 'dominated by positivism and scientism' and 'accepted to a large extent even by the most militant members of the working class' (pp. 75-6). Thus, that *Capital* was 'a text of economic laws in which the questions of class subjectivity and human alienation become suppressed', Shortall argues, 'was a concession to his readership, that was in awe of the advance of the natural and positivistic sciences' (p. 75). Yet, Shortall hints there is somewhat more to this when he notes that this ideological hegemony was accepted to a large extent by militant workers 'and perhaps to a lesser extent by Marx and Engels themselves' (p. 76).

This is not the only suggestion of a shortcoming in Marx's own thought. Shortall contrasts to Marx the position of Proudhon and Bakunin, who 'clearly recognized money and the state authority as the hostile will of the bourgeoisie and as a consequence ... resolutely set themselves against them.' Marx's failure to grasp what the anarchists did, however, 'opened the door to Marx's authoritarian statism, and subsequently to Marxism's commitment to state socialism' (p. 164). Shortall praises in this respect Bakunin, whose 'more immediate and imminent perspective of class antagonism places him in a far more perceptive position than that of the more sophisticated and "scientific" Marx of *Capital*' (p. 164).

For the most part, though, it is the weakness of the revolutionary workers' movement itself that produces the limit in Marx's thought. Shortall cites approvingly Debord's comment that:

> The weakness of Marx's theory is naturally the weakness of
> the revolutionary struggle of the proletariat of his time ... The
> fact that Marx was reduced to defending and clarifying it
> [revolutionary theory] with cloistered, scholarly work, in the
> British Museum, caused a loss in the theory itself. (p. 2)

The situation, Shortall proposes, is that the existence of only an 'embryonic workers' movement' (p. 80), the fact that the proletariat had not yet emerged fully as a class directly opposed to capital (p. 136), meant that 'while Marx could see the full development of the *dialectic of capital* he could not see the development of the *counter-dialectic of class struggle*' (p. 146). He understood tendencies in relation to the side of workers which were emerging but 'the embryonic state of such tendencies restricted his analysis of them and could therefore remain only implicit within his theory' (p. 136). Marx, in short, did not explore the way in which workers through their struggles place limits on capital simply because he was not *able* to go further: 'The historical context within which Marx lived and wrote, therefore, restricted his ability to make the great reversal within his broad thematic, from the dialectic of capital to the counter-dialectic of class struggle' (p. 140).

Although Marx himself was among the first to recognise the effects of historical change upon the development of theory, Shortall's comments about how the immaturity of the workers' movement limited Marx's theory simply do not stand up. Rather, for example, than it being 'too remote and speculative' (p. 139) for Marx to discuss the possibility of rising real wages in 1865, Shortall's musings on this matter ignore not only the rising real wages of the period but also Marx's own explanation as to why he was assuming them fixed until the book on wage-labour, as well as the places in *Capital* and other writings where he addressed these very questions.[18] Much, indeed, of Shortall's discussion of Marx's limits is gratuitous and a digression from the main thrust of his argument. Certainly, the unsupported charge about 'Marx's authoritarian statism' will appear quite strange to anyone familiar with Marx's writings on the French state, in particular, his *The Civil War in France* (or his notes on Bakunin). If Marx did not go beyond 'the dialectic of capital', it was not because the limitations of the epoch prevented it – as his writings other than *Capital* testify.

The dialectic of *Capital*

So, let us return to Shortall's main theme – the logical necessity for (provisional) closure. Where and how did Marx enact this closure in *Capital*? It all begins, apparently, with the starting point – the commodity. Whereas Marx's *Grundrisse* discussion starts with money (Negri's preferred point of departure), Shortall proposes that, in opening with the commodity-object, *Capital* proceeds from the result of capitalist production – a result which testifies to the subordination of the will of the worker who produced the commodity and to the triumph of the capitalist's will as owner (pp. 165-6). 'By starting with the commodity, Marx comes to close off the question of the subjective, and with this the counter-dialectic of class struggle' (p. 199). Once, too, labour-power is purchased as a commodity and subsumed as variable capital, 'a mere quantitative and objective element of productive capital', another critical step has been taken in the presentation of worker as object: 'right from the start of Marx's theory of surplus-value, we can see how Marx closes off the subjective by emphasizing the objective and reified relations of the capitalist production process' (p. 253).

---

[18] See Lebowitz 1992.

Shortall returns to this theme of the worker as object on a number of occasions in his discussion of Volume I, noting, for example., how in capitalist production the act of labour is not the means by which the worker realises herself 'but is rather the means through which capital comes to realize itself as such' (p. 281), how 'with the completion of the process of production, the worker and her living labour appear as merely a *vanishing moment* in the movement of capital's self-expansion' (p. 293), and how in the theory of accumulation the working class is 'mere object regulated by the rhythms of the objective laws of the dialectic of capital' (p. 261). He brings out well how Volume I – in direct contrast to Marx's discussion in the *Grundrisse* and the 'missing sixth chapter' where 'the subjective conditions of the worker are far more to the fore' (p. 299) – suppresses the standpoint of the worker in order to trace the logic of capital. In this respect, he makes a valuable addition to the literature on the one-sidedness of *Capital*.

Yet, it comes as a bit of a surprise that the bulk of Shortall's extended discussion of the three volumes of *Capital* focuses *not on the missing side of workers* but, rather, on a *different* closure – the suppression of crisis in *Capital*. For Shortall, this is not a digression because these closures are not separate: 'the closure of rupture and crisis is intrinsically linked to the closure of the counter-dialectic of class struggle as two aspects of a *two-fold* closure' (p. 346). The precise connection between the two, however, cannot be grasped fully without probing this concept of the dialectic of capital.

In *The Dialectic of Capital* (1985), Tom Sekine argued that the dialectic of capital (which his mentor Kozo Uno designated as the 'theory of a purely capitalist society') 'forms a self-contained theoretical system'.[19] It 'envisions a purely capitalist society in which the reification of social relations is supposed to be complete' and which is 'mentally constructed just as Hegel's metaphysical system is'.[20] And, although '*Capital* falls short of presenting a pure dialectic of capital' because it discusses 'both the inner logic of capitalism and its historically particular manifestations as if they were the same thing',[21] it contains within it the 'objective knowledge of capitalist society which Marx discovered in essence'.[22]

Thus, for Sekine (and the Uno School of Marxism), the point of the dialectic of capital is to distinguish between what is logical to capitalism and what is merely contingent. A clear conception of pure capitalism, Sekine argued, is the necessary first step before any concrete analysis:

---

[19] Sekine 1984, 15. Shortall (p. 468) dates Sekine's *The Dialectic of Capital: A Study of the Inner Logic of Capital* as 1985 and credits it for the attempt 'to relate the structure of Marx's critique of political economy to the logic of Hegel' but makes no other reference to the work – none, at least, that could be found in a book without an index. A briefer and more accessible account of this theory may be found in Sekine's 'An Essay on Uno's Dialectic of Capital' in the appendix to Uno (1980).
[20] Sekine 1984, p. 39.
[21] Sekine 1984, p. 17.
[22] Sekine 1984, p. 18.

'it is both futile and foolhardy to discuss such questions as class struggle and socialism without a prior grasp of what capitalism is all about'.[23] Accordingly, the dialectic of capital is intended to provide the logical exposition of capitalism: 'The purpose of the dialectic of capital is to demonstrate the logical possibility of capitalism once its historical existence is presupposed ...'[24]

Although Shortall does not follow the details of Sekine's construction, he accepts fully its general theme that Marx's main concern in *Capital* was to establish 'the ontological basis for capital' (p. 244). Shortall asks, *'what makes the capitalist economy possible'* (p. 202)? To explore this question and to set out the dialectic of capital, he proposes, Marx necessarily put to the side (as premature) all those elements which negate the possibility of capitalism – even though the negation, *'the impossibility of capitalism'*, repeatedly emerges (p. 249). Thus, for Shortall, capitalism contains within in it both possibility and non-possibility, both positive and negative; the one-sidedness of *Capital*, then, is not simply that it excludes the side of workers as the negation of capital but, rather, that its presentation of capital as a self-contained, self-reproducing system marginalises *any* elements which suggest the non-reproduction of capital. Accordingly, Marx's suppression of crisis and rupture emerges as equivalent to the eclipse of the 'counter-dialectic of class struggle' as the result of Shortall's conception of the dialectic of capital as 'the objective and positive logic of capital' (p. 121).

Thus, Shortall proceeds to trace this second closure. While the possibility of 'rupture and crisis' in the circulation of capital surfaces first with the discussion of money as mediator in C-M-C, it is closed off as Marx chooses instead to emphasise the 'unity of opposition' (p. 235). At every step, Shortall proposes, we see Marx stress the unity of commodity and money over their *'opposition and separation*, and the consequent *question of crisis'* (p. 244) – all in order to develop logically the nature of capital. This closure is especially marked throughout Volume II where Marx constantly must defer discussion of rupture and crisis – even though by Part III 'it reaches the point of insurrection [and] ... threatens to break out and disrupt the very line of development of Marx's exposition' (p. 307). Indeed, by the time we see the 'very precariousness of the conditions of social capital's reproduction' in Marx's reproduction schemes, it appears that 'in delineating the *possibility* of the overall circulation of social capital Marx comes to posit its very *impossibility'* (p. 345). And, the 'imminence of crisis and rupture' surfaces 'more and more violently' in Volume III (p. 346, p. 349), where the provisional closure that Marx has imposed in order to stress the unity of capital 'becomes exhausted'.

Here again, in Volumes II and III, the point of suppressing crisis and rupture is to permit Marx to reveal the dialectic of capital, 'the

---

[23] Sekine 1984, p. 87.
[24] Sekine 1984, p. 270.

objective and positive logic of capital'. Shortall notes the manner in which different aspects of capital emerge in these volumes: whereas Volume II explores the particular forms that capital takes in its circuit and ends by exploring the unity of capital-in-production and capital-in-circulation, the theme he identifies as especially important in Volume III is its focus upon individual capitals in competition and the manner in which they execute the inner laws of capital in general. The significance Shortall attaches to this particular odyssey of capital becomes clear when we situate properly the concept of the dialectic of capital.

As developed within the perspective of Sekine and the Uno School, the dialectic of capital treats capitalism as an eternal, self-contained and reproducing totality which is the counterpart of Hegel's dialectic of the Absolute. The dialectic of capital, indeed, is the dialectic of the Absolute [God], tracing out the same logical structure.[25] 'The exact correspondence between the dialectic of capital and Hegel's *Logic* can scarcely be doubted'.[26] Just as Hegel's discussion in the Book of the Notion in his *Logic* 'copies the self-revealing wisdom of the Absolute', so also does the dialectic of capital reveal the subject-object identity in capital as it 'follows the self-synthesising logic of capital'.[27] 'There is clearly no escape,' Sekine announced, 'from the conclusion that what Hegel believed was the Absolute was in fact capital in disguise'.[28]

Much the same picture can be found in Shortall's development of the concept of the dialectic of capital. Here, too, capital 'emerges as the identity of both subject and object' and as a historically specific, self-reproducing totality (p. 455, p. 463). As with Sekine, Shortall draws a direct link between Hegel's *Logic* and *Capital*, attempting to show that the steps in the *Logic* have their counterpart in *Capital*. Thus, he ends his discussion of *Capital* with a comparison of its structure of closure to that in Hegel's *Logic*, arguing (pp. 445–55) that the three volumes of *Capital* correspond to the three moments of the doctrine of the Notion in Hegel's *Logic* (universal, particular and singular).

This brings us, then, to the final closure in *Capital*. Just as 'Hegel argues that out of the conflicting designs of human beings the Cunning of Reason comes to reveal the absolute knowledge of God' (p. 459), so also does Marx in Volume III demonstrate how individual capitals in competition are compelled to act as 'capital-in-general' – thereby revealing how capital is 'constituted as a self-reproducing whole out of its dissociated parts'. Marx now has taken his exposition as far as it can go:

> Marx brings his dialectic of capital to a close. It therefore
> appears as the mere materialist inversion of Hegel's dialectic

---

[25] Sekine 1984, p. 35, p. 51, pp. 56–7.
[26] Uno 1980, p. 150.
[27] Sekine 1984, p. 56.
[28] Sekine 1985 proposes that 'sometimes the correspondence is so close that ... it is as if Hegel already had a complete knowledge of the dialectic of capital ...' (p. 51).

> – and this is reflected in the structure of *Capital*. A dialectical
> process that finally finds itself at rest with its ultimate, and
> ever reoccurring, identity in difference. (pp. 465–6).

We know capital, thus, through its works – a general equilibrium system in which the goal of capital is realised through the subjective self-seeking of individual capitals. With the revelation of an Invisible Hand, the logic of capital comes to an end. And, in this world that capital makes, there is no place for the negative – neither the struggles of workers (and their effects upon both circumstances and themselves) nor ruptures and crises. Unlike Sekine, however, as a critic of closure, Shortall does not consider this vision to be an adequate description of capitalism. Nevertheless, he *does* believe that this is *Capital* – ie., that the dialectic of capital is an accurate representation of the main theme of Marx's *Capital*. In this sense, Shortall ultimately explains closure as the result of Marx becoming trapped within Hegel's *Logic*.

Shortall's closure

Where, indeed, could Marx go from this point? And how? Having pursued the dialectic of capital to its end, Shortall proposes that the only way out for Marx now was to reverse himself. If the whole problem begins with the commodity as starting point and with the suppression of the possibility of rupture in simple commodity exchange, then to go beyond the dialectic of capital 'would have required Marx to have retraced his steps right back to the commodity-form in order to now stress *difference and divergence* rather than the *unity* of capital' (p. 430). To go beyond *Capital* 'to consider the incoherence of capital, its crisis and rupture', he argues, points to the need for a reversal – 'a reversal that repeatedly, and ever more incessantly, demands to be made within the text of *Capital*. But it is a reversal that Marx never made' (pp. 483-4).

Nor could he do so, Shortall argues. Discussing the conclusion of Volume III and the possibility of reopening the closure, he explains:

> Such a task was a formidable one, far greater than simply
> completing a chapter as such; it was a task that was clearly
> too great for the ailing Marx. Thus we find *Capital* inscribing
> a two-fold closure within Marx's thematic of capitalism and
> its overthrow. (p. 431)

The task does seem formidable. But, given that Shortall raises this in the context of the incomplete chapter on class in Volume III – material drafted almost two decades before Marx's death, the matter of Marx's health is somewhat besides the point. Rather, the problem is that, having argued that Marx suppressed critical elements in order to follow the dialectic of capital, Shortall appears to offer no clear guidance as to the way beyond – other than the need to go right back to the starting point. 'The tangential moments of *Capital*', he advises, 'must be bent back together to form a new presentation' (p. 467). How that is to be done – ie., how those elements of 'the counter-dialectic of class struggle' and crisis are to be developed, however, remains a mystery. And, an important part of the reason is that, in structuring his argument around this concept of the dialectic of capital, Shortall himself has become trapped.

All Shortall's judgements begin from the premise that Marx's project in *Capital* is to demonstrate, through his dialectic of capital, that capital constitutes itself as 'a self-reproducing whole' – ie., a system which produces all its own premises. This again is precisely the argument that E.P. Thompson made – that Marx introduces an organic system, a system of 'closure', in *Capital*, where all is subsumed within the circuits of capital.[29] Yet, as I have argued in *Beyond Capital*, there is no organic system presented in *Capital*; rather, the side of wage-labour must be elaborated in order to establish adequate conditions for a reproducing whole.[30]

This was *always* Marx's understanding. It certainly can be seen in his earliest writings, when he criticised political economy for its one-sidedness in considering the worker only as an object for capital and where he declared that capital and wage-labour were antitheses and constitute a whole.[31] Yet, it also is apparent in his *Grundrisse* projections when he indicated that the book on wage-labour would complete 'the inner totality' and that this was to be followed by 'the concentration of bourgeois society in the form of the state', the 'concentration of the whole' in the book on the state.[32]

Precisely because the book on *Capital* was not about capitalism as a whole, the whole question of movements in the level of workers' needs, Marx noted in his *Economic Manuscript of 1861–63*, does 'not belong here, where the general capital-relation is to be developed, but in the doctrine of the wages of labour'. In order to understand the nature of capital, 'the only thing of importance is that it [the level of workers' needs] be viewed as given, determinate'.[33] And, this is why *Capital* assumes the standard of necessity to be given, an assumption designated for removal in the book on wage-labour, a book that Marx still made reference to in *Capital*;[34] it allows Marx to demonstrate that capital is the result of exploitation.

Yet, as Marx knew perfectly well, that standard of necessity is not given; rather, like the length and intensity of the working day, it is determined by two-sided class struggle, where, contrary to the efforts of

---

[29] Thompson 1978, p. 163, p. 167.
[30] Lebowitz 1992.
[31] Cf. Lebowitz 1992, p. 9, p. 60.
[32] Marx 1973, p. 264, p. 227, p. 108.
[33] Marx 1988, pp. 44-5.
[34] Marx 1977, p. 683.

the capitalist, the worker 'constantly presses in the opposite direction [and] the matter resolves itself into a question of the respective powers of the combatants'.[35] Class struggle on the part of workers, in short, is required to determine an essential premise for capital. There cannot be a self-reproducing totality in *Capital* because the necessary presuppositions for capital are not all results of it itself but, rather, depend on something outside of capital as such.[36]

Shortall, through his embrace of the dialectic of capital, has himself imposed a closure upon *Capital*. Although he understands that there is something outside of *Capital* that is critical (which he assigns to the unexplained 'counter-dialectic of class struggle') and that the categories of that book by itself are one-sided, his acceptance of the concept of the dialectic of capital prevents him from seeing the opening contained in *Capital*. As a result, the way to incorporate the other side, the side of wage-labour, in a logical extension (rather than a reversal) of the argument in *Capital* is also obscured for him.[37]

However, it is not simply through its assumption of a self-contained, self-reproducing totality that the dialectic of capital leads Shortall into an impasse.[38] Given his argument that Marx must suppress the question of rupture in order to trace out the 'objective and positive logic of capital', crisis and rupture become the subject for much of his discussion of *Capital*. The question of crisis not only 'repeatedly serves to drive Marx's exposition forward' (p. 244) but it also 'reaches the point of insurrection' (p. 307). While there are definite insights (such as the link to the distortion of Marx's value theory) as the result of this focus on the suppression of rupture, the dialectic of capital deflects attention from the worker as subject in order to stress this second closure.

Can a closure with respect to rupture and crisis, however, compare in significance to that enacted in *Capital* with respect to the side of workers? Indeed, the place of crisis in Marx's theory is far more complex (as Shortall recognises) than merely a challenge to the possibility of capitalism: 'Crisis emerged from the very conditions that ensure the coherence of capitalism just as subsequently the coherence of capitalism is re-imposed by means of crisis' (pp. 481-2). Despite his acknowledgement of the corrective aspect of crisis, Shortall proposes that, in addition to their common characteristic as threats to the

---

[35] Marx 1985, p. 146.
[36] Lebowitz 1992.
[37] See the discussion in Lebowitz 1992, which is extended further to explore the capitalist state in Lebowitz 1995.
[38] It should be noted also that this so-called dialectic of capital, with its intimations of eternity, is an integral element in a perspective which explicitly rejects the materialist conception of history (Sekine 1984, pp. 12-15, pp. 72-86). Pursuing the 'objective and positive logic' of capital, it differs substantially from Marx's (1977, p. 103) own concept of dialectics, which itself 'includes in its positive understanding of what exists a simultaneous recognition of its negation, its inevitable destruction', and it abstracts entirely from Marx's discussion in *Capital* of the process of *becoming* – both the becoming of capitalism but also the becoming of its transcendence.

possibility of capital, the two closures (or 'two aspects of a *two-fold* closure') are linked in another way. The development of the working class into a class-in-and-for-itself, he argues, 'requires the mediation of crisis, the development of temporary centrifugal forces in the dialectic of capital that can break up and rupture the smooth operation of its objectification and reification' (p. 430). Indeed, these ruptures and crises appear to be not only the necessary but also the sufficient condition for subjectivity: 'The dialectic of capital, through its inherent ruptures and crises, produces the objective conditions for the emergence of the counter-dialectic of class struggle which holds within it the possibility of the revolutionary overthrow of capitalism and thus of a future communist society' (p. 454).

Certainly the establishment of a direct connection does seem to be necessary – once these are identified as the two aspects of that two-fold closure that the dialectic of capital requires. Unfortunately, Shortall merely asserts this linkage and does so in a way that contains more than a hint of the automatic Marxism he elsewhere criticises. Further, the focus of his discussion of crisis is on the *possibility* of crisis, not its *necessity* – ie., why crises in capitalism are inevitable.[39] Not only, then, does his emphasis upon rupture and crisis as a second aspect of closure effectively marginalise consideration of the worker as subject but Shortall's attempt to relate directly the two aspects of this two-fold closure seems to leave the worker as object of crisis, the subjective as reflection of the objective. For a work explicitly oriented toward the recovery of the subjective and the dialectic of human praxis, this is no small irony.

The fate of the dialectic of human praxis

Shortall's goal in *The Incomplete Marx* is to contribute to a return to Marx – a Marx freed once and for all from the scientific and deterministic readings of orthodox Marxism. He looks to a 'return that would be free to reconstruct a true Marxism based on a theory of human praxis and aiming for the full liberation of humanity in communism' (p. 488, p. 491).

At the core of this vision, clearly, is the dialectic of human praxis – 'the self-development of human beings in their relation to each other and nature' (p. 119). Self-development because, through their own activity, people change both circumstances and themselves: 'In transforming the world in accordance with their own subjective will and purpose they come to transform themselves as natural and social beings'. Shortall understands that this dialectic, which he describes (p. 261) as 'the ontological basis for the entire Marxian project,' contains within it the potential for a society based upon the association of free

---

[39] For a discussion of the distinction between the possibility and necessity of crisis, see Lebowitz 1994.

and equal producers, one which permits the free development of human beings.

How was it, however, 'that the revolutionary theory of Karl Marx which had originally aimed at human liberation ended up as a conservative state dogma which sought to liberate the productive forces at whatever human cost' (p. 485)? Shortall's answer, as we have seen, begins with Marx himself – that Marx imposed, indeed was forced to impose, a closure in *Capital* in order to develop the dialectic of capital. What was for Marx a *provisional* closure, however, became for Marxism 'a *final* closure' as Marxists proceeded to consider *Capital* a closed book rather than one which pointed beyond itself (p. 469).

While there are many who share responsibility for the eclipse of Marx's revolutionary theory of human praxis, Shortall blames, in particular, Engels. He argues that Engels vulgarised Marxism – that by rooting the dialectic in the natural world, 'Engels had come to discard the theory of praxis and human alienation' (p. 487). Given, too, that Engels's influence was key in shaping the Marxist orthodoxy of the Second International and that Soviet Marxism retained the economic determinism of the Second International (pp. 486-7), what became known as Marxism was, largely, what Shortall calls 'the Engelist degeneration of Marxism' (p. 488).[40]

And, yet, Shortall makes a strikingly familiar point in his discussion of Engels's distortion of dialectics. He argues that Engels' 'simple materialist inversion of Hegel led him to preserve the Absolute Idea (God) in the guise of the forces of production which must constantly seek their highest expression in the course of human history' (p. 487). However, as noted above, Shortall had earlier concluded (p. 465) that Marx's dialectic of capital 'appears as the mere materialist inversion of Hegel's dialectic – and this is reflected in the structure of *Capital*'. So, why should we not acknowledge that the real problem was that Marx, having become trapped within the premises of political economy or Hegel's *Logic* or positivism and scientism, himself discarded the dialectic of human praxis, the concept of revolutionary practice?

Certainly, the picture that Shortall offers of Marx's work in *Capital* – one in which capital ultimately reveals its eternal order through the workings of the Invisible Hand – is rather removed from a thematic of the self-development of human beings. As noted earlier in this essay, the evidence for Marx's continuing focus on human praxis is there; rather than revealing this, however, Shortall's preoccupation with the limiting concept of the dialectic of capital only serves to obscure this critical theme.

---

[40] The proposition that Engels discarded the dialectic of human praxis does gain some credibility when we consider one example of his editing of Marx. After Marx's *Theses on Feuerbach*, he dropped one phrase from a passage in the third thesis. The passage Marx wrote was 'The coincidence of the changing of circumstances and of human activity or self-change can be conceived and rationally understood only as *revolutionary practice*.' The phrase missing in Engels' version is 'or self-change'. Marx 1976, p. 4.

Given Shortall's goal of restoring the dialectic of human praxis to its appropriate place in a renewed Marxism, this is unfortunate. It can be said that a working class in motion will redirect attention to what is present in Marx; however, simple dialectics tells us it is the other way around, too.

References

Barker, Colin 1997, 'Some Reflections on Two Books by Ellen Wood', *Historical Materialism*, 1: 22–65.

Lebowitz, Michael A. 1992, *Beyond Capital: Marx's Political Economy of the Working Class*, London: Macmillan.

Lebowitz, Michael A. 1994, 'Analytical Marxism and the Marxian Theory of Crisis', *Cambridge Journal of Economics*, 18, 3: 163–179.

Lebowitz, Michael A. 1995, 'Situating the Capitalist State', in *Marxism in the Postmodern Age: Confronting the New World Order*, edited by Antonio Callari et al., London: Guilford Press.

Lebowitz, Michael A. 1997, 'The Silences of *Capital*', *Historical Materialism*, 1: 134–46.

Marx, Karl 1973, *Grundrisse*, New York: Vintage Books.

Marx, Karl 1975, 'Economic and Philosophical Manuscripts of 1844' in *Collected Works, Karl Marx and Frederick Engels*, Volume 3, New York: International Publishers.

Marx, Karl 1976, 'Theses on Feuerbach' in *Collected Works, Karl Marx and Frederick Engels*, Volume 5, New York: International Publishers.

Marx, Karl 1977, *Capital*, Volume I, New York: Vintage Books.

Marx, Karl 1979, 'Revelations Concerning the Communist Trial in Cologne' in *Collected Works, Karl Marx and Frederick Engels*, Volume 11, New York: International Publishers.

Marx, Karl 1985, 'Value, Price and Profit' in *Collected Works, Karl Marx and Frederick Engels*, Volume 20, New York: International Publishers.

Marx, Karl 1988, 'Economic Manuscript of 1861–63' in *Collected Works, Karl Marx and Frederick Engels*, Volume 30, New York: International Publishers.

Marx, Karl and Engels, Frederick 1976, 'The German Ideology' in *Collected Works, Karl Marx and Frederick Engels*, Volume 5, New York: International Publishers.

Negri, Antonio 1991, *Marx Beyond Marx: Lessons on the* Grundrisse, New York: Autonomedia.

Sekine, Thomas T. 1984, *The Dialectic of Capital: A Study of the Inner Logic of Capitalism*, Vol. I, Tokyo: Yushindo Press.

Thompson, E.P. 1978, *The Poverty of Theory*, New York: Monthly Review.

Uno, Kozo 1980, *Principles of Political Economy: Theory of a Purely Capitalist Society*, Brighton: Harvester Press.

Workers in a Lean World. Unions in the International Economy
Kim Moody
London: Verso, 1997

Reviewed by Adrian Budd

Flexible in their chosen methods, ruling classes everywhere are inflexible
in their attempts to bind workers to their rule and prevent the
generalisation of alternative ideas about how society might be organised.
Having won the Cold War, the West's rulers talk less of freedom (save
when they need to demonise a dictator) and more of the market. We are
told that not only is there no alternative to the market (witness the
collapse of the USSR and the renaissance of capitalism in China) but
that the 'globalisation' of market forces has rendered hopeless all
attempts to tame them via state action or labour movement activism. On
the Left, tragically, few seem willing to accept Ellen Meiksins Wood's
characterisation of 'globalisation' as 'the heaviest ideological albatross
around the neck of the left today' and an excuse for defeatism and
retreat from anti-capitalism.[1] Kim Moody is one of them, referring to
globalisation as 'an amorphous, all-encompassing analytical device that
frequently concealed more than it explained' (p. 37).

Much 'globalisation-speak' mystifies the continuities in the essence
of exploitation and accumulation beneath the shifting phenomenal
forms assumed by the capitalist world order. But there have been real
developments in the international economy over the last two decades
which the Left ignores at its peril. Lenin's argument that the immediate
phenomenal form of the world is just as real/objective as the essence
remains valid, yet a more complete understanding requires a dialectical
approach to the relationship between appearance and essence. The Left
must address what has changed while holding on to what remains the
same.

Last summer's World Cup final provides a metaphor for the
changed relationship between workers, big business and the state. A
young, flexible, although highly paid, worker, Ronaldo, has a convulsion
and four hours later is sent out to play, allegedly under pressure from
Nike, Brazil's multinational sponsor whose $125 million deal allows it
to determine who and where the team play. Tostao, a finalist in 1970,
remarked: 'in my time it was the army generals running Brazil who tried
to pick the team... Today it's the sponsors, the businessman, the media
moguls'.[2] This is a change but we must beware drawing superficial and
one-sided conclusions. Nike has sponsored a national (state) team
which remains dependent on skilled labour and, crucially, is inserted
into a system of international competition. Within that system

---

[1] Wood 1997a, p. 23.
[2] Smith 1998, p. 22.

transnational capitalist organisations still require the support of, and attach themselves to, states.

In *Workers in a Lean World*, Kim Moody has provided a nuanced account of the dialectic of continuity and change in the international economy. His purpose is not academic nit-picking, or to bemoan the plight of the victims of capitalist restructuring, but to emphasise workers' resistance, and the possibilities for a shift in the balance of class forces in favour of the working class.[3] This, he asserts, requires a fighting trade unionism that places itself at the head of the class as a whole, workers and the unemployed, concentrated or dispersed in sweated trades, urban and rural, male and female, black and white, North and South. The task of what he calls 'social-movement unionism' is to encourage a class in itself to become conscious as a class for itself at an international level. His class instincts are unquestionable, but I will argue that what we can call Moody's international syndicalism ultimately fails to deliver a viable project for the sort of change he wants.

'Globalisation'

The first half of *Workers in a Lean World* addresses, under the headings 'capital's offensive' and 'capital's cops', the contradictory nature and unevenness of the internationalising tendencies in the world economy and the various modes of regulation employed by capital and its states. Moody's view of 'globalisation' (chapter two) contributes to a growing backlash among sections of the Left against 'ultra-globalisation', much of which he berates as so much 'globaloney'.[4] Recognising that foreign direct investment has accelerated since capitalism returned to its classical boom-slump cycle in 1973–4, Moody acknowledges that 'today's world economic integration is both deeper than and different from either of the two major epochs (1870–1914 and 1914–45) that preceded it' (p. 48). He nevertheless argues that the international economy is not a seamless whole but is criss-crossed by the jurisdictions of nation-states, which remain central to the accumulation process. Thus, in the advanced economies something like 70 percent of employment/output is in services serving a local market (education, insurance, retailing, etc.) which cannot be simply shunted off-shore to low-wage economies, even if they had the appropriate infrastructure. According to Wood, 'foreign branches of multinational corporations account for about 15 percent of the world's industrial output, while 85 percent is produced by domestic corporations in single geographical

---

[3] For an angry, humorous account that does concentrate on the victims of restructuring, see Moore 1997. For a recent sociological account, see Sennett 1998.

[4] See, inter alia, Harman 1996, Hirst and Thompson 1996, and a series of contributions in recent issues of *Monthly Review*.

locales'.[5] These companies, more accurately described as transnationals (TNCs) than multinationals, continue to operate from a home base. Furthermore, Moody's analysis of uneven development in chapter three emphasises that internationalisation is not uniform and that 'far from some sort of global homogenisation, the spread of capitalism has created even more economic fragmentation. The increasing openness of markets does not remedy this, it compounds it' (p. 65).

Capitalist states, while being the product of various contradictions, engage in a perpetual effort to smooth those contradictions. Marxists have often seen these as operating primarily within nation-states. Thus, the provision of a system of property law, education and training, infrastructure, banking supervision, measures to secure social stability, mediation of the internal conflicts between capitals etc., 'form the irreducible core of the modern capitalist state and the reason why it will not disappear' (p. 136). This is true as far as it goes, but states have always existed, like capitals, in the plural, within an inter-state system. In the circumstances of the internationalisation of the law of value, where the 'external' dovetails with the internal logic of states, their imperative as guarantors of the conditions of accumulation and mediators of that internationalisation is intensified. Evidence of a deepening internationalisation of trade, production and finance in response to the crises of accumulation and profit rates since the early 1970s, far from contradicting this assertion of the centrality of the state as ultra-globalisers argue, actually reinforces it. The danger of the state's exposure to working-class interests has lead the world's ruling classes to shift elements of regulation upwards to international bodies like the IMF and the WTO, but their remit is the product of negotiation and accommodation by those same ruling classes. Internationalisation of markets means the internationalisation of competition and therefore increased exposure of individual capitals and national economies to a dense web of potentially destabilising interactions. Just as the exposure of the neurotic's conflicts to the perceived hostility of the outside world requires countervailing defences, so capital's contradictions demand the defence of states. States may have ditched some of the roles acquired in the hey-day of Keynesianism, such as direct production, but they cannot be ditched by big capital and remain at the heart of capital's contradictions.

In chapters four and five Moody analyses the restructuring of capitalist production, via strategies of lean production, management by stress, casualisation, downsizing, just-in-time production, out-sourcing, etc. These, he shows, have been dependent upon the generalised defeats inflicted on the working class by the combined powers of individual capitals and states since the mid-1970s.[6] Thus 'much of the loss in jobs

---

[5] Wood 1997a, p. 24.
[6] These include, inter alia, the Social Contract in Britain, various social pacts after the death of Franco in Spain, most notably the Moncloa Pact of 1978, the crushing defeat of the FIAT strike in 1980 which allowed the bosses to re-claim control over the labour process throughout Italy, and the defeat of the air traffic

and income among workers in the North is not the direct result of the export of capital or jobs, *per se*, but of a combination of neoliberal policies and cost-cutting within the North itself' (p. 53). Nowhere were attempts to dismantle the post-war class compromise more imperative for capital than in the twin laggards of the post-war boom, Britain and the United States – hence the deeper impact of neo-liberalism in those countries. But while many erstwhile leftist academic scribblers have accommodated to the market and Blairism's 'modernised' pro-market version of social democracy, some of those closer to the heart of the beast, including many who not long ago were in the vanguard of neo-liberalism, show a greater flexibility in defence of their system. Chastisement of the Japanese state for not doing enough to restore the health of its economy is now commonplace. Just as the volatility and instability of the 1930s and 1940s spawned theorists like Keynes and Polanyi, and a new interest in capitalist regulation, so today's crisis has placed state intervention back on capital's agenda. State-led restructuring of Japanese financial institutions and the bail-out of US hedge funds, even the virtual nationalisation of the South Korean Kia Car Company before re-privatisation to Hyundai and the imposition of capital controls by Malaysia's maverick leader Mahathir, may be just the tip of the iceberg.

The main thrust of Moody's analysis of 'globalisation' seems to me incontrovertible. Academic theorists of ultra-globalisation are clearly wrong about the footloose character of capital and the decline of the nation-state, and Moody rightly argues that internationalisation, or even 'triadisation', are preferable terms to 'globalisation'.[7] Problems emerge, however, when Moody sets out his proposals to combat capital's 20-year ascendancy.

Unions in the international economy

In the second half of the book, Moody explores 'labor's response' to internationalisation and restructuring. Against postmodernists and assorted end-of-class theorists, Moody is uncompromising in his commitment to class politics: 'academics and futurists can write the working class off because it is diverse and changing along with the sweeping changes in work. Working-class people themselves have no such luxury, given the crises that have invaded their lives' (p. 146). He is also consistently optimistic about the possibilities of working-class resistance to corporate agendas, for instance in the organisation of what bureaucrats see as unorganisable workers. And he rightly argues that

controllers under Reagan. The term 'Japanisation', which subsumes lean production and associated management techniques, is the result of the earlier defeat of a militant union movement in the 1950s which paved the way for company unionism and the host of methods lately copied by capital internationally. On post-war Japanese capitalism see Itoh 1990.

[7] On triadisation, see Ruigrok and van Tulder 1995.

the 'failed parties of the left' can no longer be relied upon, if they ever could, to secure improvements in workers' lives.

He starts from the Marxist view that capital's ascendancy can never be complete because capital is not a thing but a social relation between dead and living labour. Certainly capital and its states can inflict defeats on the working class, and capitalist restructuring can have a devastating impact on workers' lives. But living labour has consciousness, traditions, memories, feelings and aspirations at odds with the needs of capital and out of these it can develop organisation and a willingness to fight. Well might Henry Ford bemoan the fact that whenever he wanted a pair of hands he got a human being. When workers do fight they find that capital remains dependent on their labour-power. The international production chains constructed in the last decades have the appearance of decentralisation but actually increase the need for centralised control and coordination by TNCs. As Moody puts it: 'what emerges, then, is not some disorganised fragmentation of capital into tiny units or isolated production sites. Rather, a clear hierarchy of control dominated by a small number of corporate giants becomes visible' (p. 78). Objectively, at least, workers are united internationally as never before in production chains that are highly vulnerable to stoppages in one part of the chain. Thus, the 1990s have seen the whole of GM in North America closed down by strikes starting in individual plants in the US, while the threat to Renault's Vilvoorde site in Belgium met a response across Europe. Again objectively, it is not just the workers within these chains that are affected. The pay and conditions of local road sweepers and school cleaners, for example, are ultimately subject to the same cost-cutting measures as those producing directly for TNCs. Moody is clearly right to insist that internationalisation fosters the objective conditions for the international unity of the class.

Moody's account has other strengths, too. He is suspicious of traditional trade union bureaucrats, who form a conservative layer at the top of the labour movement and whose raison d'être is not social change but negotiation. To ward off the worst effects of restructuring, they have followed the path of business unionism, concessionary bargaining, accommodation to lean production and just-in-time methods, and sought 'social partnership' with the capitals located in 'their' nation-states. In the context of the post-1973 crises this strategy has been disastrous: in the advanced countries corporatism no longer suits ruling classes seeking the marginalisation of unions to force down costs. In the US, where concessionary bargaining has gone furthest, the passive union strategy of 'buy American' has coincided with the replacement of GM as the country's largest employer by Manpower Inc., an employment agency specialising in one-day contracts.

Yet, despite the essentially accurate assessment of the processes of 'globalisation' and the objective possibilities for international action by the world's working class (now more numerous than ever), and his distrust of the possibilities of union bureaucracy leading such action, the strategic response Moody champions for the workers' movement is at variance with his analysis and fails to convince. For one who so strongly asserts the continued centrality of the state the almost total omission, indeed avoidance, of politics is a serious weakness. The retreat from politics amongst Marxists since the collapse of the state capitalist regimes is reproduced here, and Moody offers us no serious reflection on the renewal of the Left. Instead we get a confusing and abstract commitment to international syndicalism.

Working-class internationalism must be central to any Marxist politics and Moody rightly argues, in chapter ten on 'official labor internationalism in transition', against a bureaucratic internationalism which simply reflects the national, and sometimes regional, structures of capitalism: 'linking together weakened, bureaucratic, conservatized unions will not limit the power of TNCs' (p. 4). He has in mind bodies like the European Trade Union Confederation (ETUC), deeply involved in social partnership with the EU Commission, which part funds it, and the European bosses' association (UNICE), while 18 million Europeans languish on the dole. Moody recognises that capitalism is an international system and that socialism in one country, or even one region, is an impossibility. But, while he does not argue against domestic struggles, the tenor of his book tends towards an abstract internationalism. Thus his argument that 'the day they [the world's workers] unite ... is the day the alternative will become clear' (p. 8), while correct in principle, echoes the static thinking of the trade union leaders that Engels condemned, waiting for the day that union coffers were full before considering action. In reality, the relationship is more dialectical. As Ellen Meiksins Wood argues, domestic struggles against the common capitalist logic (restructuring, etc.) of all the world's states can 'be the basis – in fact, the strongest basis – of a new internationalism'.[8]

At issue here is not just generalising internationally the positive message that fighting back is possible, or demonstrating a concrete alternative, as against the gloom of common suffering, although that is, of course, vitally important, and the exchanges of information via international workers' networks clearly have a role to play in it. Yet domestic struggles are the key to the development of a thoroughgoing internationalism, rather than vice versa. Not only do they enable us to concentrate our forces, thereby maximising the chances of victory from

---

[8] Wood 1997b, pp. 16–17. The experiences of the Third and Fourth Internationals are instructive here. Lenin proclaimed 'long live the Third International' at the outbreak of the First World War but only set about building it after the victory of the Russian revolution. Even then it degenerated in parallel with the Stalinists' defeat of the revolution *within* Russia. Trotsky proclaimed the Fourth International during the darkest days of the century in a valiant attempt to concentrate his dispersed supporters. Only the most blinkered Trotskyist would regard the latter as anything other than a failure. For a few years after the Russian Revolution internationalism became a mass current within the labour movements of the world; without a national success from which to generalise, the internationalism of official Trotskyism was simultaneously grandiose and a caricature.

which workers internationally can learn, but, by their very nature, they pose the sharpest challenge to one of the central political mechanisms used by states to bind workers to the interests of national ruling classes, namely nationalism.[9] Moody is acutely aware of divisions within the working class (see chapter seven, 'Pulled Apart, Pushed Together') but any strategy of renewal on the Left which fails to address nationalism must, despite its author's intentions, leave an open field for ruling-class ideas.

There is a danger, flowing from a preoccupation with the capital-labour relation and struggles against individual units of capital, and the concomitant relative neglect of wider political issues, of dissipating our energies on grandiose schemes and international workers' networks in anticipation of a resurgence of worker's activism. On the experience of the Liverpool dockers, for example, Moody writes: 'the bold campaign of the Merseyside dock workers to field world-wide actions against a major user of the scab-run Liverpool docks gives us a glimpse of what is possible when the ranks are organized, persistent and daring' (p. 267). Moody is not alone. Chris Bailey began coordinating the British-based Internet site 'LabourNet' during the Liverpool strike. Like Moody, his commitment to working-class internationalism is paramount. But he, too, puts the cart before the horse. Bailey writes:

> the most important question facing the working class is the realisation that we have re-entered a situation, like that of the 19th century, where gains can only be made and defended through internationalism. In turning to international work the dockers were recognising the global nature of the transformations in the port industry and were posing the only way to fight back for dockworkers everywhere.[10]

Note that this is 'the only way'. Now it is clearly dangerous to suggest that workers can win reforms from national states without intense class struggle. The reversal of Mitterrand's earlier reforms in 1982–3 clearly demonstrated this, and it would be surprising if, in the absence of mass mobilisations to support them, the tax plans of the new SPD government were not whittled down by the German bosses. In left politics, social democracy, not Marxism, has been the chief casualty of the processes of internationalisation. But the opposite formulation, that internationalism is the key to winning domestic struggles, is equally dangerous. More localised actions, whether they be stopping the closure of a school or defeating a major employer like UPS, can produce positive results. It is this partial blindness to the possibilities of victory when our forces are concentrated that produces the fulsome praise for the dockers' initiative in launching the campaign of international solidarity, which, although it did deliver magnificent support, failed to

---

[9] For a recent Marxist discussion of nationalism see Löwy 1998.
[10] Bailey 1997, p. 236.

prevent the dockers' defeat.[11] Moody writes not one word on that defeat, nor on alternative strategies that might have brought victory by concentrating the dockers' energies on British ports which would have both caused greater inconvenience over a much smaller area and, potentially, posed the question of state power much more acutely.

That this is the result of an abstract internationalism, and not of any weakening in Moody's commitment to working-class struggle bears repeating. As Trotsky said in the Third International's debates, syndicalists not only want to fight capitalism but really want to tear its head off.[12] It is for this reason that Moody is sensitive to the changes that have taken place within the unions internationally in recent years: breaks from the government-recognised Federation of Korean Trade Unions, which in turn is 'transforming itself from a state-controlled bureaucracy into an ordinary right-wing trade union bureaucracy'; the establishment of more militant independent unions in France; the development of a 'critical sector' in the Spanish Comisiones Obreras; a 'Union Opposition' amongst Swedish car workers; etc.[13] Developments such as these are important, and encourage rank-and-file union members, creating opportunities to argue for, and legitimate, a more combative style of unionism.

Moody is aware that changes of leadership in traditional unions can only have limited effects. Although he writes about the possibilities opened up by the election of a more aggressive leadership, the 'New Voices' team around John Sweeney, in the AFL-CIO in 1995, he recognised that the leadership itself combined the rhetoric of fighting unionism with the (continued) practice of business unionism.[14] Today Sweeney 'is seeking partnership with the No. 1 union-buster in the US, General Electric CEO Jack Welch' and claims that the aim of labour-management cooperation should be 'a process between leaders of labor and leaders of business which will eventually be perceived as a legitimate and high-minded one by other significant stake-holders in society'.[15] Furthermore, despite Sweeney's commitment to recruit to the unions, and a ten-fold increase in funding to achieve it, US union membership fell by 157,000 last year to below 10 percent of the workforce for the first time in a century. More frightening still is the fact that 'more than 60 percent of workers in recognition elections in the last seven years

---

[11] In a personal communication Terry Barrett, one of the Liverpool dockers, gave an example of worker internationalism: Liverpool dockers were visiting a port in French-speaking Canada but, not speaking French, began to explain their case in English. Their 'audience' carried on working until one docker came over and said 'you're strikers from Liverpool aren't you'. He then called his mates over to listen to a meeting in scouse on the grounds that 'I'm a docker first, a French-Canadian second'.
[12] For a Marxist analysis of the trade unions, see Cliff and Gluckstein 1986. On bureaucracy and syndicalism see Trotsky 1990. See also appropriate sections of Hessel 1983.
[13] Gyoung-hee 1998, p. 44.
[14] See Mort 1999 for a wildly over-optimistic assessment of the 'New Voice' campaign and the prospects of Sweeney's leadership.
[15] *Socialist Worker* (Chicago), 23 October 1998, p. 11.

have voted against unions – despite the fact that unions request elections only if they have a solid majority of a shop's workforce on record in favour of unionising'.[16]

This is an unwelcome antidote to Moody's excessively rosy picture of change in the unions internationally. But both are one-sided and present a false image of what is happening in the world and the possibilities for renewal of the Left. Their common error lies in ignoring the impact on workers' consciousness of political change outside the work-place. Without this wider view, socialists can be seduced by a rise in the class struggle from a very low ebb (which is, of course, to be welcomed) and, like Moody, can write of a global awakening of the class. Alternatively we can be thrown into a slough of despond when activism dips temporarily or when unions suffer defeats. And most importantly, without a wider concept of politics, we can miss the opportunities to build an anti-capitalist current within the labour movement.

In *Wages, Price and Profit*, Marx wrote that workers ought 'not to be exclusively absorbed in these unavoidable guerrilla fights incessantly springing up from the never-ceasing encroachments of capital or changes of the market'.[17] Trade unionism is, in Rosa Luxemburg's words, a labour of Sisyphus; a necessary labour but one that cannot breach the limits of capitalism. For that we need to recognise the uneven consciousness within the class, and, as the Bolsheviks did, link economic struggles with politics. Of course, they did not always get the balance right, especially at the beginning. To take an example from a strike on the Baku oil-fields, described by Cecilia Bobrovskaya, a Bolshevik committee member in the region. A 'very good agitator' from the Menshevik faction 'was never tired at mass meetings of discussing minor questions like the provision of aprons, mitts, etc., by the employers without touching upon the real significance of the strike'. The Bolsheviks meanwhile adopted a rather academic approach to the strike such that Bolshevik speakers 'were often interrupted by uncomplimentary shouts about the Bolsheviks who instead of demanding mitts and aprons demanded the overthrow of the autocracy'. This failure to connect the struggles of the class to wider questions, this desire to run them parallel rather than together meant that when, in 1905, the overthrow of autocracy assumed real importance, 'the Bolsheviks were, to a large extent, not in a position to provide real leadership'.[18]

That they quickly learnt the lesson contributed in no small measure to the success of the Russian Revolution in 1917, when for the first time the limits of capitalism were transcended, whatever the subsequent fate of the revolution under Stalinism. Moody argues insistently against the separation of economics and politics characteristic of capitalism, and of

---

[16] See Palast 1998.
[17] Marx 1958, p. 446–7.
[18] LeBlanc 1993, p. 90.

its social-democratic defenders, and, as we saw above, recognises that the state's 'irreducible core' continues to shape all aspects of workers' lives. But the syndicalist orientation of his politics prohibits him from fully accepting the unity of the two. Ultimately, syndicalism becomes the flip-side of the social-democratic coin: on the one face, politics; on the other, economics.

Syndicalism, justifiably impatient with business unionism, bureaucratic compromises and the capitulations of political reformism, attempts to unite the working class as a whole across the divisions of gender, race, craft, section and politics. Now slogans like that of the Industrial Workers of the World, 'no race, no creed, no colour' are, at one level, entirely correct. But syndicalism tends to posit a primordial, almost mythical, unity of the working class which will re-emerge triumphant in strikes. Clearly strikes do begin to break down divisions, but there is no automatic process by which every trace of the ideological muck of ruling-class ideas is thrown off. Only by actively engaging with and challenging the divisions that have debilitated our movement can we hope to fashion real unity. That requires not a mythical conception of class unity, but a dialectical approach that recognises the working class, to borrow a term from Lukács, as a differentiated unity. Indeed, as Trotsky argued, the more successful the unions are in organising the greatest number of workers, the greater the potential weakness arising from differentiation, from uneven consciousness. Differentiation becomes more of a hindrance to class unity, not less, the longer it is ignored and backward ideas not challenged.

Instead, regarding the Transnational Information Exchange (TIE), the sort of operation Moody sees as a key component in social-movement unionism, Moody writes: 'for people to create a functional international network they had to keep what divided them to themselves and share what they had in common – the global analysis and the activist approach to the workplace' (p. 256). The habitual reflexes of ruling-class ideas such as freedom, democracy, nationalism, superiority/inferiority, etc., that seek to legitimise or render opaque the core operations of its power, are left largely undisturbed.

Moody explores and champions social movement unionism in chapters nine and eleven and in the conclusion. But its inherent problems become transparent the moment that he illustrates it, by drawing on the experience of Brazilian and South African unions. Indeed, Moody himself seems half aware of its limitations, and even presents evidence of them, but his politics prevent him from reaching adequate conclusions. In Brazil the Workers' Party grew out of militant trade unionism, while in South Africa a new-style fighting trade unionism in the 1980s saw the creation of COSATU. Yet, Moody is quite aware that the PT has become little more than a mainstream social-democratic electoralist party, with a right-wing social-democratic minority wing. COSATU, without an independent politics separate from the stages solution of the ANC (capitalist democracy first, the struggle for socialism relegated to some far-distant future), has proved incapable of resisting the pro-business line of the ANC-led government's Reconstruction and Development Programme. Indeed, some fifty or so COSATU leaders actually entered political office after the 1994 elections.[19] Today, mass discontent and the bureaucracy's own anger at its declining influence has pushed it into confrontations with the government, which have been met with brutality. COSATU is nevertheless under enormous pressure to accommodate to big business and government plans for economic restructuring. Meanwhile, unemployment is estimated to be running at close to 40 percent.

Moody himself writes that '...the experience of both South Africa and Brazil reminds us that political direction is not something that can be taken for granted even where strong social-movement union has taken root' (p. 212). Furthermore, that 'these unions, too, face a tendency towards bureaucratisation. But the members have enough experience in union affairs to resist this trend' (p. 277). This is a serious underestimation not only of the structural powers of any bureaucracy, even one initially committed to struggle, to control the base and/or incorporate it into the logic of negotiation and conciliation, but also of the more general limits of trade unionism. This applies even to a type of unionism that seeks to connect with broader working-class interests beyond the work-place in the streets and communities, and with previously unorganised groups of workers within out-sourced production chains.

Conclusion

As capitalist crisis is superimposed onto two decades of restructuring, there is widespread evidence of mounting anger at the base of unions internationally. This is not always manifest in actions to shift the bureaucracy from the path of 'social partnership'. In Britain, just before September's TUC in Blackpool a poll of bosses and unions showed increasing industrial unrest and predicted an increase in strikes. The TUC responded by rejecting the poll's findings: 'Yes, ballots are used more widely, but few lead to industrial action'.[20]

In his classic study of revisionism in the German SPD, Schorske wrote that 'the trade-union bureaucracy was anti-revolutionary *in Permanenz*, by virtue of its corporate interest in the existing order. The working class was not similarly committed...'[21] This assessment remains true today and is equally applicable to the new bureaucracies of the unions that Moody asserts represent the future of the labour movement and the way out of the impasse of capitalist restructuring at workers'

[19] Callinicos 1996.
[20] 'TUC Scoffs at Winter of Discontent Prediction', *The Observer* 13 September 1998.
[21] Schorske 1955, p. 110.

expense. Trade unionism as such, and especially syndicalist social-movement unionism, can take us a good way down the road towards socialism and is still a training-school for working-class struggle. But it does not pose a political alternative to capitalism. That requires a form of Marxist politics that not only orientates directly on trade union issues and struggles but also challenges workers politically and presents a Marxist answer to the pressing issues of the day.

To return to our earlier metaphor about football, Moody has produced a book of two halves. The first half on 'globalisation' and restructuring pulls ruling-class defences apart and exposes their weaknesses. But the fight against capitalism does not stop at half-time and unfortunately Moody's second half tactics are too defensive: holding out for a draw on capitalism's home ground means he misses opportunities for victory. Moody has good class instincts and really wants to win, but the depth of the crisis today requires him to make the shift towards Marxist politics that so much of his analysis cries out for.

References

Bailey, Chris 1997, 'Towards a Global LabourNet', *Labor Media 97*, conference papers, Seoul, pp. 229–37.

Callinicos, Alex 1996, 'South Africa after Apartheid', *International Socialism*, 70: 3–46.

Cliff, Tony and Gluckstein, Donny 1986, *Marxism and Trade Union Struggle: The General Strike of 1926*, London: Bookmarks.

Gyoung-hee, Shin 1998, 'The Crisis and Workers' Movement in South Korea', *International Socialism*, 78: 39–54.

Harman Chris 1996, 'Globalisation: A Critique of a New Orthodoxy', *International Socialism*, 73: 3–34.

Hessel, B. (ed) 1983, *Theses, Resolutions and Manifestos of the First Four Congresses of the Third International*, London: Pluto.

Hirst, Paul and Thompson, Grahame 1996, *Globalisation in Question*, London: Polity.

LeBlanc, Paul 1993, *Lenin and the Revolutionary Party*, Atlantic Highlands, N.J.: Humanities Press.

Löwy, Michael 1998, *Fatherland or Mother Earth? Essays on the National Question*, London: Pluto.

Itoh, Makoto 1990, *The World Economic Crisis and Japanese Capitalism*, London: St. Martin's Press.

Marx, Karl 1958, *Karl Marx Selected Works*, Volume I, Progress Publishers: Moscow.

Moore, Michael 1997, *Downsize This*, London: HarperCollins.

Mort, Jo-Ann (ed) 1999, *Not Your Father's Union Movement. Inside the AFL-CIO*, London: Verso.

Palast, Gregory 1998, 'Workers Win the Battle – But Bosses Win the War', *The Observer*, 13 September.

Ruigrok, Wyn and van Tulder, Rob 1995, *The Logic of International Restructuring*, London: Routledge.

Schorske, Carl 1955, *German Social Democracy 1905–1917. The Development of the Great Schism*, New York: Harvard University Press.

Sennett, Richard 1998, *The Corrosion of Character: The Personal Consequences of Work in the New Capitalism*, London: Norton.

Smith, David 1998, 'The Mysterious Shadow of the Ronaldo Affair', *The Independent*, 7 August.

Trotsky, Leon 1990, *Trade Unions in the Epoch of Imperialist Decay*, London: Pathfinder.

Wood, Ellen Meiksins 1997a , 'Capitalism, Globalization, and Epochal Shifts', *Monthly Review*, February: 21–32.

Wood, Ellen Meiksins 1997b, 'Labor, the State, and Class Struggle', *Monthly Review*, July–August: 1–17.

The Art of Interruption: Realism, Photography and the Everyday.
John Roberts
Manchester: Manchester University Press, 1997

Reviewed by Giles Peaker

A significant part of the history of photography consists in its role as a site for debates about realism. John Roberts's book is both an examination and an important transformation of these debates, which appears at a time when their import is all but forgotten. It performs a critical recovery of a range of photographic practices from canonical orthodoxies, Left and Right, and advances a critical approach, dialectical realism, capable of understanding both photographs and the arguments around photography as complex social objects.

The book does not aim to be a comprehensive historical study of photography, although it is structured to give a near continuous historical account from the Russian Revolution to the present. Instead, after a theoretical introduction, there follow a series of analyses of specific moments of photographic theory and practice – those most closely involved with debates on realism and representation. These accounts can be read independently, but also form a complex historical narrative of cultural politics. At the centre of Roberts's analyses is the category of the 'everyday'. The shifts in the concept of the everyday (or *quotidien* or *byt*) following its intense politicisation in the period of the Russian Revolution are the starting points for his rich and suggestive commentaries. It is, for instance, by tracking the shifts and positionings of the concept that the book manages convincingly to rescue some anti-fascist value for New Objectivity photography from the established Brecht/Benjamin derived condemnation of its aestheticising positivism. (Although, at the same time, Benjamin's interest in August Sander is merely noted. The sense in which Benjamin saw Sander's photographs as functioning as a form of training involves a somewhat different version of the everyday to that of the Brecht/Benjamin axis discussed in the rest of the book.) The concentration on the 'everyday' enables Roberts to open photography into socio-political history because it is not 'an ontological category, but a discursive and tropological one'. The concept of the everyday is both the means by which photography constructs its relationship to the world and an active product of socio-political history.

Beneath the historical account of the everyday there is an ontology, one which is suggested in the introductory discussion of realism. Roberts defines his use of the term 'realism' as meaning a dialectical realism:

the theory of the contradictoriness of things. Contradictions
are the essential nature of all social objects and their relations;
however, dialectical realism explains such contradictions
ontologically as the expression of more fundamental divisions.
(p. 12)

Realism, for Roberts, is not an aesthetic question, nor an 'untheorised
account of representation'; instead 'it represents a continuing
philosophical commitment to the application of dialectical reason to the
problems of cultural production' (p. 11). (The book's discussion of the
historical construction of the concept of realism can be confusing – a
realist analysis of realism. Some distinction of the terms would have
helped as the two can threaten to slide into each other.) Robert's close
attention to the relationship of the form and content of the photograph
and the conditions of its production, distribution and reception enables
a subtlety of analysis which opens up photographs as embodiments of
socio-historical conditions without ever losing sight of their active
participation in their world. The photographs are seen as made out of
social contradictions, but are never just a product.

The work that Roberts is primarily interested in is work that is either
'realist in effect' – work which 'consciously foregrounds the
contradictions out of which it makes its meaning' – or works which, by
making visible 'certain states of affairs through the countering of
mystification or prejudice could be said to produce realist effects' (p.
12). There is an interesting fusion made here. On the one hand, in the
works which foreground contradiction, there is the heritage of a
somewhat Benjaminian version of avant-gardism. On the other, there
are works which need to be read in terms of their relation (or
opposition) to dominant ideologies and the situation of their production
and consumption in order for a realist effect to be the result. One of the
great strengths of this book is that this fusion is generally successfully
and productively achieved in the analyses. Jo Spence's photographs of
her 'damaged body', for instance, are not taken as a simple 'counter-
archive' or factography. Instead, the photographs are both associated
with the 'confessional' narcissism and abject displays of 1980s/1990s
spectacles and distinguished from them through Spence's engagement
with 'non-artworld audiences'. Directed towards 'groups in education
and sections of the labour movement', the works' reception can involve
a critical process of despectacularisation. However, a question might be
asked. Given the essential nature of contradiction for all social objects
and their relations, is there not the possibility of producing a realist
effect in the reading of any photograph? Roberts's analyses are intended
to foreground the contradictory as, in a sense, an aim of their objects,
hence his claim that Walker Evans's *American Photographs* should be
read as a 'progressive critique of congealing FSA ideology in the late
1930s, despite the Modernist "privatised" nature of the work' (p. 6) (or
rather, because of it). The demand that Roberts makes of the work is
that it should somehow exhibit contradiction. But if it is necessary to

situate the work in order to establish a demonstration of contradiction, as is the case with the museum-oriented Walker Evans, then what makes this different to a potential analysis of any potential photograph?

One answer would be tactics. Roberts's book is, in one sense, a history of tactical positions. The claims of the 1920s are themselves given a tactical gloss in relation to the emergence of Stalinism, and the subsequent history is that of attempts to sustain a commitment to an engagement with the everyday as the site of a lived experience, attempts which are inevitably determined by a relation to representational orthodoxies and the politics of cultural production. A commitment to the everyday is likely to give rise to work marked most strongly by contradiction and thereby useful to a dialectical realist analysis. It is this approach which underlies Roberts's recent work on the Young British Art scene and his formulation of the concept of the philistine, which is not, unfortunately, addressed in this book.

A history of tactics is also largely a history of difficulty and retreat, inevitably so, given the political and social history of the twentieth century. The options increasingly close down. Beginning with the confidence of the revolutionary avant-gardes in their portrayal of and intervention in a working class everyday, the history takes us through the turning of interventionist artforms into culture and of factography into documentary. That this can be acknowledged as a loss is, Roberts claims, partly due to the 'recovery' of the avant-gardes in the 1970s. However, this recovery is no mere restaging, instead it involves a process of 'identification and critique' in response to very different social and political circumstances. Amongst these are the apparent fragmentation of collective experience and the absence of links between photography and an organised working class. John Berger and Jean Mohr's attempt in the 1970s to show a narrativised, collective experience in *A Seventh Man* and *Another Way of Telling,* here given a rich and broadly sympathetic reading, can only find a basis in peasant life. What is apparently necessary, a shifting of attention *'away* from the industrial working class', functions, it could be argued, less as 'a view from below' than a view from outside or at least from a border. Jeff Wall's version of realism, despite or because of its claim to the 'demotic' of genre, can only suggest the everyday as a point of tension or disruption in the smooth surfaces of the 'dominant fictionalised experience of the "everyday" within advanced media-based culture' (p. 188), thereby, perhaps, revealing them as politically structured abstract spaces. As Roberts puts it, 'the crisis states of consciousness that Wall creates point to a sense of self directed outwards towards the world' (p. 197). The Anglo-American 'rise of theory' in the 1980s results, for Roberts, in an abandonment of the everyday in its 'separation of discourse from material interests' and its sacrifice of concrete experience to ideology.

A history of tactics must also include this book. It is intended as a 'history from below'. Rather than putting forward a grand theory of critical photographic practices, this is cast as a 'redemptive critique', releasing its objects from official histories and reassessing them from the standpoint of the present. The account of surrealism, posed in part against its current post-structural revision, is a strong example of this. Whilst acknowledging some of the strengths of the revision of Surrealist photography undertaken by Rosalind Krauss and Hal Foster, for instance in its rescue of the full range of surrealist practices from their 'high art' appropriation, Roberts criticises the effectively formalist version of both Bataille and surrealist photography that is the result. Against this, he argues for a montagist and interruptive basis for surrealism, following Aragon's early assertion that 'the marvellous is the eruption of contradiction within the real' (p. 109). The book overall constructs its arguments against what Roberts takes to be the two main strands of contemporary criticism. 'Critical deconstructionism', which includes post-structural and postmodern approaches, receives repeated and often acute criticism on a range of grounds – in particular its failure to acknowledge dialogism and the relation of meaning and social exchange. 'Left aestheticism' is the target of much of the introduction, couched in terms of a critique of Adorno. Roberts's critical approach perhaps shares rather more than he would like to acknowledge with Adorno, for example in the sense of truth (or realist effect) emerging at the level of commentary or reflection:

> The "realist-effects" of works of art are not reducible to any pre-given set of contents or forms but the product of a discursive reconstruction of a given work of art's claims to 'truth'. (p. 11)

There might also be a commonality in the apparent, although not explicit, historical shift from the positive depiction or construction of a working class everyday to a more negative maintenance of contradiction as a symptomatology of the 'everyday'. The iconicity of the photograph perhaps comes to perform a similarly irreducibly contradictory role to that of beauty in Adorno's work of art, although in many ways it is its opposite. In any case, Roberts is certainly right to reprove Adorno for his 'downgrading' of photography and in the implied criticism of the total reification thesis.

Both critical deconstructionism and, to some extent, left aestheticism, Roberts suggests, judge works in separation from the everyday. Against this he poses a critique, influenced by Henri Lefebvre, which does not aim to judge the work but to find in it the contradictions of everyday life and in doing so to find the resources and possibilities for the critique and transformation of that life. Dialectical realism's task is 'to discover and explain the rational potential of an object' (p. 12). The book's final chapter makes this clear. It mounts a timely and strong critique of the claims made for the digital technologies. The proclamation of the burial of the real, technological utopians and dystopians receive a dialectical examination which poses the fantasies of the technological against their socio-economic determination. The 'free floating' – utopian or dystopian – remains tied to the material. 'Technological transformation, then, is always a concretisation of the contradictions of the capitalist mode of production' (p. 226), its possibilities for a changed social organisation are substituted by changes in the use-value of technology in an unchanged social structure. That the digital will bring about changes in production and consumption will not mean that the digital will be free of contradiction and so realism, in Roberts's sense, remains vital.

Realist criticism, of course, is as much *performed out* of the contradictions of everyday life' (p. 9) as its objects. Roberts acknowledges this, but the possibilities and role of the realist critic are not discussed in any detail. If the problem of how 'a critical photographic culture [might] intervene into everyday life in conditions where advanced commodified social relations separate historical knowledge from social practice' (p. 11) remains, then the same question is true of realist criticism. In a sense, though, the book performs part of that discussion. It is an intervention in a debate; however, the book is not aimed as a contribution to it, rather it is a dialectical critique of the debate's very grounds. Although there is much that some may want to argue with in Roberts's particular historical analyses – for me, for instance, his effective dismissal of Lefebvre's critique of surrealism avoided the issue of surrealism's deeply touristic relation to working class Paris – any response must approach that critique. The book might not be 'an answer' – the demand for such a formula rightly meets with Roberts's criticism – but as an attempt to recover and transform things that may be useful, to refigure a concept of the everyday and realism for now, it is an important and valuable work.

Radical PHILOSOPHY

93 Jan/Feb 1999 £3.95/$7.00

92 Nov/Dec 1998

Subscriptions

individuals: (6 issues)
UK £21 Europe £25 ROW surface £27/$44 airmail £33/$54
(12 issues) UK £37 Europe £45 ROW surface £49/$80 airmail £61/$100
institutions: (6 issues)
UK £44 Europe £48 ROW surface £50/$82 airmail £55/$91

Visa, Access/Mastercard, Eurocard, Money order/Cheque payable to *Radical Philosophy Ltd*
Central Books (RP Subs), 99 Wallis Road, London E9 5LN
rp@centralbooks.com   http://www.ukc.ac.uk/secl/philosophy/rp/

Dissolution: The Crisis of Communism and the End of East Germany
Charles Maier
Princeton: Princeton University Press, 1997
The Politics of Economic Decline in East Germany, 1945–1989
Jeffrey Kopstein
Chapel Hill: University of North Carolina Press, 1997
Varieties of Transition: The East European and East German Experience
Claus Offe
Cambridge: Polity, 1996

Reviewed by Gareth Dale

Introduction

On 7th October 1989 East German leaders gathered at the 'Palace of the Republic' to celebrate the fortieth birthday of their state – one which Charles Maier describes as 'a repressive little state built on public self-congratulations and pervasive policing' (p. xii). Despite the pomp and pageantry, all was not well. Gorbachev was in town, and his name was chanted by demonstrators outside, as a symbol of hopes of political reform. The first open signs of division in the politburo had just appeared. The assembled guests were nervous. Suitably dark jokes circulated. One went as follows: after the sinking of the Titanic, three countries began to work on its salvage, each with a keen motive. The USA was after the gold in the safes. The USSR was interested in the technology of the machinery. And the GDR? Its leaders were desperate to find out which pieces had been played – so bravely – by the orchestra as the ship went down.

The three books reviewed here discuss some of the key questions concerning the causes and processes of the sinking of the GDR. Why did its leaders refuse to change course? Why did much of the population mutiny, and what was the historical significance of their uprising?

Each author brings a distinctive angle to these issues – reflected in the questions they ask and how they are answered. Jeffrey Kopstein focuses on the interaction of structural constraints with the strategies of the ruling élite; his main theme is the mediations between economic decline and political strategy. Beginning from the constraints on policy – in the shape above all of workers' resistance, Soviet domination, and East Germany's insertion into the world economy – he demonstrates how the SED leadership's strategic choices, though rational in the short term, proved ultimately irrational. In attempting to explain why the 'irrational' course was maintained, his analysis illuminates the structural preconditions of the 1989 revolution. His theme is not the revolution as such – not the process, nor the actors, nor the outcome. For Kopstein, the protestors are simply assumed to be driven by the desire for a Western lifestyle, as a result of their experience of 'relative deprivation'. The outcome of the revolution, German unification, is inscribed in the sheer fact of the East's material poverty; it requires no further elucidation.

Charles Maier, by contrast, has a keen curiosity in situations of widening historical choice, as exemplified in the process of revolution. If Maier consistently produces works of profundity and scope, it is doubtless due to his sharp sense of history but also because his standard is the spirit and ideals of the American revolution, against which the real world seems so terribly corrupt. 'As a citizen of the United States', he begins his discussion of 1989, he is 'proud that the values which my country has represented – at least in its best moments – proved so contagious' (p. xx). For Maier, the 'Citizens Movements' of Eastern Europe are worthy inheritors of the values of liberty, equality and fraternity – those 'founding principles' of the USA (which 'will hopefully retain their attraction' in years to come).

Though sharing Maier's commitment to the ideals of bourgeois society (particularly the 'rule of law'), Claus Offe's account of 1989 is decidedly different, imbued with fatalism and pessimism. Although rarely explicit in this volume, the background to this is surely Offe's pioneering of the 'new social movement paradigm' in the 1980s. For Offe, 'new social movements' (NSMs) are crucial buttresses to the pillars of bourgeois democracy. They 'focus on overcoming some of the built-in biases, deficiencies and blind spots' (p. 42) of the major political and economic institutions. Thus he writes 'At the beginning of the eighties ... on the occasion of the marriage of the new social movements, the general prediction [i.e. Offe's prediction] was for a trend towards a post-industrial society in which the significance of "materialist" realms of politics geared towards guiding values such as growth and [social security] would recede', giving way to 'postmaterialist' movements based on issues such as peace and ecology which should 'lend a strong impetus to a "post-industrial Left"' (p. 197). Now, however, the NSM paradigm lies in tatters.[1] Offe wrote the volume considered here during a period when it was becoming clear that his 'speculative position [had] proved to be completely erroneous'. One has a strong sense that Offe's disappointment in the stillbirth of the post-industrial Left applies equally to the NSM-like Citizens Movement organisations of 1989, as they floundered in the face of political crisis, before being rapidly overtaken by the 'materialist' movement for German unification.

---

[1] For more on the NSM paradigm, see Barker and Dale 1999.

The constraints of SED rule

I begin with Kopstein's geometry of 'confining conditions'. He concentrates on three spheres which constrained the strategic choices available to the SED: industrial relations, military rivalries and alliances, and economic competition.

On industrial relations, Kopstein's book fills something of a gap, at least in the English literature. In his account, East German rulers, following World War II, faced a working class which had gained a considerable degree of control over much of industry and, to a surprising extent, resisted the competitive culture demanded by the imperatives of accumulation. Especially where 'enterprise councils' were strong, the prevailing shop floor ethic was 'egalitarian, co-operative, defensive, and geared toward survival rather than the maximization of gain' (p. 21). As economic growth resumed the labour market tightened, and was exacerbated by booming demand from West Berlin. 'Such market conditions', with workers 'chang[ing] jobs relatively freely', notes Kopstein 'gave the working class a power of sorts' (pp. 156–7) – and presented managers and officials with major headaches. Their response, in the late 1940s and early 1950s, centred on intensive efforts to undermine solidarity and raise productivity through raising differentials and the introduction of 'a rigorous Taylorist labor régime'. The competition inscribed in the labour market was complemented by the granting of differential rewards related to performance (piece work etc.) and political loyalty. Schemes of 'socialist competition' were introduced in which workers (and work brigades) were pitted against one another – and were obliged in the process to commit themselves ritually to 'the party and its production goals'.

This employers' offensive faced widespread and tenacious resistance, many examples of which are provided by Kopstein. Thus, '[w]here management stiffened its resolve to increase wage and consumer good differentials, workers often spontaneously evened out the differences by purchasing goods for each other' (p. 27). According to SED reports, 'many foremen could not be stopped from putting all the piecework tickets in a common urn in order to ensure equality of reward' (p. 29). 'Workers and enterprise councils spontaneously eliminated piecework and often removed time clocks at plant entrances as symbols of work speedups and other distasteful aspects of capitalist (and Nazi) [sic] industrial life' (p. 27). Those who did go along with managerial ideals of 'activism' and norm-busting 'tended to be despised and isolated by the rank-and-file employees' (p. 33).

It is at this point in the story that the second of Kopstein's 'confining conditions' – geopolitics – intervenes. In his opinion, '[t]he cat-and-mouse game' of industrial struggle might have continued as a war of attrition 'had the cold war not taken a new turn' (p. 35). In its earliest phase East Germany had existed as a paradox and a problem for the USSR. Raising its flag over the Reichstag in Berlin marked the historical high-watermark of the Kremlin's power; yet the territory occupied, being a small fraction of pre-war Germany, was not envisaged as a viable entity. It was intended by Stalin simply as a bargaining chip to be exchanged for the neutralisation of Germany. The Soviet zone was substantially weaker than its western twin: its economy was disproportionately cramped by the division of Germany, and, rather than receiving Marshall Aid, it was subjected to years of intensive plunder by Moscow. Far from being the triumphant outcome of a German revolution, it was nothing but naked geopolitical (and geo-ideological) rivalry – the developing antagonism between the USA and Russia – which 'locked the Russians into reinforcing East Germany's national status' (Maier, p. 23). Part of this process involved cementing it into a keystone of Soviet empire. In emulation of the economic model of the conquering power, a powerful heavy industrial base was reconstructed beneath a sturdy military machine. In 1952, in Kopstein's words, '[u]nder Soviet orders the East Germans committed themselves to building up their armed forces and defense industry at a cost of 1.5 billion marks, to be financed from reductions in social spending coupled with higher taxation' (p. 35). The upshot of such austerity was a rapid deterioration of living standards for much of the population. Together with deepening divisions in the Soviet leadership, which catalysed U-turns and vacillation in the GDR and generated confusion throughout the institutions of rule, a revolutionary crisis developed, culminating in a mass strike and uprising in June 1953.

The uprising, though eventually crushed by Soviet troops, starkly reminded the SED of its limited room for manoeuvre on the industrial front. As Kopstein remarks it 'effectively crippled the régime on the shop floor', (p. 37) with the result that the SED was forced to proceed more cautiously. In the following decades, 'fearing a repetition of the June events, labor peace could be bought only at the price of long-term stagnation in labour relations, wage structures, and productivity incentives' (p. 18). Except for the construction of the Berlin Wall, which 'tourniqueted the flow of skilled labor and stabilized the political situation' (Maier, p. 87), the SED scored few major successes in its battle to weaken what Kopstein describes as workers' substantial 'tacit power'.[2]

Organizing stability

By crushing the 1953 uprising and backing the building of the Wall, Moscow demonstrated a 'fraternal solidarity' with its German creature that was to grow in strength.[3] These acts of brute intimidation doubtless

---

[2] 'It was not the power to strike, organize or bargain collectively, but as the [high] rates of absenteeism illustrate, it did entail the power to withhold services.'
[3] 'Paradoxically,' Maier notes (p. 23), 'uncertainties within the Soviet bloc strengthened the Soviet commitment to the East German state. Any notion of trading it for neutralization of a united Germany became far too adventurous for

helped to promote deference (or 'legitimacy'). They represented a determined assertion of class power which helped to lay the basis for domestic and international stability, and thereby (typically, if ironically) for a growing recognition of the GDR as a sovereign state. However, the techniques of rule are invariably more intricate than the language of concrete and lead. Maier's distinctive take on this is what he calls the 'corruption of the public sphere'. His use of the term is broad, and not unlike Gramsci's: 'Between consent and force stands corruption [which aims to] sow disarray and confusion', for example by 'procuring the demoralisation and paralysis of the antagonist (or antagonists)' (p. 80). Maier applies the term liberally – for instance to familiar phenomena in Western democracies such as 'the growing role of private wealth for political participation, the replacement of debate with simplified slogans and images of personality' as well as other symptoms of media power such as the increasing prominence within political discourse of 'the interaction of television audiences and interpretors of public opinion' (p. 41).

In the East German case, corruption of the public sphere centred on the ramified forms of the state's imposition into everyday life by exploiting its command over resources. The state sought to govern through private bargains with citizens, attempting to transform citizens into clients so as to encourage an attitude of needy subordination. Above all the distribution of resources was used as an instrument of division. Although nominally based upon solidarity, 'the régime survived precisely by undermining solidarity with differential rewards such as travel and education, even by dividing up its supposedly loyal proletarian supporters into competitive work brigades, and by rewarding snooping' (p. 39). In Maier's account, East Germany was a great pork barrel: those who bowed and scraped gained privileges, with the régime hoping to reap loyalty in return.

Even the Stasi's activities, suggests Maier, can be better understood as corruption than repression (p. 47). Its officials saw themselves 'as much as social workers as policemen', often sincerely believing that the 'objects of investigation should be grateful for the tutelage provided' (p. 48). Its true function consisted less in the information gleaned and the uses to which it was put than in the opaqueness it created for the régime – a power of mystification and secrecy upon which the ability to corrupt independent action and stifle dissent depended. It 'wove large numbers of East Germans, over 1 percent of the whole population, probably over 10 percent of the adult "intellectual" population, into a network of corrupting complicity, [making] complicity a key principle of governance' (p. 48).

---

even the reformist Khrushchev, once the Polish and Hungarian upheavals shook Eastern Europe in 1956'

Economic reform

The third pillar of SED rule – apart from force and corruption – was economic growth. Given the intensity of geopolitical and geoeconomic competition (above all with the FRG), and given the wage pressure from what Kopstein describes as 'a highly skilled and mature labor force', (p. 157) competitive productivity growth was the key priority of the nomenklatura. Even a casual glance at SED documents, Kopstein suggests, 'reveals how obsessed the leadership of the SED was with improving economic performance and how focused it was on comparisons with production and consumption levels in the West' (p. 1).

In the 1950s and 1960s, Maier notes, growth was rapid, especially in the spheres of investment and rearmament (pp. 81–8). More significantly, 'growth rates from the 1950s through the 1960s and into the 1970s were comparable with those in the West'. Such indicators of success, however, conceal a widening productivity gap with the FRG which, notes Kopstein, was particularly painful and politically sensitive (p. 4). Worried by this productivity slippage, sections of the ruling class developed plans for major economic reform. Against the background of détente – in which a relaxation of orthodoxy became more thinkable – and drawing on Soviet reform ideas and recent texts on Western management (Kopstein, p. 49), plans were drawn up to introduce market mechanisms and to grant greater autonomy to firms. Over seven years some of these plans were put into practice, in what was known as the New Economic System (NÖS).

The results were hardly promising: they ran up against problems of three sorts. The first, Kopstein argues, was opposition by workers and managers (p. 11). Following years of resistance to Taylorisation, and in the wake of the 1953 uprising, the SED had been forced to give workers 'a virtual veto power over wages, prices, and work norms', thereby conceding to them a degree of ability 'to restrict the range of plausible reforms at a later period'. One plank of the NÖS, due to begin in trial form in 1966, involved a refocus on profitability as the determinant of investment decisions; as such it would necessarily entail closures and lay-offs. Kopstein relates how in one trial scheme '[t]hose threatened with transfers to new work put up stiff resistance. Coal miners and their managers in Zwickau brought the situation to the edge of revolt. In the face of these prospects, plans to close down certain parts of the coal mine were quickly dropped.' (p. 62) The trial scheme was effectively scuppered.

The second problem was that reform decreased the ability of the central planning authorities to ration demand, giving rise 'to bottlenecks and stagnation of consumer goods ... energy crises ... and an unavowed inflation' (Maier, p. 92). More significantly, economic devolution, through attenuating the state's control over the economy – for example by allowing enterprise managers to engage directly in foreign trade –

raised the spectre of centrifugal forces undermining the power of the central authorities and, by extension, of the power of the Kremlin's hegemony over Eastern Europe. The fate of the reformist government in Czechoslovakia highlighted the latter question. It is this constraint that leads Maier to explain the termination of NÖS in 1970 as reform falling 'victim to the logic of imperial control' (p. 89).

Economic decline

For Maier, the termination of NÖS was a pivotal mistake. Despite the (hardly promising) example of reformist Hungary, he suggests that market reforms could have rescued the profitability of the East German economy. Whereas most 'Western economic analysts' – including Kopstein – 'have maintained that the final crisis of communism merely culminated its insoluble long-term contradictions' Maier sticks his neck out and 'proposes an alternative scenario, namely that socialist policy makers might have evolved toward more flexible production in the 1960s, but then put off reforms for a fateful decade or more' (p. 79).

Whatever the merits of such speculation, it is certainly true that the early 1970s mark a watershed in East Germany as well as elsewhere in the Soviet bloc and beyond. For one thing, these were the years when '[c]apitalism and communism together left behind the period of rapid and relatively easy capital accumulation that marked the quarter century after World War II to enter a far more troubled era' (Maier, p. 81). But more significantly, although 'many of the difficulties of communism also assailed the West' – where 'painful' restructuring was attempted – in the East, relative decline evolved into drawn-out and worsening crisis.

Why was this? Maier's explanation centres on the relation between the peculiar structures of the Soviet economies and the world economy. The USSR had become locked into a particular complex of structures – economic, political, geopolitical – that had in mid-century been innovative and singularly conducive to capital accumulation, enabling it to achieve regional hegemony, recover from war, rearm, and rebuild an industrial base, but these, now replicated throughout Eastern Europe, were becoming fetters on further growth. 'Mobilized' societies aiming to overtake western rivals became 'siege' societies stuck in a vicious circle of decline. In the East German case, being relatively small and advanced, the contradictions were felt especially painfully.[4]

Maier develops his case in two different ways. The first is a rather loose and speculative argument. It suggests that command economies have an affinity to the stage of development which characterised the industrialised world from 1930 to 1970, 'because the preponderant technology of the era seemed to be based on large productive units and

---

[4] Kopstein's figures (p. 198) suggest that by 1980 East Germany, of all the Eastern European countries (except Yugoslavia) had advanced least when compared to the pre-war level.

heavy industry' where efficiency was conceived in terms of the 'mechanized output of standardized products' (p. 97). Communism subscribed to 'the romance of coal and steel', a type of product which is, he assumes, peculiarly amenable to central planning.

In advancing this case Maier points to real phenomena – the ecologically disastrous commitment of the SED to expanding lignite production, the extreme emphasis on heavy industry, and 'soft budget constraints' which enabled once-competitive sectors to be maintained when world conditions had long rendered them obsolete. But do such 'inefficiencies' emanate from an affinity of central planning with an outdated (simple and heavy) stage of technological development? And has the world economy really shifted to a new 'flexible' phase based upon smaller units and greater complexity? By some measures the opposite would seem to be the case. The size of firms in many sectors is now larger than in mid-century – making many East German 'giants' seem like dwarves.[5] Meanwhile the developing division of labour continues to underwrite tendencies to greater standardisation of mass production, and to simplification of processes at the micro level.

Maier's second angle relates to these developments. He highlights how the Comecon economies were structurally organised to resist 'the encroaching world market' (p. 104). In order, however, to benefit from the possibilities of international trade and production, and forced, indeed, by the imperative of matching the scale, resources and reach of the world's leading firms, intensive engagement in the world economy was all but inevitable. The longer resistance lasted, the greater would be the pain of restructuring when integration came. In Maier's version of this thesis the world market operates essentially as a selection mechanism. His case would be stronger, however, if he posited the difficulties of integration into the burgeoning international division of labour as itself the chief cause of the relative decline which underlay the process of 'deselection'.[6]

'Westwards pull'

Although the end of NÖS and the replacement of SED leader Ulbricht by Honecker in 1971 were both linked to what Honecker himself described as the need to beware the '"pull to the West"' (Kopstein, p. 71), and were followed by a recentralisation of decision-making, this by no means resulted in an end to closer integration into the world economy. Trade with the West continued to grow. Import-export firms were set up in the West to sell East German commodities, to speculate

---

[5] In the vehicle industry, for example, the largest East German players employed under one tenth as many workers as General Motors; the gap was larger still if measured by turnover.
[6] For an exposition of such a thesis see Callinicos 1991.

on stock markets, and to channel proceeds back to the hard-currency-starved domestic economy.

Western imports comprised consumer goods, but also capital goods required to upgrade production. Import-led growth was a strategy that Ulbricht had already championed during the economic crisis of 1970, in the following terms: '[I]t is straightforward: We get as much debt with the capitalists, up to the limits of the possible, so that we can pull through in some way. A part of the products from the new plants must then be exported back to where we bought the machines and took on debt' (Kopstein, p. 68). Under the sign of détente and Ostpolitik, the expansion of trade (particularly imports) and debt was striking. Net indebtedness to the West, according to Kopstein, increased during the latter half of the 1970s by more than 20% annually (p. 84)!

If the low cost of borrowing in the 1970s encouraged the strategy of import-led growth (and thus the deferral of restructuring and austerity), its rise as the decade ended provoked a major crisis – in East Germany as in Mexico, Poland and elsewhere. Investment geared to western markets was devalued when those markets slumped; accumulated levels of debt proved unsustainable when interest rates soared. As Nigel Harris has put it: 'the whip to speed growth could as easily turn into a noose to strangle' (p. 192).

Under the pressure of crisis and the pull of the world market, Comecon began to fracture. By 1981, notes Kopstein, 'the Soviets were no longer in a position to do what they had always done when necessary – bail out the SED' (p. 92). From effectively subsidising its allies with cheap oil, the oil price began to approach world market levels and its supply became less assured. The grave – or perhaps tragicomic – political effect of this was exemplified when Moscow diverted oil from East Germany to Poland in 1981. Honecker, painfully aware that over a billion DM had been invested in equipment to refine Soviet oil on the assumption that it would remain cheap and on tap, complained to Brezhnev that the reduction 'undermines the foundation of the GDR's existence' (Kopstein, p. 92).

East Germany, like the rest of Eastern Europe, was in a double-bind. It was caught between closer integration into the world market (spelling debt and politically dangerous dependency), and retrenched orientation to the Comecon bloc (which promised stagnation). Greater integration with the world economy spelt heightened vulnerability to fluctuations of world demand, interest rates, and to the dictates of 'hard' world standards and prices which exposed more starkly the GDR's lagging productivity. Integration could therefore, paradoxically, tend to worsen the trade prospects of weaker, sheltered economies such as the East German, pushing them back towards 'soft markets' and autarky.

These smouldering economic contradictions and crises of the 1970s and 1980s highlight Kopstein's reasons for positing the 'international political economy' as the third imperative, or 'confining condition' (after workers' resistance and geopolitics) which delimited the strategic choices of the SED leadership (p. 12). Inevitably, these broader imperatives which competed for political priority contradicted one another. For example, even as the 'social contract' of the 1970s was being prepared, in order to maintain peace on the labour front, the state planning commission produced a report which insisted such measures could not be afforded. 'The effect, the paper argued, would be increasing indebtedness to the West and a ballooning domestic monetary overhang, as well as declining rates of capital accumulation' (Kopstein, p. 82). Of course, such clashes over priorities are the everyday currency of politics. But as underlying contradictions accumulate, political conflicts tend to become sharper. Maier highlights a dramatic case in 1988: when the Chief Planner proposed austerity measures (with his eye on ballooning debt) he was sharply attacked by Mittag, the Head of the Economy, (whose eye was on social stability). Maier reports that in the aftermath the Stasi's economic unit 'warned how demoralizing an effect Mittag's attack was exerting on economic debate within party ranks' (Maier, p. 72).

In microcosm, this clash represents a sea-change within the nomenklatura. Whereas, in the 1960s, leaders exuded confidence, and Ulbricht could even assert that the GDR could 'succeed politically' by overtaking its Western rivals 'on the economic front' (Kopstein, p. 67), by the 1980s a growing awareness that the confining conditions were closing in led to general demoralisation. The nomenklatura, notes Maier began to 'lose faith'; they began to 'share their critics' sense that the economic and social stalemate could not continue, but they did not know how to extricate themselves or devise decisive reforms' (p. 57).

With this cascade of contradictions in mind, and the resultant diminished room of manoeuvre experienced and perceived by policymakers, one can get to grips with the question as to why the iceberg was not avoided, why contradictions were not resolved, why the SED leadership was driven to make what with hindsight appear to be 'mistakes', and why 'the political élite return[ed] time and again to the same solutions that did not work?' (Kopstein, p. xii). In contrast to Maier, who sees the 'renewed wager on orthodoxy' of the 1970s as a serious mistake (p. 94), Kopstein provides an intriguing explanation of why ruling classes are driven to make such 'mistakes'. His emphasis is on the constraints upon policy, and how choices 'may be rational in the short run but irrational over the long run' (p.105). In the case of the GDR, the constraints on reform included – apart from the lack of regularised régime change and the sheer inertia and complacency that tends to imbue every successfully established régime – the 'pull to the West', dependence upon the USSR, as well as the close interlocking of economic, political and cultural institutions, between economic structure and geopolitical alliance which meant that even piecemeal reform might catalyse the dissolution of the GDR, given its precarious economic and national status. By the late 1980s, then, 'even if

Honecker and company had wanted to "reform" the economy ... they would not have had an easy time of it. They were hemmed in by the choices both they and their predecessors had made at critical junctures in their state's history' (Kopstein, p. 104). To recap, these included the Kremlin's decision to build East Germany as a front-line state, which required a massive rearmament programme which, in turn, catalysed the 1953 uprising. This, together with East Germany's front-line situation, heightened the imperative of pacifying the working class, and this entailed measures which were to lower the chance that NÖS would succeed. This failure, in turn, limited Honecker's room for manoeuvre in the 1970s.

This was the (domestic) context in which the revolution of 1989 occurred. In Maier's words, 1989 witnessed a ruling élite feeling 'overwhelmed by social complexity' (p. 38). In fact it was not complexity that overwhelmed, but rather their weakness and lack of cohesion in the face of ever more aggravated contradictions. As the revolutionary crisis set in, that demoralisation visibly increased. With details emerging of unprecedented levels of debt (Maier, p. 59), and with Gorbachev making contradictory pronouncements on the fate of East Germany (Maier, p. 156), SED confidence crumbled. The only plausible reaction to such paralysing circumstances was, it seemed, to sit tight. In Kopstein's words '[t]he SED élite believed that it faced an extreme version of the Tocquevillian paradox: unpopular governments become unstable when they start to reform themselves' (p. 104). Though none may actually have read Tocqueville, 'their conversations in the final years reveal an intuitive understanding of their predicament. Reform seemed to be both necessary and unimaginable.'

Accidental breakdown?

What sense should be made historiographically of this breakdown of the SED ancien régime? On this subject a rather headstrong claim is made by Offe, who argues that the 'breakdown of the GDR cannot be explained in terms of ... a coming to a head of long-inherent crisis tendencies, but must be accounted for in terms of a contingent and rather "accidental" chain of events', a chain which includes first and foremost Gorbachev's rise to power and the opening of the iron curtain (p. 24). Certainly Offe is correct to argue that there is not automatic progression from economic crisis to revolution. Nevertheless, his case for contingency is equally untenable and rests on two misconceptions. The first is empirical. Offe asserts that the East German economy benefited from 'an immunity to crises' (p. 141); but anybody with a closer understanding of it would agree by and large with Naumann and Trümpler's view that serious crises in fact occurred in 1948/9, 1953,

1956, 1961, 1970/1, and 1979/80, not to mention 1989.[7] Related to this misconception is the belief, which Offe shares with currents of thinking amongst Greens and the SED (though demonstrably not East German workers), that '[t]he supply of consumer goods has been adequate and even relatively good since the 1960s' (p. 18).

The second problem is methodological. Offe's rigid distinction between determination and contingency makes little sense when applied to actual historical processes. That Hungary opened the iron curtain may be 'contingent', but that it did so was surely linked to the 'pull to the West' outlined above. It seems to me that a more helpful conception of the role of contingency is indicated in Trotsky's intriguing formulation: '[t]he entire historical process is a refraction of historical law through the accidental. In the language of biology, we might say that the historical law is realized through the natural selection of accidents'.[8] Although each particular revolution may seem on the face of it to be the outcome of a chain of accidents, the prevalence of revolutions and other sharp ruptures of political form is surely connected to the general processes whereby changes in productive forces and relations of exploitation take the form of, and are conditioned by, changing complexes of economic and political organisation. These structures comprise an intensively uneven and combined, and intrinsically competitive, global capitalism. When economic contradictions, and/or conflicting imperatives upon states may develop into economic, social and/or geopolitical crisis, and are interpreted as and acted upon as such, established structures become 'audited', subject to intense scrutiny.[9] At such times leaders and supporters of failing institutions are liable to come under fire from challengers; the scope of strategic possibilities and the apertures of historical vision swiftly widen.

It is then, when old orders become subject to internal scrutiny and serious fracture, that the scope for collective action 'from below' also broadens. For the imperatives, the 'confining conditions,' that occupy centre-stage in structuralist analysis of the Kopstein kind are not externally articulated but internally related. Capitalism, as I have written elsewhere, (with Colin Barker), is best 'understood as a system with a dual core set of relations: as simultaneously competitive and exploitative accumulation. The heart of the accumulation process is the continuous extraction of surplus labour using ever new methods, a process fuelled by the competitive relations existing among the various centres or units of accumulation, and constantly resisted by those subjected to it'.[10] When accumulation, and/or the political structures that regulate it, enter crisis, the interests of the exploited are directly affected; the soil for mass collective action is watered. It is to this that we now turn.

---

[7] Naumann and Trümpler 1990, p. 5.
[8] Cited in Carr 1987, p. 102.
[9] 'Audit' is adapted it from Barnett via Hay 1996.
[10] Barker and Dale 1999.

Was it a revolution?

In what sense was 1989 a revolution? The three authors give very different answers. Kopstein's is Skocpolesque. His lens is sharply focused upon structural contradictions, but lacks the flexibility to shift focus onto agency when breaking crisis moves its role to centre-stage. The outcome of revolution is assumed to be immanent in the crisis itself. Accordingly, Kopstein proclaims his framework as an alternative to those that highlight the 'mobilization of civil society'. Mobilisation, he implies, is nothing but the steam that rises from the heat of structural clashes; it is merely 'one stage in the revolutionary process, and one that appears relatively late in the game' (p. 13).

If Kopstein is dismissive of mobilisation in general, Offe directs his fire specifically at those who champion the mobilisations of 1989. His case is that it was not a revolution, and for two main reasons. First, by defining revolution in a peculiarly strict way, as entailing 'the construction of a new order built upon new ideas', he can conclude that '1989 was not a "revolution" ... but just the crumbling of an old régime' (p. 187). His logic is pristine, but one wonders if he realises that it also rules out the French or Russian examples, built as they were upon such well-worn ideas as Liberty, Equality and Communism. Second, in explaining the 'crumbling' of the régime, Offe accords sole explanatory force to institutional change and none to social movements. In the case of the Soviet reform process, his reference points are purely institutional, and never those agents of collective resistance – from Solidarnosc to the Mudjahedin – which helped to kick Gorbachev et al. into considering possibilities of reform. In Offe's account of the East German case, the implosion of SED authority occurred essentially because the ruling élite had lost confidence in the economy, followed by the raising of the iron curtain, Gorbachev's indications that Soviet military support could not be counted upon, and the consequent immobilisation of the repressive apparatus (p. 12). 'The demise of the régime was thus caused', Offe insists, 'by the loss of repressive pressure, not the rise of counter-pressure' (p. 20). Evidence for this is that mobilisation occurred only after 'the collapse of the régime's ability to use repression was already well underway, and thus the citizens' movement could unfold in a relatively risk-free way'. 'It was not the movement that brought about victory', Offe concludes, 'It was just the opposite: the obvious weakness of the state apparatus encouraged and triggered the growth of a democratic movement' (p. 21).

This sort of one-eyed, deterministic thinking is discussed perceptively by Maier, who is worth quoting at length. He inveighs against his 'West German colleagues [who] have talked of an "implosion" of East Germany as if some worn-out machine finally just broke down' (p. xiv). They,

> argued that no revolution had occurred. Instead, they claimed
> that the GDR had collapsed as a result of its inner difficulties;
> it had suffered 'systems failure' or 'imploded.' These
> judgments were occasionally condescending. To a degree, the
> East German popular movement seemed actually
> embarrassing to some West German social scientists [who]
> were used to thinking in terms of abstract processes, and the
> powerful intrusion of crowds and demonstrations seemed
> vaguely threatening ... The East German protestors were like
> obstreperous children at an adults' dinner party (p. 119).

In Maier's treatment, the weakening of the state and the burgeoning of
social movements were mutually enhancing processes. Far from being a
walk-on part, 'at each critical juncture, the East Germans' collective
action – no matter how hesitant at first, and how filled with doubts later
– impelled decisive accommodations or allowed new initiatives' (p. xiv).
He describes several of these critical junctures. First were the
demonstrations by would-be emigrants. These culminated in early
October when trainloads of westward-bound emigrants passed through
Dresden, and 15,000 people besieged the station in an attempt to get on
board. The police managed to thwart them in this aim, but failed to stop
them regrouping to form a permanent demonstration (of fluctuating
size) which wound through the city, periodically scuffling with police,
for a marathon eighty hours. A few days later in 'Plauen, also on the
route of the emigration-trains, 10,000 demonstrators took to the streets
and barricaded the mayor in his city hall' (p. 145). The thrill of these
days consisted in the dramatic and unexpected demonstration of the
potential of collective mobilisation to resist suppression. The state's
omnipotent image was decisively punctured. Second came the
demonstrations for political change, initially culminating in Leipzig on
October 9th. On that day, bloodshed seemed inevitable, with twenty-
eight army divisions present. But the sheer scale of the demonstration,
which overawed and demoralised the local SED leadership and security
forces, undermined any inclination to open fire. Of all the critical
junctures this was a breathtakingly close call. No blood was shed, but
had it been, the course of the revolution could have been entirely
different. It was only now that the old régime really began to 'collapse',
ie. only after a showdown with an already highly mobilised movement. It
is considerations such as this that lead Maier to judge that 'at a critical
instant, the crowds of Leipzig and Berlin pushed the process of
Communist concession and erosion beyond the point of return' (p.
120). *Pace* Offe, the movement did make a difference, striking fear into
the SED leadership, reconfiguring the political agenda, and accelerating
the pace of the crisis and collapse of the Soviet order, and then the pace
of German unification. Moreover, Maier insists that the crowds 'were
revolutionary': at least in the first month of protest they 'were bonded
by a vision of an alternative public sphere; they shared a fraternal

identity ...; they demonstrated the exaltation of will that social theorists such as Durkheim ... have emphasized; they helped bring down a régime' (p. 166).

Dynamics of revolution

A common narrative of 1989 is that the protest movement was united for the first month or so, after which it began to divide – between the original organisers of protest (the 'Citizens Movement') and a nationalistic movement for unification. The former is seen as radically democratic – in Zizek's terms, 'authentic' – the latter as inauthentic, conservative, and motivated chiefly by the 'seduction' of Western commodities. As to the régime, its backbone was cracked by the protests after which it gave in to popular demands, replacing the head of state, opening the Wall, and paving the way for elections and unification – in short, both régime and state 'collapsed'.

This interpretation is, as I shall indicate, as simplistic and misleading as it is common. The Citizens Movement (CM) was in fact only one of the early organisers of protest in 1989, the other being the emigration movement. Its leaders' attitude to protest was ambiguous; many, such as Rainer Eppelmann 'viewed the mass demonstrations in Leipzig with some uneasiness and called for their end once representatives of the régime were willing to talk' (Maier, p. 175). They were reluctant to call the SED's monopoly of power into question; their goal was not to force the régime from power but to pressure and persuade it to reform, within the framework of an SED-CM 'dialogue'. But as Maier points out, this was a strategy that sought as much to brake as to mobilise protest: '"dialogue" set limits on the protestors. Although the presence of tens of thousands of demonstrators on the streets made the situation volatile, to appeal for dialogue was to accept for the short-term a self-limiting role for the crowd and to renounce any seizure of the state' (p. 176). A classic justification by one CM leader, Jens Reich, is cited by Maier: 'We never wanted power. It would have conflicted with our commitment to legality'(p. 169). 'Self-limitation' was the order of the day. When delegations from major workplaces approached CM leaders to propose strike action in support of democratic demands the response was negative. When demonstrators sought to occupy SED and Stasi buildings, CM groups organised to prevent entry. When popular pressure brought down the Wall, many CM leaders were shocked. One 'suggested that what remained of the Wall should "exist a bit longer"' (Maier, p. 199), while another even considered appealing for its reconstruction.

Nor was the 'collapse' as straightforward as is often imagined. When Maier proclaims that '[p]ower passed to the streets' he is voicing a common misconception (p. 120). In fact, neither régime nor state simply 'collapsed'. It is certainly true – and was glorious to witness –

that the supposedly omniscient Stasi was unable to contain mass emigration or protest. However, all the key institutions of power remained intact, even if some heads rolled. Some sections of the nomenklatura quickly came to realise that transformation was unstoppable, but saw that if reforms were made and the CM were courted revolution might be restricted to the 'passive' kind, with limited popular protest and only minimal changing of the old guard.[11] Under Hans Modrow, the SED set about wooing CM leaders, offering them a morsel of 'responsibility' in return for a dampening of protest. The olive branch was accepted. Thus, when popular mobilisation built towards its zenith – not, as usually assumed in October, but in December and January – CM leaders entered a 'crisis-management' alliance with the régime, at first around a 'Round Table', and subsequently in government.

Maier describes the round tables as the institutional expression of 'self-limitation'; they aimed to realise 'an armistice between protesters and state', and served as 'a surrogate for the constituent assembl[y] that the transition process never convoked' (p. 184). However, this ghostly surrogate was practically powerless. Moreover, it lacked legitimacy, so failed to conclude the armistice. Rather, it came to be seen as indicating the CM's complicity with the SED, and thereby exacerbated the gap between the CM and the bulk of the protest movement. The demands of the latter now became directed more and more towards the corruption and greed of the nomenklatura, the shameless persistence of the Stasi, and the demand for German unification. The growing force and militancy of this movement, combined with continued emigration, underwrote what Maier refers to as 'the sudden erosion of credibility for the East German government in mid-January' (p. 255).

This was the highpoint of the revolution, with protestors emboldened by success, raising demands which directly challenged the rule and institutions of the SED, and even the existence of the state itself. It is also the point at which the sympathy of liberals tends to expire – as exemplified by Maier's depiction of angry protestors storming a Stasi headquarters as 'ugly and on a rampage' (p. 164).

How, though, should the split in the movement be assessed? Maier refers to 'the divergence of two streams of protest: the one emanating from dissident groups and the church-oriented; the other based on the ... working class, fed up with urban overcrowding and material and ecological privation' (p. 374). As we have seen, the former tended to prioritise 'dialogue' while the latter relied exclusively on public protest. Regarding goals, the latter generally supported German unification. But, as Offe argues, the nationalism displayed was hardly that of an 'emotionalized *Volk*', but was essentially 'instrumental' in nature – aimed at eliciting economic support from the FRG (p. 16). It was the

---

[11] The fear of radicalization of protest was not restricted to the East German ruling class. Helmut Kohl assured SED leader Krenz that in this respect, if no other, they were shoulder to shoulder (cf. Dale 1996, p. 108).

combination of seeing the quality of life in West Germany and hearing revelations of the extent of economic crisis and ruling class hypocrisy and corruption that 'produced a feeling, especially amongst older workers, that for years they had been betrayed of the fruits of their labour'.[12]

For such groups, Maier suggests 'absorption in West Germany was precisely the guarantee of liberty and welfare they craved' (p. 118). West Germany seemed to offer a definite, gilt-edged promise of civil liberties, democracy, and a decent living standard. The CM, by contrast, offered little. Its leaders refused even to consider the possibility of taking power, seemed to consider austerity to be a virtue, were ambiguous in their attitude to the Wall, and even entered into alliance with the SED – just as revelations of the latter's mismanagement and corruption were being greeted by resounding popular anger, and a growing clamour for an emphatic break with the ruling class – party, state and all. This was the basis of the movement for unification. It was certainly nationalistic, but that should not imply that the divergence of the two streams was between nationalism and internationalism. Rather, it expressed a choice of nationalisms. Some key currents of the CM defended the existence of the GDR and identified with it as the valid nation; an identification that, in turn, spurred the developing diversion of mass support from CM to FRG.

Finally, the split in the movement was also reflected culturally. In one of the most vivid sections of his book, Maier reflects upon the linguistic aspect of the divergence. Despite a preoccupation with 'communication' between 'state and society', CM intellectuals often spoke the same language as state spokespeople. An abstruse and systems-theoretical jargon was, on the one hand, 'invoked both by the régime and by the intellectuals who would transform it. On the other hand, a rhetoric of primeval popular assembly – the language of "antistructure," of shoulder-to-shoulder community – arose anonymously from the crowd. This second language was the more potent; like Joshua's trumpets it brought down the Wall' (p. 134).[13]

Why was the CM like this? Why did its rhetoric converge with that of the régime and diverge with that of the crowds on the streets? Offe offers a perceptive insight here, suggesting that the CM's predecessors, the opposition groups of the 1980s, had effectively been 'sealed off from the rest of society' (p. 141). In this context, they had developed in a 'new social movement' direction, which rendered them 'unable, with their issues and strategies, to gain support or sympathy from within the industrial working class' (p. 21). Offe's case is a strong one. If little

---

[12] Hoffman and Rink 1990, p. 120. Evidently, motives for demanding unification were strongly linked to perceptions of exploitation, thus refuting Kopstein's suggestion that the 'revolutions of autumn 1989 ... were largely political actions of dissatisfied consumers, not, as Marxian social theory would have us expect, of dissatisfied producers' (p. 192).
[13] 'But' he adds 'it would have been too much to expect that it might become a durable hegemonic discourse'.

else, the SED had mastered the techniques of the management of dissidence. Oppositionists had been fairly successfully quarantined within the walls of the church, with extra-church activity heavily repressed. The church acted as a container, in both senses of the word – functioning as a host to dissidence, but also as a severe steward of its boundaries. Both church officials and undercover Stasi agents acted to theologise and individualise dissent, and to smother political activity, ensuring that if organised opposition could arise at all, it was heavily skewed towards pious moderation.

The outbreak of revolution revealed that the organised opposition had internalised the limits of the status quo more deeply than most of the popular movement. Their disorientation in the face of rapid political change, their readiness to engage in 'dialogue' with a corrupt régime, their defence of a state that had clearly lost all popular support, and their astonishment that the working class would rise up at all, were all products of an internalisation of those narrow limits to action and thought that had become institutionalised over the years in which gradualist pragmatism had seemed the only viable strategy. It is a poignant irony that the former oppositionists, despite years of courageous defiance in the face of repression, ultimately placed greater trust in the SED than did the bulk of the protest movement.

Where now for Germany and the Left?

With the dust of battle now cleared, how have the revolutions of 1989 altered prospects for democracy, for the Left, for Germany? For Offe, 1989 represented the closing down of alternatives. With the end of the Cold War prospects for the Left are worse than ever (p. 190). His book reads as a phlegmatic affirmation of the inevitability of actually existing capitalism, which, in its liberal form, at least has the virtue of embodying a civilised mode of social regulation based upon constitutionalism and the rule of law.

Maier's case is crisper. Whereas Offe bases his fatalism on a diagnosis of communism that emphasises its opposition to capitalism, Maier insists 'that it advances our understanding to compare the problems of late communism with the contemporaneous difficulties faced by the advanced capitalist countries' (p. 329). Thus, the breakdown of communism represents, not the closing of historical alternatives, but a reminder of the sorts of contradictions that also confront otherwise more successful regions. 1989 did not simply represent the triumph of democracy but closed a decade which had seen an immense upwards transfer of wealth, a saturnalia of inequality and exploitation which 'might yet prove as corrosive to democracy as the fall of communism was beneficial' (p. 201). His concluding chapter, 'Anschluss and Melancholy', ends with a cautionary juxtaposition:

> The harsh pressures of relative backwardness brought down
> the Soviet system in the 1980s and helped to liquidate the
> East German state that incorporated Russia's claim to have
> shared post-1945 leadership with the West. The pressures
> encroaching on the capitalist world from the 1970s to the
> 1990s led to the end of full employment, ... increasing
> inequality, and increasing dissension over economic
> integration. Thus the unease that East Germans brought to
> united Germany came to be increasingly matched by the
> malaise emerging in the wider society (p. 329).[14]

For this reviewer, Maier's comparison of crisis East and West is a
welcome antidote to the familiar End of History refrain. Since 1989
Western Europe, especially Germany, has seen a marked increase in
instability and social polarisation. One aspect of this was an electoral
'pink tide' which culminated in the best general election result ever
achieved by parties of the German Left, against which Offe's
despondency seems almost quaint. With this in mind, one can reread
1989 as a source of inspiration and invaluable insights into the algebra
of revolution. Although the movement in East Germany was fairly
successfully contained within bourgeois limits by established and
reformist political forces – from Modrow to Kohl to the CM – it
nevertheless gave a glimpse of the potential that arises when established
order breaks down in the face of collective protest. Despite the dead-
weight of the decades in which open resistance had been unthinkable,
within a few weeks all was transformed. Breaking the power of the
security forces opened up manifold possibilities for meaningful
intervention 'from below'. In the face of one of the most extensive
security apparati in the world, demonstrations were organised,
democratic space forced open, and Honecker's régime overthrown.
These things were done with growing wit and panache, displayed on
countless placards, or in countless confrontations with advocates of 'law
and order'. Aims and strategies were proposed, developed, defended
and rejected; organisations were initiated, built, or abandoned, all
during a four month-long conflagration of popular democratic debate
and initiative. In short, ordinary East Germans seized the political
agenda, and even shook the international sphere – forcing rapid

---

[14] If Maier's concluding chapter ends with a warning of malaise and portending
crisis, his epilogue – which centres on the avant-garde artist Christo's wrapping
of the Reichstag – is bizarrely upbeat. Wrapping the German parliament in
Berlin, he reckons, has 'liberated the building's parliamentary potential from the
incubus of earlier failures of representative government. Unveiled, it might be
born anew' (p. 332). The born-again building – released from its 'heavy legacy'
– symbolically seals Germany's transition from a tortuous *Sonderweg* to liberal
normality. As if that is not enough, 'the wrapped Reichstag suggested' to Maier
'that these diverse Germans could be friendly as well as challenging'. Quite apart
from the condescension of this statement, it is striking that an author with such
insight into the severity of Germany's current social contradictions can come up
with sanguine speculation that bears as scant relation to German reality as the
'Diana effect' did to Britain.

unification, and knocking any remaining diplomatic cards out of Gorbachev's hands.

In the process, and particularly during the radicalisation in December and January, a glimpse was given of the potential displayed by movements in revolutionary crises to deepen, accelerate, and change direction, and to reveal in the process hitherto unsuspected collective capacities, and to expose historical switching-points, times when collective organisation and political consciousness come to the fore as determinants of historical change.

References

Barker, Colin and Dale, Gareth 1999, 'Protest Waves in Western Europe: A Critique of "New Social Movement Theory"', *Critical Sociology*, March.

Callinicos, Alex 1991, *The Revenge of History*, Cambridge: Polity.

Carr, E.H. 1987, *What is History?*, Harmondsworth: Penguin.

Dale, Gareth 1996, 'The East German Revolution of 1989', in *To Make Another World*, edited by Colin Barker and Paul Kennedy, Aldershot: Avebury.

Gramsci, Antonio 1971, *Selections from the Prison Notebooks*, London: Lawrence & Wishart.

Harris, Nigel 1983, *Of Bread and Guns*, Harmondsworth: Penguin.

Hay, Colin 1996, *Re-Stating Social and Political Change*, Buckingham: Open University Press.

Hoffmann, Michael and Rink, Dieter 1990, in *Leipzig im Oktober*, edited by Jürgen Grabner et al., Berlin: Wichern.

Naumann, Gerhard and Trümpler, Eckhard 1990, *Von Ulbricht zu Honecker*, Berlin: Dietz.

Vietnam: Anatomy of a Peace
Gabriel Kolko
London: Routledge, 1997

Reviewed by Kenneth J. Hammond

Northwest of Ho Chi Minh City, the former Saigon, in Long Anh province lies the district of Cu Chi. Here, during Vietnam's long war against the Americans in the 1960s and early 1970s, a massive system of tunnels was constructed which allowed major forces of the Liberation Army to operate in close proximity to the nerve centre of the American military-sponsored régime. Thousands of soldiers and cadres of the National Liberation Front worked and lived in these tunnels, suffering under harsh jungle conditions, repeated incursions by American and ARVN units, and relentless bombing from unseen B-52s.

In July 1997, I visited Cu Chi and observed two very different legacies from the wartime era. The tunnel complex has been turned into a kind of theme park for tourists, mostly foreigners. The tunnels themselves have been widened to accommodate the girth of Western visitors, and lined with concrete to spare travellers the dirt and dampness of the underground world. A firing range has been set up to allow returning veterans or the merely curious to shoot off bursts of bullets, getting the 'feel' of war, and lending a surreal soundtrack to the scene. Cu Chi was the only place in Vietnam, North or South, where physical signs of the war could still be seen – craters from B-52 bombs dot the jungle, looking almost as if they have been preserved to maintain the ambience of battle. The tunnel site is a favourite, almost a mandatory destination for tourists, and the souvenir stands and soda stalls were packed with sweaty Caucasians.

Just next to the tunnel site, but not on the itinerary for visiting foreigners, is a brand new memorial to the 50,000 or so Vietnamese who died in the Cu Chi district during the war. Built in the style of traditional village *dien*, or spiritual halls, but on a much larger scale, this imposing edifice was a beautiful but sobering reminder of the reality of war, and the incredible suffering and sacrifices endured by the Vietnamese people. It was sacred space, not to be profaned by the cameras and sneakers of casually curious travellers. It stood in stark contrast to the scene at the tunnels. This contrast reflects the deeply divided reality of Vietnam today, a reality presented in clear and sombre prose by Gabriel Kolko in his new book.

Kolko has long been a scholar of Vietnam and its struggle for independence. His earlier masterwork *Anatomy of a War* is an excellent overview of the war between Vietnam and United States, tracing in exhaustive detail the course of the war and the political and military complexities on both sides of this epic conflict. Kolko maintains high standards of evidence and objectivity, while nonetheless clearly supporting the Vietnamese in their quest for freedom from foreign domination – French, American, or Chinese. The victory of the Vietnamese in this protracted war in 1975 was seen by Kolko, and by progressive forces around the world, as a great moment, and as setting the stage for post-war reconstruction and socialist development.

The reality of Vietnam in 1997, however, is very different from what might have been expected in the wake of the triumph of April 1975. In the course of two weeks in Hanoi, Ho Chi Minh City, the Mekong Delta and Tay Ninh province that summer, I was repeatedly told by representatives of the Vietnamese government, members of the National Assembly, local officials, and boosters of the Ho Chi Minh City chamber of commerce, that Vietnam has embarked on a course of economic 'reform' which takes as its foundation the creation of a free market, with foreign investment aggressively sought under the guiding hands of the World Bank and the International Monetary Fund. In Hanoi, and much more so in Ho Chi Minh City, petty capitalist enterprises were to be seen everywhere. Small shops, restaurants, repair services for bicycles or watches, flower vendors, fruit hawkers, and the ever present cyclo drivers all testified to the dynamism and extent of profit-seeking hustle in Vietnam's cities. Construction cranes, looming office blocks and hotel towers showed that international capital was also pouring in to the country. Bars and brothels catering to foreign businessmen and returning Vietnamese or ethnic Chinese have sprung up as well.

How has this come about? How did the promise of socialist revolution, which fuelled the liberation struggle in Vietnam and the solidarity of people around the world, come to be replaced by this explosion of capitalism? And how complete has this change of course been? These are some of the questions Kolko seeks to address in his new book.

The key to this puzzle for Kolko is the problematic nature of the leadership of the Vietnamese Communist Party. Ironically, in Kolko's view, the same factors which helped the Party win victory in the war undermined its ability effectively to construct a socialist society once the war was over. The geography of Vietnam, the extreme conditions of decentralisation enforced by prolonged warfare, and the rapidity of the final collapse of the Saigon régime once American military support was withdrawn, combined to create a situation by mid-1975 in which the Party found itself in possession of all the territory of Vietnam, but without either a sufficiently large body of cadres or a coherent plan for administering and developing the newly recovered provinces of the south. The central leadership of the Party had grown used to delegating large degrees of autonomy to provincial and local-level Party committees during the war, and this made strong central leadership difficult to create in the new conditions of post-war Vietnam. Large numbers of new Party members were recruited in the months and years immediately after liberation in the south, and many of these proved to be opportunists or worse, using their new status as Party members to shield themselves from political or economic changes, and eventually turning lower-level Party organisations into private enterprises and corrupt sinecures.

Almost as important as structural problems within the Party were the international entanglements in which Vietnam committed major resources to the invasion and occupation of Cambodia, and to resisting the Chinese 'punishment' campaign of 1979. The Cambodian involvement in particular became an ongoing haemorrhage, draining off resources desperately needed for economic recovery and socialist development at home. Just when Vietnam began to extricate itself from Cambodia, the collapse of the Soviet economy and termination of Soviet aid struck a further blow at the Vietnamese economy.

In 1986, a new generation of leaders began to dominate the Politburo of the Vietnamese Communist Party. Vo Van Kiet, Nguyen Van Linh, both southerners with technocratic backgrounds, along with Do Muoi, came to constitute the top echelon of Party and government. Along with individuals such as Nguyen Xuan Oahn, who had risen to prominence in the post-war period – despite his earlier collaboration with the Japanese, the Americans, and his work for the International Monetary Fund – advising the Saigon régime in the 1960s, these new leaders decided that socialism simply would not work in Vietnam, and that the economic crisis the country was facing could only be solved by turning to the free market and the international capitalist system. This turn to the capitalist road, however, was not to include any diminution of the power of the Party. As Kolko sees it, these twin themes, free-market reforms and the preservation of the Party have become the foundation of official policy in Vietnam from the late 1980s to today.

This does not mean, though, that all Vietnamese have abandoned their hopes for a more just and equitable society free of foreign domination. Indeed, the erosion of social services in education, public health, and the status of women which has accompanied the program of market reform has made the goals of socialism all the more requisite for many people in the countryside and in the cities who have not prospered in the new competitive marketplace. Millions of Vietnamese families continue to suffer from losses they sustained during the war. Veterans and rank-and-file Party activists have resisted the leadership's reform efforts from below. Peasants have protested, sometimes violently, against grain-marketing policies designed to extract rice from the countryside for sale on the international market in order to raise foreign exchange. Pro-reform officials boast about Vietnam's new status as a top rice exporter, but this has been achieved at great social cost to the traditional base of peasant support for the Party.

Vietnam today is caught between a Party leadership which continues to press for greater 'reform' to bring Vietnam in line with the demands of the World Bank and IMF, and many social and lower-level political forces which resist these reforms and press for a return to what they have conceived of as the socialist road. This conflict lies behind the difficulty the Party has had in bringing another 'new generation' of leaders to the top posts in the government and Party. Efforts in 1996 were unsuccessful, and the younger technocrats selected in the late summer of 1997 have yet to assume real power.

Kolko presents the complexities of Vietnam's present crisis with profound sympathy for the people who fought so hard and gave so much to win their country's independence. This book is filled with a sense of righteous indignation, while still maintaining the rigorous mode of analysis characteristic of Kolko's work in general. He delineates the various interests at work, within the Party and outside it, pulling and pushing the society and economy of Vietnam in many different directions. And he argues strongly that the land question will ultimately prove to be the crucial determinant of the future of Vietnam's development. Without a return to policies which directly and materially benefit the peasants, the current leadership will not be able to maintain its dominant position.

Kolko clearly grasps some of the fundamental questions facing Vietnam today. Yet the very intensity of his focus leads him to neglect some important matters. He has little to say about the situation of women, and, aside from the Chinese, does not address the role of concerns of ethnic minorities. Nor does he discuss the possible impact of Vietnam's membership in ASEAN on the balance of forces within the country, or the relationship between Vietnam and China. These are all important issues, and their inclusion would have given Kolko's book an even more comprehensive perspective.

More problematic is the absence of a clear sense of how the Vietnamese Party got into its current dilemma, or of how it might be able to extricate itself from its contradictions. Kolko's perspective is essentially populist, without addressing what organisational or institutional measures could move the country and the Party in the direction of positive change. Lacking any sense of programmatic prospects, the future for Vietnam seems poised between the stark polarities of continuing authoritarianism or systemic collapse. Further, there is no attempt to connect the course of events in Vietnam with the larger pattern of the recent history of socialist régimes around the world. The collapse of the Soviet Union, the adoption of market-oriented reforms in China, and the general abandonment of the model of top-down state-driven socialist development are missing from Kolko's universe. Vietnam's particular situation is no doubt the product of specific historical and material realities, but it is difficult to conceive that these have come about in complete isolation from the struggles and failures of revolutions and counter-revolutions elsewhere.

Indeed, the populist nature of Kolko's analysis prevents him from digging down to the real basis of the crisis in Vietnam – the question of how socialism could ever have been constructed on the ruins of a peasant agrarian economy and society. Engagement with this question would have drawn Kolko into the mainstream of the history of socialism in the 20th century, in which the critical problem of the accumulation of social capital under conditions of scarcity has plagued every attempt to build an alternative to capitalism. By focusing on the contradictions, substantive as they may be, within the Vietnamese Communist Party, rather than on the fundamentals of the Vietnamese economy and the obstacles in the way of basic reconstruction, let alone the creation of socialism, Kolko has let slip the opportunity to go beyond the polarity of Party authoritarianism versus a vague populist egalitarianism.

Such concerns notwithstanding, this is a very important book. It presents the post-war history of Vietnam clearly and analytically, and contributes greatly to our understanding of the changes which have taken place, and which may lie ahead there. For those of us who fought against the American war in Vietnam, and who saw Vietnam's socialist revolution as a major reason to support the Vietnamese people in their fight for independence, the apparent abandonment of the socialist road has been a troubling anticlimax. Gabriel Kolko has made the contradictory realities of post-war Vietnam more comprehensible, and manages to leave a glimmer of hope in the continuing resistance of many in Vietnam to the betrayal of the revolution by leading Party technocrats. Whether this resistance can go beyond a return to a hypothetical, more democratic form of statism, and lead the Vietnamese towards a truer form of liberation, remains very much to be seen.

Analytical Marxism: A Critique
Marcus Roberts
London: Verso, 1997

Reviewed by Christopher Bertram

It is perhaps fitting that the first footnote of Marcus Roberts's critique of analytical Marxism should refer to Perry Anderson. It is now nearly a quarter of a century since, on the publication of *Lineages of the Absolutist State*, Anderson's creative juices became exhausted. But Anderson's trademark olympian dismissiveness does not lack for imitators and Marcus Roberts – himself published by the great man's own house – provides us with some splendid examples of the style. The neatly placed *bon mot*, the witty little parody, the deft use of a clever quotation, and the ironic use of the rhetorical question: all are deployed with verve. The hazard of deploying this rhetoric, however, is that one leaves oneself vulnerable to more of the same: as a certain thinker once wrote, '*de te fabula narratur*'.

Which is not to say that this is a bad book, by any means. On the contrary, Roberts gives broadly accurate summaries of the main theses espoused by both G.A. Cohen and John Roemer and has something to say about a number of the other analytical Marxists – particularly Erik Olin Wright and Adam Przeworski. Critical as he is, though, of what all of these thinkers have to say, the book betrays a deep ambivalence towards their thought. The more he reads, the more Roberts confronts what Lord Denning might have called an 'appalling vista'. Namely, that the analytical Marxists may have – despite themselves – undermined rather than reconstructed the central claims of Marxian social science. If so, then what remains? Many of the original analytical Marxists have concluded that we can divorce the ethical commitments of socialism from the social scientific claims of Marxism and that attention must be given to clarifying and examining those commitments. Does Roberts dissent? It is hard to tell. Certainly, he thinks that ethical arguments are rather feeble weapons in the face of global capitalism (and who would disagree?). But, although a total theory of the type classical Marxism proclaimed itself to be would – if true – be both useful and reassuring in the face of our current political predicament, it is precisely that truth that is at issue. Lenin may have proclaimed, in one of Louis Althusser's favourite sayings, that 'Marxism is all powerful because it is true'. What of its power if it is not?

In the 'Preface' to this work, Roberts addresses himself to these questions, but does not give any satisfactory answer. He tells us that some of his readers have suggested that his arguments presuppose the health of some alternative, non-analytical, Marxism. His readers are right about this: he does often write as if there were some other Marxist school (unnamed) which is – unlike analytical Marxism – in good order. But when the question is posed explicitly, Roberts denies that he believes any such thing. This ambiguous attitude marks and in the end mars the book.

What is analytical Marxism?

The first problem that must confront someone contemplating a critique of analytical Marxism is that this 'school' displays an alarming lack of unity. It is not just that the main protagonists of analytical Marxism disagree about the 'analytical' part, with some pursuing a slash-and-burn programme of methodological individualism, whilst others permit a mild anti-reductionism. Some of the 'analytical Marxists' aren't even (do not even pretend to be) Marxists. This is true, for instance of Philippe Van Parijs who is misdescribed as an exponent of analytical Marxism on p. 207. On the methodological front, commitments range from enthusiastic to sceptical concerning 'rational choice' theory and are sufficiently heterodox to allow for the inclusion of Erik Olin Wright, despite his penchant for the work of Althusser. As Roberts himself points out, one of the most methodologically aggressive of the original analytical Marxists – Jon Elster – is, in a number of works, also one of the most trenchant and sophisticated critics of that approach.

So what is, methodologically speaking, distinctive about analytical Marxism? My own view is that it is it best to emphasise the negative: analytical Marxism denies that Marxism is methodologically distinct from 'bourgeois' social science. It does not employ any special methods or logic of its own and claims that those attempts that have been made to do so have been part of immunisation strategies designed to shield Marxism from the kind of critical reflection that should be applied to any body of knowledge.

Now, of course, what the standards for evidence and argument ought to be may be a moot point. But, and here is the key point, whatever they ought to be is a matter for epistemology and the philosophy of science, and Marxism – as Marxism – has (or rather ought to have) nothing whatever distinctive to say on those matters.

What does Roberts himself think? It is hard to tell. The most sustained discussion of the philosophy of science in the book takes place at pp. 63–72 in the context of a critique of Cohen's allegedly positivist account of science. Roberts quotes approvingly from both Sean Sayers – who contrasts a dialectical method to that employed by positivism – and Richard Miller who is, arguably, himself an analytical Marxist. But what is meant by 'positivism' here? Again, it is hard to tell, since Popper is mysteriously enlisted to their ranks (which would have been news to Carnap et al.). The apparent target of Roberts's remarks is Cohen's adherence to the deductive-nomological model promoted by Hempel and Nagel and we are told, rather sniffily, that 'the leading Analytical Marxists have signally failed to engage with recent work in the philosophy of science: the work of Kuhn, Feyerabend and Lakatos appears altogether to have passed them by' (p. 69). An inspection of p. 46 on *Karl Marx's Theory of History* (*KMTH*) demonstrates that Kuhn and Feyerabend had not passed Cohen by (he just disagreed with them). In any case, their work is hardly 'state of the art' (p. 68) either – *de te fabula narratur*. What Roberts needs, and fails, to show is that Cohen's work depends on his espousal of a particular model of law and explanation which should be abandoned in the light of more recent work *on those questions*. This would be an interesting problem to address, but it is not approached here.

Roberts's grip on the philosophical background to analytical Marxism is, in any case, pretty loose. He makes much of the supposedly non-progressive nature of analytical philosophy and writes of analytical Marxists as 'a group of theorists self-consciously allied to a philosophical school founded upon the insistence that everything is what it is and not something else' (p.217). This is doubly problematic. First, it is clear that the analytical Marxists do not, as 'a group', subscribe to any particular methodological or philosophical position. But, second, that characterisation of analytical philosophy is inaccurate and anachronistic. On p. 12, Roberts writes of 'the "analytical" tradition, understood in a broad sense'. If that tradition is understood in a 'broad' sense, then Wittgenstein and his admirers form only a narrow part of it and any specific doctrine of his a still narrower part. But a reading of Wittgenstein's dictum that on p. 13 is described by Roberts as 'cavalier' has, by p. 217, become characteristic of the entire tradition! Roberts tells us 'A philosophical school capable of such prep school parochialism and spontaneous chauvinism would hardly seem to be conducive to the reconstruction of the theories of a German theorist who had been inspired by the greatest of all German metaphysicians' (pp. 12-13). *De te fabula narratur* , as they say.

Historical materialism

About half of the book is taken up with an exposition and critique of the central claims of Cohen's *KMTH*. The reader is presented with a reasonably accurate picture of much of Cohen's work on historical materialism and there is a useful summary of some of the main lines of critique. Once again, though, Roberts gets carried away with his own polemic and is at crucial moments careless in his exposition.

The chief symptom of this carelessness is that Roberts is often so keen to get in his critique that he neglects to consider the background against which some claim of Cohen's is to be understood and, crucially, the nature of the question which Cohen is seeking to answer. Yet in any interpretation, sensitivity of this kind is going to be crucial. To use an old example: the question '*Why* did Eve eat the apple?' is significantly different from the questions, 'Why did *Eve* eat the apple?' and 'Why did

Eve eat the *apple?*'. If you misunderstand, by failing to get the right contrast class, then you will end up giving an inappropriate answer. Both when Roberts attempts to problematise Cohen's insistence that the material productive forces can by characterised independently of the social relations of production and when he mounts his critique of Cohen's 'primacy thesis' he makes errors of this kind.

Let me take the question of material productive forces first. As Roberts writes:

> ...whether or not something can properly be designated as a productive force *cannot* be determined other than by reference to the *specific* mode of production within which it is – or is not – being used. As Cohen readily concedes, whether or not a tool is a productive force will depend on the use to which it is being put: if a spade is being employed in order to produce vegetables, then it is a productive force; if it is being used as a weapon, then it is not. Consider the question of whether or not a spade is to be included amongst the productive forces. Cohen answers that it should be included just so long as it is being used in order to produce something. (pp. 65-6)

What can we say about this passage?[1] What of the foisting on Cohen of the claim that for something to be a productive force it has to be being used to produce something? While some of the formulations that Cohen employs in the crucial chapter 2 of *KMTH* could be taken the way Roberts suggests, it is clear from context that they are to be governed by the canonical definition that Cohen gives at p. 32 of *KMTH* where he tells us that to qualify as a productive force 'a facility must be capable of being used by a producing agent in such a way as production occurs (partly) as a result of its use ...' When Cohen later writes of 'Our restriction of productive forces to what are used to produce things ...'(*KMTH*, p. 32) it is clear that the relevant contrast is with entities (such as law or morals) that are not and *cannot be* directly used in production to produce something. When Cohen writes at p. 177 of *KMTH* that 'Existent forces are fettered when, for example, capitalist depression makes plant and labour idle', he is saying something that would be plain incoherent on Roberts's reading. Idle machines and misused spades remain a part of the material productive powers available to the human race, even when social relations dictate their idleness and misapplication.

---

[1] The inclusion of the phrases 'As Cohen readily concedes' and 'Cohen answers' might lead the reader to believe than some specific text of Cohen's is being addressed and criticised. While this may indeed be so, Roberts does not give us chapter and verse to guide the reader and those who look so far as the footnotes between the bottom of page 63 and the top of page 72 will find multiple references to Sean Sayers and Richard Miller, but none to *KMTH*. Certainly this reviewer has been unable to find this 'ready concession' in Cohen's own work and, indeed, it would be very much contrary to his theoretical purposes to make the move that Roberts attributes to him.

Second, let me take Cohen's 'primacy thesis'. According to this thesis, a society has the social form it has because, at a given level of development of the productive forces, that social form has a propensity to develop those productive forces.[2] Roberts picks up on a key problem with the primacy thesis, namely that it has grave difficulties in accounting for the transition from one social form to another and that the reason why one social form gives way to another often seems to have little to do with the propensity the replacing form has to develop the productive forces fettered by its forerunner. As Roberts (following Brenner) notes, it is implausible to attribute to historical agents the knowledge and motivations necessary to have them acting to replace their existent social relations with new ones in order to foster the development of their productive powers. It is implausible to think that people bring about capitalism to tap its developmental potential, so it looks as if that developmental potential does not explain capitalism's emergence. Primacy, what primacy?

A number of people have proposed a 'Darwinian' strategy to preserve the primacy thesis, whereby the emergence of a mutant capitalist strain of social relations destabilises feudalism and then spreads through the population of societies.[3] Whatever the merits of such a strategy, Roberts insists that if the primacy thesis is to be preserved, someone, somewhere has to introduce capitalist social relations for the right reasons: namely to foster development. But it is hard to see why he thinks this. My guess is that he fails to appreciate the nature of the 'why' question that the primacy thesis is responsive to. The question 'Why did capitalism replace feudalism?' is very open-ended and admits of various elaborations including ones that call for essentially narrative answers that say little about the development of the productive forces. (It is also a question that, depending on emphasis, admits of answers like 'Because the productive forces weren't developed enough for socialism' and 'Because coexistence between the two systems would be unstable.) But the question 'Why do (nearly) all modern societies have capitalist social relations?' is one to which it is perfectly in order to respond (in line with the primacy thesis), 'Because capitalism develops the productive forces (at a certain level of their development) faster than any other social form'. The Darwinian strategy explains capitalism's triumph in terms of that propensity, but can afford to be perfectly agnostic about why some people adopted capitalist social relations in the first place.

---

[2] Now Cohen's *KMTH* does exactly what it says on the cover: it provides a defence (and exposition) of Karl Marx's theory of history. Cohen shows that the primacy thesis can plausibly be attributed to Marx and offers some arguments in its support. It would be odd, in a critique of a book which purported to be a defence of, say John Stuart Mill's *On Liberty* to address oneself exclusively to the substantive questions of individual freedom it discussed and to refer hardly at all to Mill's text. Amazingly, this is Roberts's procedure. The key chapter four, where the primacy thesis is attacked contains *not one* citation of a text by Marx!
[3] I do this in Bertram 1990, and, as Roberts notes, it is a significant part of Carling 1991.

I am sure that some readers – and Marcus Roberts himself – will not be satisfied with that answer. Roberts tells us that proponents of the Darwinian move need to show both that it is reasonably likely that capitalist social relations will emerge somewhere within feudal society *and* that, once established, such relations will be able to spread by outcompeting or otherwise dominating surrounding feudalisms. Roberts is highly dismissive of Alan Carling's attempts to do these things, but this would appear to be because he, Roberts, has a highly idealised and unrealistic picture of feudal societies. Even if we do term all medieval societies 'feudal' (a highly implausible thing to do) there were plenty of societies where market relations were significant and well established and others where feudal lords had nothing like the effective power that ideal theory would attribute to them. In other words, there was plenty of 'space' for proto-capitalist relations to emerge *somewhere*. Maybe Roberts is right that an ideal feudal society could insulate itself effectively from the spread of these new social relations (and Japan tried pretty hard!) but most of the neighbours of these 'interstitial zones' where proto-capitalist social relations might emerge, would themselves be rather impure and messy feudalisms. 'Darwinians', like Carling, have, in any case – as Roberts realises – got another string to their bow. If the attraction to their neighbours of making things better, faster and with less effort is not enough, capitalist societies might spread (and resist) through military means. Again, Roberts is dismissive 'the political and military power is only accidentally related to the development of its productive forces' (p. 106). I confess I find it hard to react to this claim other than with incredulity. The resistance of the Dutch to the Spanish empire, the remarkable emergence of England as a world power and the ability of Commodore Perry to force the Japanese to reopen their society, were these only 'accidentally' related to the development of the productive forces made possible by the emergence of capitalist social relations?

Conclusion

There is much to Roberts's book that cannot be covered in a review of this length. Among other things, he gives us summaries of Roemer's views of exploitation and of Przeworski's explorations in political sociology and these are not without merit. The reader who is already well-acquainted with analytical Marxism will find much that is stimulating, provocative (and sometimes irritating) in this book and such people are its ideal target audience. Those wanting a more dispassionate and indeed (in both good and bad senses) academic treatment of the material will probably do better to look at Tom Mayer's *Analytical Marxism* instead. Mayer is less fun than Roberts and less obviously *engagé*; Roberts has a better sense of the *political* importance of his subject that Mayer does. This is a book that could have done with another draft and the assistance of a competent editor to help iron out the inconsistencies, but it remains an exciting potential.

References

Bertram, Chris 1990, 'International Competition in Historical Materialism', *New Left Review* 183, November–December: 116–28.
Carling, Alan 1991, *Social Division*, London: Verso.
Cohen, G.A. 1980, *Karl Marx's Theory of History – A Defence*, Oxford: Oxford University Press.
Mayer, Thomas 1994, *Analytical Marxism*, London: Sage.

Gordon Finlayson responds to Ben Watson's review of current Adorno literature in *Historical Materialism* 2

From his 'review' of Simon Jarvis's book on Adorno (*Historical Materialism* 2, pp. 165–183) it is clear that Ben Watson does not know how to write one. Watson's puerile, *ad hominem* rant could not pass for a polemic, let alone a book review. He tells us virtually nothing about the substance of the book, omits to compare it to other introductions to Adorno eg., those by Gillian Rose and Rüdiger Bubner and he fails to judge the work immanently, by standards appropriate to the kind of book it claims to be. If Simon Jarvis's book is really as worthless as Watson tries to make it out, then he should not be wasting his time (and your space) reviewing it. If it is worth reading and worth reviewing, then he ought to be able to say why. To the extent that he cannot, he indicts himself as a reviewer and as a reader.

Watson seems incapable of grasping the specific demands posed by different genres. He rebukes Jarvis for not writing his introduction in the same aphoristic and self-consciously dialectical prose as Adorno, as if Jarvis intends his own work to be a replacement for, rather than a supplement to Adorno's. Most students of Adorno, at least those who want to learn something about his ideas, will be thankful for the change of idiom, for the 'colourless pedagogic prose' (p. 165) that Watson ridicules. Besides which publishers, mindful of their audience, usually insist on it. Undaunted by such prosaic considerations, Watson berates Jarvis for having situated Adorno's work in the tradition of philosophical sociology between Weber and Durkheim, thereby 'degrading critique into the shopping mall of options' (p. 167). He rebukes him for having made 'patient' and 'careful' comparisons of Adorno with Kant, Hegel, Heidegger, Husserl and Habermas, and yet for having omitted to compare him with (surprise, surprise) Voloshinov and Sloterdijk. So Jarvis's heinous crime is successfully to have written an introduction to Adorno's philosophy that students and non-specialists will be able to understand, one that traces the major influences on Adorno's work and situates it within Adorno's own intellectual horizons, and his heinous omission is not to have written the book that Watson would have. The book Jarvis wrote is condemned for its 'scholastic gibberish', 'academic idealism' and for 'the pseudo-objectivity of academic discourse' (p. 166).

The rest of Watson's criticisms achieve a banality of truly undergraduate proportions. It does not seem to have occurred to him that, if, on Jarvis's interpretation, Adorno's materialism does not turn out to be the kind of materialism that can 'build a picket line' (p. 167) this might have more to do with Adorno's metaphysics than with his interpreter's ideological prejudices. The same can be said of Adorno's reluctance (as he saw it) to subjugate praxis to theory. Arguably this reluctance is symptomatic of a deeper difficulty in his thought. The Hegelian conceptual apparatus of subject/object fails to capture the difference between two relations: that between descriptive propositions and the world they describe and that between rational thought and human action and feeling. Whether Adorno's theoreticism is really a symptom of a deeper underlying problem can only be established by the kind of philosophical arguments Watson repudiates. Instead of abstract philosophical arguments he demands a 'political' reading of Adorno which provides the reader with 1) a method 2) a world view; and 3) an unqualified statement to the effect that the philosophies of Heidegger and Derrida are vacuous (p. 169), cut and dried like the answers to the questions posed by meetings at the SWP's *Marxism* annual event. Jarvis's work fails to deliver these articles of faith, thus demonstrating that it is 'crippled by academic respectability'. Let no one say that Watson's review be guilty of such an error!

Watson's savage and singularly uninformative 'review' raises the wider question of whether *Historical Materialism* is or is not concerned with academic respectability *per se*. If it is not, that explains why it is content to publish reviews that merely rubbish and do not recense. But if, as the quality of the articles in the first two volumes suggests, it does see academic respectability as one thing (among others) worth aiming for, if, unlike Watson, it believes that to be deserving of intellectual and academic recognition is at least not inconsistent with the aim of achieving radical social-political change, it ought not to let such dross past the editors. A book review should review a book, not serve as an opportunity for dropping shit from a great height. Whatever one's reservations about the academic 'establishment', there is still something to be said for the ideal of academic respectability; it is incompatible with the pretentious, pseudo-populist, journalistic bullshit which Watson so generously contributes. In case you think this unfair, I offer one of several egregious examples. 'The term "academic", after all, derives from the institution of the musical academy', Watson declares knowingly (p. 169). Unless Watson has privileged and hitherto undiscovered evidence of an ancient Greek academy of music, I think I am right in saying that the term derives from the Greek word Ἀκαδημικο' [Akadêmikoi] for the students who met in the Ακαδημα [Akademía], the place outside Athens where they discussed philosophy with Plato. True, it is only a detail, but the detail exemplifies the whole review; *faux* intellectualism betrays itself as stupidity. There again, stupidity, as Adorno once wrote, is a social phenomenon not the private property of an individual: 'Stupidity is nothing privative, not the absence of intellectual ability, but rather the scar of its mutilation'. If Adorno is to be believed, Watson's review might just be a casualty of the capitalist order it criticises.

Ben Watson replies

I'm surprised the editors of *Historical Materialism* are bothering their readers with Gordon Finlayson's letter. He nowhere shows any grasp of the elementary principles I take to be the basis for debate among

Marxists. He states that an *ad hominem* (or 'personal') attack is beyond bounds. For those who hold that social being determines consciousness, a certain *ad hominem* slant to debate is inevitable: explanation of error by reference to the class interest of the author is a standard weapon in the Marxist arsenal, found in the writings of every classical Marxist. But perhaps Finlayson's letter can serve a purpose: it provides a sample of the indignant bluster with which liberals greet the suggestion that thought might be something more than a passport to professional status.

In seeking to exclude me from debate as some kind of beyond-the-pale barbarian, Finlayson avoids engagement with the particular points I made. Instead, he provides the unpleasant prospect of someone trying to rabblerouse his colleagues with news of a dangerous animal let loose. Everyone – however ignorant of Adorno or modern music – can rush to the defence of civilised values. If Marxist scapegoats are used for such appeals to the banality of professional self-interest, however, they usually butt back.

Finlayson claims I have no idea of the genre Simon Jarvis is working in, no interest in introductory works on Adorno. He does not seem to have finished my article, whose entire second half consists of praise for Max Paddison's introductory work, *Adorno's Aesthetics of Music*. My argument is that because Paddison has a deep interest in the material Adorno most frequently and fruitfully returned to – music – his study avoids Jarvis's otiose canonisation. For Adorno, musical and artistic form is the subjectivity he wishes to analyse with historical objectivity (thus transcending the Kantian divide). Jarvis's emphasis on Adorno's concepts – rather than the things conceived – downgrades the urgency and bite of his ideas. By restricting his brief to description, Jarvis lays the ground for a passive reception of Adorno's critique: a typical case of what the situationists called 'recuperation'. In contrast, because it develops Adorno's thought – and suggests tasks for it to do – Paddison's book is a better example of the 'introductory genre'. Paddison's Marxism may not be mine, but it has the virtue of the partisanship that makes intellectual discussion something more than a parlour game.

After much strenuous abuse – designed to obviate the necessity of anyone in the charmed circle of 'academic respectability' needing to investigate what I'm actually saying – Finlayson's philosophical professionalism was evidently too exhausted to reach the kernel of my critique. I point out that that in order to accommodate Adorno's ideas to class society, Jarvis betrays Adorno's materialism (he claims Adorno made subject and object 'more or less' equivalent [Jarvis, p. 205]). Still, anyone who can say without blushing in a Marxist journal 'the Hegelian conceptual apparatus of subject/object fails to capture the difference between two relations: that between descriptive propositions and the world they describe and that between rational thought and human action and feeling' is evidently confusing long sentences with analytical perception. Everything Marx and Engels wrote and did was predicated on Hegel's Kant-critique, and hence the success of his 'conceptual apparatus of subject/object' – or, as we call it on the left, dialectics. If Finlayson wishes to establish his intellectual credentials to the readers of *Historical Materialism*, he could do better than start by denying the very proposition that should unite us and allow for constructive intellectual exchange.

What Finlayson so graciously calls my 'pretentious, pseudo-populist, journalistic bullshit' was not written to flatter or entertain anyone – least of all members of the political party to which I belong – but as a blow in the current struggle over Adorno's legacy. It opposes the reduction of his critique of music and capitalism to just another philosophical option for unfortunate students – doubly unfortunate, it seems, in the vicinity of Finlayson, whose phrase 'a banality of truly undergraduate proportions' reveals a casual arrogance any conscientious teacher should be ashamed of.

Nor was my aim in the review exclusively destructive. Academic musicology is today reeling from a barrage of postmodernist attacks. A new populism has emerged, insisting that Mozart should be replaced by Madonna (but not by Mingus). It talks 'anti-élitism' while celebrating the rule of the market and the victory of capitalist relations. My article in *Historical Materialism* was the first in a three-pronged critique of these developments – from someone long involved in non-classical music scenes – which I hope will have a genuine impact. A polemic against pop-studies guru Simon Frith will appear in *Living Through Pop* (a collection edited by Andrew Blake for Routledge); and a polemic against Georgina Born's now-standard study of IRCAM, *Rationalizing Culture*, will appear in *Parallax*.

I am no stranger to controversy. In presenting the latter at 'Popular Music Talks Back' at the Conference of Critical Musicology (Kings College, London, 19 April 1996), my paper was closed down after Dr Born heckled and walked out. For presenting facts about the state of the world economy (ones that will hardly be revelations to the readers of *Historical Materialism*, about global capital's attacks on the working class during the 1980s, and the growing gap between rich and poor), I was branded a 'Neanderthal Marxist' and told to shut up. Truths acknowledged in some academic disciplines are anathema in others – particularly if they burst the rosy illusion of many tender souls that the expansion of commercial multiculturalism and the decline of state-sponsored culture constitute unalloyed 'progress'.

Of course border-disputes between academic disciplines are endemic – whether pursued respectably or not, and without necessarily any contributions from Marxists – even assaults on their right to exist. As thinkers who seek to understand the natural and social totality, Marxists are duty-bound to criticise the academic division of labour. If they cause controversy to erupt by reminding academics in one pleasure-dome about what they're telling each other in another, well and good.

However, once again, I insist this is neither wilfully destructive nor obstreperous. Like Max Paddison, I believe that a musicology based on Adorno's materialism is uniquely capable of analysing non-classical music, far superior to approaches based on positivist sociology or post-structuralist irrationalism. As to the question of 'academic respectability' – simple genuflection to which would surely signal the failure of any self-respecting Marxist journal – I should point out that if Finlayson knows any millionaires wishing to set up an Institute of Materialist Music Studies (with the obverse of Theodor Adorno's deathmask carved into the paving-stones of the quad as a Hoheisel-style 'negative monument'), this underpaid music critic would have no qualms about becoming as 'respectable' as any other arrogant and abusive dunderhead in the faculty.

NB: In the preparation of *Historical Materialism* 2, some of my footnotes went astray. In the interests of the aforementioned academic respectability, I should like to take this opportunity to append them:

p. 166 'the concept does not exhaust the thing conceived', Adorno 1973, p. 5

p. 167 'on-the-one-hand and on-the-other-hand', Marx 1975, p. 187

p. 176 'Art can become a strong ally of revolution only in so far as it remains faithful to itself' is not Paddison, but Trotsky 1970, p. 114.

p. 178 'form is sedimented content', Adorno 1984, p. 209.

p. 181 'the civilisational constraints ...', Adorno 1963, 'Culture Industry Reconsidered' cited in Paddison 1993, p. 203.

p. 181 'beyond the stalemate of serialism', Paddison 1993, p. 270.

p. 181 'has a relevance for the pluralism ...', Paddison 1993, p. 274.

Notes on Contributors

Christopher Bertram teaches philosophy at the University of Bristol and is the author of a number of papers on political philosophy. He is currently working on a study of Rousseau's *Social Contract*.

Werner Bonefeld teaches at the Department of Politics, University of York. He is a member of the editorial board of *Common Sense* and co-editor of the *Open Marxism* series by Pluto Press.

Adrian Budd teaches Politics at South Bank University and is currently researching globalisation and the state.

Paul Burkett, teaches Economics at Indiana State University, Terre Haute, Indiana, US. His research focuses on Marxism and ecology, and the political economy of finance, inflation, and economic crises. A member of the Conference of Socialist Economists and the Union for Radical Political Economics, his work has appeared in such journals as *Science and Society*, *Capital and Class*, *Organization & Environment* and *Studies in Political Economy*.

ecburke@scifac.indstate.edu

Howard Chodos is currently a postdoctoral fellow at the School of Public Administration, Carleton University, Ottawa. He has taught political theory at the University of Ottawa and has written numerous articles on Marxist theory. Prior to completing his PhD, he worked for fifteen years at a variety of jobs in the graphic arts industry, and has been active in the Canadian and Quebecois left since the late sixties, including a stint in a Leninist party. He is the co-editor of the *Socialist Studies Bulletin*.

Simon Clarke is Professor of Sociology in the Centre for Comparative Labour Studies at the University of Warwick. He has written and edited a number of books, including *Marx's Theory of Crisis*; *The State Debate*; *Keynesianism, Monetarism and the Crisis of the State*; *Marx, Marginalism and Modern Sociology*. Since 1991 he has been working on and with labour and trade unions in Russia, where he is Scientific Director of the Institute for Comparative Labour Relations Research (ISITO).

Gareth Dale co-edited *Migrant Labour in the European Union* (with Mike Cole; Berg, 1999), and is a member of the SWP.

c/o hm@lse.ac.uk

John Ehrenberg is Professor and Chair of Political Science at the Brooklyn Campus of Long Island University in New York City. He has written extensively on various aspects of Marxist and democratic political thought. His *The Dictatorship Of The Proletariat: Marxism's Theory Of Socialist Democracy* was published by Routledge in 1992, and *Civil Society: The Critical History of an Idea* is appearing in early 1999 from New York University Press.

Kenneth J. Hammond is Assistant Professor of East & Southeast Asian History at New Mexico State University, Las Cruces, New Mexico, US. His research interests include the cultural & social history of early modern China and East Asia; and East Asia in the early modern global economy. Recently he has published 'The Decadent Chalice: A Critique of Late Ming Political Culture', *Ming Studies* 39, Spring 1998.

Colin Hay is a Lecturer in the Department of Political Science and International Studies at the University of Birmingham. He is the author of *Re-Stating Social and Political Change* (Open University Press, 1996) which was awarded the Philip Abrams Memorial Prize, and *The Political Economy of New Labour: Labouring Under False Pretences?* (Manchester University Press, 1999). He is also co-author (with David Marsh et al.) of *Postwar British Politics in Perspective* (Polity, 1999), editor of *Demystifying Globalisation* (Macmillan, 1999) and co-editor (with Martin O'Brien and Sue Penna) of *Theorizing Modernity* (Longman, 1999). He is a member of the editorial board of *Sociology*.

Peter Hudis is an independent scholar and activist who has written a number of critical essays on Marxist theory. He edited *The Marxist-Humanist Theory of State-Capitalism* and has published in such journals as *Humanity and Society, Socialism and Democracy*, and *Against the Current*. He is currently a member of the national editorial board of the US publication *News & Letters*.

Jonathan Joseph has written a PhD on hegemony and critical realism and has produced a number of articles in these areas. He is also a regular contributor to the journals *What Next?* and *Workers' Action*.
Jmj6@netscape.net

Michael Lebowitz lives in Vancouver and teaches Marxian economics at Simon Fraser University. He is an editor of *Studies in Political Economy* and a contributing editor to *Science & Society*. His publications include *Beyond Capital: Marx's Political Economy of the Working Class* (1992); 'Is "Analytical Marxism" Marxism?' *Science & Society* (1988); 'The Socialist Fetter: A Cautionary Tale' (1991), in the *Socialist Register*;

and 'Kornai and the Vanguard Mode of Production', *Cambridge Journal of Economics* (forthcoming). He is currently working on a book with the provisional title, *The Socialist Economy and the Vanguard Mode of Production*

mlebowit@sfu.ca

John Molyneux is a senior lecturer at the University of Portsmouth. He is the author of *Marxism and the Party, Trotsky's Theory of Revolution* and *What is the Real Marxist Tradition?* He is a member of the Socialist Workers Party.

Giles Peaker is a lecturer in Art History and Critical Theory at the University of Derby. He is currently working on a study of Walter Benjamin and avant-garde aesthetics and has published on Benjamin, Alois Riegl and contemporary art.

G.Peaker@derby.ac.uk

John Roberts is the author of a number of books on art and cultural theory and has contributed to various journals and magazines including, *New Left Review, Third Text, Art Monthly* and *Oxford Art Journal*. His *Art of Interruption: Realism, Photography and the Everyday*, was published by Manchester University Press in 1998.

jorob@btinternet.com

Alan Shandro teaches political philosophy at Laurentian University in Sudbury, Ontario. He has published articles in Marxist political theory. He is a member of the editorial board of *Science & Society*. His research, which proceeds under the working title *Lenin and the Logic of Hegemony*, is concerned with the logic of a Marxist theory of political action.

shandro@cyberbeach.net

Historical Materialism
Research in critical marxist theory

Back issues

Issue No. 1, Autumn 1997

Ellen Meiksins Wood – The Non-History of Capitalism • **Colin Barker** – Reflections on Two Books by Ellen Wood • **Esther Leslie** – Walter Benjamin's Arcades Project • **John Weeks** – The Law of Value and Underdevelopment • **Tony Smith** – Neoclassical and Marxian Theories of Technology • **Michael Lebowitz** – The Silences of *Capital* • **John Holloway** – A Note on Alienation • **Peter Burnham** – Globalisation: States, Markets and Class Relations • **Fred Moseley** – The Rate of Profit and Stagnation in the US, plus reviews by **Linebaugh, Beaumont, Teschke**

Issue No. 2, Summer 1998

China Miéville – The Conspiracy of Architecture: Notes on a Modern Anxiety • **Gregory Elliott** – Velocities of Change: Perry Anderson's Sense of an Ending • **Andrew Chitty** – Recognition and Social Relations of Production • **Michael Neary & Graham Taylor** – Marx and the Magic of Money: Towards an Alchemy of Capital • **Paul Burkett** – A Critique of Neo-Malthusian Marxism: Society, Nature, and Population • **Slavoj Zizek** – Risk Society and its Discontents • **Ben Watson** on Adorno and Music • **Mike Haynes** on Popular Violence and the Russian Revolution • **Esther Leslie** on Walter Benjamin • **Elmar Altvater** on David Harvey • **Martin Jenkins** on Althusser and Psychoanalysis • **Geoffrey Kay** on Freeman & Carchedi • **Henning Teschke** on Amsterdam Benjamin conference

---

For back issues (£7 + £1 p+p each) please write to

The Editors, *Historical Materialism*,
London School of Economics,
Houghton Street, London, WC2A 2AE, UK
Email: hm@lse.ac.uk

Historical Materialism
Research in critical marxist theory

Future issue

Issue No. 4, Summer 1999

Symposium on Robert Brenner & Marxist Crisis Theory with contributions by **Werner Bonefeld** • **Robert Brenner** • **Alex Callinicos** • **François Chesnais** • **Simon Clarke** • **Guglielmo Carchedi** • **Gérard Dumenil & Dominique Levy** • **Alan Freeman** • **Chris Harman** • **Michel Husson** • **Michael Lebowitz** • **Fred Moseley** • **Anwar Shaikh** • **Murray Smith** • **Neil Smith** • **John Weeks** • *Plus more, including* **Edwin Roberts** on Marxism and Pragmatism in the US • an interview with **Slavoj Zizek** • **John Roberts** on Adorno's Aesthetic Theory

For information about future issues please write to

The Editors, *Historical Materialism*,
London School of Economics,
Houghton Street, London, WC2A 2AE, UK
Email: hm@lse.ac.uk

Subscription Details

Name ....

Address ....

Email address ....

I wish my subscription to start with issue No.1 / No.2 / No.3 / No.4 (please circle)

Rates for two issue subscription
Individuals
UK — **£10**
Europe — **£13 or US$20**
Rest of World (surface) — **£13 or US$20**
Rest of World (airmail) — **£16 or US$25**

Institutions
UK — **£40**
Europe — **£48 or US$79**
Rest of World (surface) — **£48 or US$79**
Rest of World (airmail) — **£55 or US$90**

Methods of Payment

Cheques, Eurocheques or bank drafts should be made payable to *Historical Materialism* and should be drawn in pounds sterling or US dollars.

Charge credit card (please tick):
Visa ☐   Mastercard ☐   Delta ☐   Eurocard ☐

Amount..
Card no..
Expiry date..................................

Signature..................................

Please send subscriptions to:
The Editors, *Historical Materialism*,
London School of Economics,
Houghton Street, London, WC2A 2AE, UK.
Email: hm@lse.ac.uk